FEDERAL CONTRACTING PLAYBOOK

FEDERAL CONTRACTING PLAYBOOK

HOW TO WIN BUSINESS USING THE INSIDE TRACK FRAMEWORK FOR INNOVATORS

JANELLE BILLINGSLEA

NEW DEGREE PRESS

FEDERAL CONTRACTING PLAYBOOK

How to Win Business Using the Inside Track Framework for Innovators

ISBN   978-1-64137-936-6   *Paperback*

    978-1-64137-736-2   *Kindle Ebook*

    978-1-64137-737-9   *Ebook*

CONTENTS

———

PREFACE   11
INTRODUCTION   15

PART ONE   ON YOUR MARKS   37
CHAPTER 1   THE FEDERAL PROCUREMENT ARENA 39
CHAPTER 2   THE INSIDE TRACK FRAMEWORK   65
CHAPTER 3   PLAYING THE GAME   83
CHAPTER 4   THE STRATEGY ZONE   91
CHAPTER 5   PLANNING YOUR ATTACK   111

PART TWO   GET SET   135
CHAPTER 6   BUILDING YOUR TEAM   137
CHAPTER 7   THE TEAMING ZONE   171
CHAPTER 8   LISTENING FOR OPPORTUNITIES   195
CHAPTER 9   THE INTELLIGENCE ZONE   217
CHAPTER 10   THE TECHNOLOGY ZONE   229

PART THREE   **GO!**   **261**
CHAPTER 11   PLAYING TO WIN   263
CHAPTER 12   DELIVERING VALUE   285
CHAPTER 13   THE PITCHING ZONE   297
CHAPTER 14   THE PERFORMANCE ZONE   319

             GO GET 'EM, TIGER!   329

             RESOURCES   **333**
             ONLINE RESOURCES   335
             LIST OF ABBREVIATIONS   339
             INSIDE TRACK TOOL TEMPLATES   343

             REFERENCES   359

*Dedicated to my coaches (especially Coach Hamey,
Coach Dixson, and Coach Helmer) and my parents.
You helped me realize the potential
I didn't know I had.*

PREFACE

My first book has been a long time in the making. In fact, as my Wikipedia page somewhat embarrassingly announces, it was originally scheduled to be released in 2008! I began work in earnest on this version in July 2019, with the support of a writing coach, and entered into the New Degree Press creator program as an alumna of Georgetown University. I originally signed up as much to ensure personal accountability for completing the book as to receive the writing help. They have given me wonderful guidance and unfailing support through every step of the process. Without them, this book would likely still be a collection of slide decks, notes, and articles on my hard drive.

I would particularly like to thank Brian Bies, head of publishing, and Professor Koester for their guidance; Christina Mallon for her comments, and Whitney Jones, Cynthia Tucker, and Caitlin Panarella for their tireless editorial support. Also, thanks to Gail Seymour for her coaching, to Lucie Schurerova for referencing, and to Natali Simonovski for illustrations. I also owe a debt of gratitude to Young Bang, Doctor J.D. Walter, Doctor Jimmie West, and Rebecca Bailey for kindly agreeing to beta read the manuscript at various stages of completion from a technical standpoint, and for their invaluable insights.

During the final stages of preparation for publication, the coronavirus crisis hit the world stage, and shortly thereafter the United States. Having only recently been brought over to the civilian side of procurement from a Department of Defense background—with the expectation of a much slower-paced, quieter life—I was called on, along with other ex-DoD colleagues, to introduce some "military structure" and restore some order into the spending chaos that was sweeping the post-corona Federal Procurement Arena with its new rapid procurement process.

The COVID-19 pandemic and the coronavirus spending and relief bills—a $2 trillion bill in March 2020 and a further $3 trillion one in May—have resulted in some eye-watering shopping lists crossing procurement desks, with line items in the billions. Fiscal caution in many ways has been thrown to the wind. Congress approved massive spending, throwing money at everything in hopes of combating this threat. We have seen an unprecedented need to procure Personal Protective Equipment (PPE), ventilators, and other critical equipment, as well as to develop effective treatments, cures, and vaccines against the virus.

I spoke to one business owner who had not been aware of the opportunities available in government contracting until he received $250,000 and $150,000 purchase orders from his county government to deliver non-medical grade masks. He realized it had taken less time and fewer resources to capture one government client than he usually expended. He would have needed to sell forty thousand individual masks to public customers to garner the same profit as from a single federal sale.

Everyone in the United States watched as General Motors won a LARGE contract to produce ventilators from the federal government immediately after the Defense Production Act was signed.[1] As the GM Defense website shows, they have over a century of experience supplying the government, and the military in particular. GM Defense supplied over 8,500 trucks to the war effort in World War I and has made considerable contributions to every war effort since.[2]

So many people and companies are going under during this crisis because their only revenue stream comes from the commercial industry. But even in "normal" times, commercial industry can be finicky and subject to the whims of the market. In contrast to the government's "spending frenzy," venture capital and startup funding from the private sector is drying up at an alarming rate. As Angus Loten of the *Wall Street Journal* says, "Capital from seed-stage funding, often the first significant source of cash for new ventures, has declined by about 22% globally since January."[3] This, he explains, means "Without funding, many startups will fail before catching the eye of corporate buyers, leaving a critical gap in the technology development ecosystem."

---

1   Department of Health and Human Services, 2020.
2   GM Defense, 2020.
3   Loten, 2020.

Even large American corporations are seeking bailouts from the US government in the wake of the coronavirus. Therefore, as an innovation entrepreneur, to be successful in an unpredictable environment, you should seek alternative funding—i.e. from the federal government.

There was already a strong need for this book to help innovation entrepreneurs navigate the Federal Procurement Arena. The government already needed to support small, flexible businesses in their endeavors to ensure America remains competitive technologically, and to keep us at the forefront of the global economy. The government has been making an increased effort to reach out to nontraditional government suppliers in recent years, but there is still a lot of work to be done. This process is still difficult for some companies to navigate, particularly when they are used to working with the private sector. But the coronavirus crisis has thrown the need for governmental support of every area of the economy and populace into sharp focus.

Make no mistake about it, fortunes will be made from this bout of spending. They will be made by those who seize every opportunity available to them and who learn to play the Federal Contracting Game. If you want to be among those who thrive and survive in this uncertain environment, you need this book. I hope you will read it, absorb its message, and act on its guidance.

INTRODUCTION

On Saturday, April 27, 2019 at the Region 3-6A Track Championship, high school senior Matthew Boling turned in a 9.98-second 100-meter dash—making him the fastest teenager in history. Unfortunately for him, on this occasion, his world-record breaking performance would not count because the race was run with a 4.2 mile per hour headwind. But it did make him an overnight media sensation.

Of course, the headline-making event was not Boling's first track outing. Nor was it a stroke of luck.

Just the month before, he had posted a 10.22-second 100-meter finish at a similar event without making waves outside the athletic community. His father describes him as having "a work ethic that I've never seen from anybody."[4] Boling also had a 20.58-second 200-meter personal best and won the long jump at the same meet with a jump of 25 feet, 2 inches.

---

4   Coleman, 2019.

For anyone who doubted his ability, he later set an official 100-meter high school world record of 10.13 seconds on May 12, 2019.

But what does any of this have to do with federal contracting?

Let me tell you about a battery company in South Carolina, and how it, too, became an "overnight success."

⊏⫯⊱ ELECTRIC FUEL BATTERY CORPORATION

Electric Fuel Battery (EFB) Corporation primarily sold batteries. One of their largest customers was the Department of Defense, but in the wake of the fiscal crisis of 2007 and 2008, the military stopped making heavy investments in older technology and started making smaller procurements of zinc air batteries. This could have been a disaster for EFB. They were in danger of going bust. Instead, they refocused. The product that turned the tide was the Soldier-Worn Integrated Power Equipment System (SWIPES.)

EFB knew the end user: soldiers stationed down range. They understood a pain point for those soldiers was the weight of soldier-worn equipment. They knew the type of equipment soldiers wore. EFB designed a modular solution that enabled all the soldier-worn equipment to be powered by a single, conformable, rechargeable battery.

As a result, soldiers no longer had to carry two to three spare batteries for each piece of equipment while on a mission. EFB knew they had a solution to a problem. In fact, the SWIPES system was voted one of the top ten military inventions of 2010.[5]

They had an early-stage prototype, but it had not been through military testing, and EFB lacked the financial resources to make that happen.

RAPID EQUIPPING FORCE

Fortunately for EFB, back in 2012, I was working for the Rapid Equipping Force (REF), a federal government procurement organization that "harnesses current and emerging technologies to provide immediate solutions to the urgent challenges of U.S. Army Forces deployed globally."[6]

As Pete Newell, co-author of *Hacking for Defense* and former REF director, explains, REF was "essentially the Army's Ferrari of skunkworks. It was a small organization that had a fairly significant budget, and it only worked for one person. That was the four-star general who was the Vice Chief of Staff of the Army, the number two guy. And their job was simply to go out and find emerging problems on a battlefield and then find emerging technologies that could be rapidly adapted and reapplied to the battlefield."[7]

In other words, I was working with a small, autonomous group of people to research and develop radical solutions to intractable problems and to plug capability gaps for soldiers, and to do it fast. Most of the soldiers and units we

---

5   Lafontaine, 2011.
6   U.S. Army Rapid Equipping Force, 2019.
7   Bova, 2018.

supported were fighting the war. We had personnel laboratories in Afghanistan, Kuwait, and Iraq.

It was my job to find a way to lighten soldiers' loads. We liked EFB's idea and had the right kind of funding to take it through the technology maturation process, all the way through to acquisition (explained in "Testing Requirements" in **Chapter 10: The Technology Zone**). I had R&D dollars and procurement dollars. That enabled me to not only fund the development and testing of an initial prototype but to make a sizable purchase, after the SWIPES solution successfully passed testing to military standards.

 ## FEDERAL CONTRACTING SUCCESS

EFB succeeded because they adapted one of their primary products (batteries) to address a new and emerging need. They targeted the right agency with a problem they could solve. They found the right government staff member with whom to work. From the outside, they became an overnight success story. After working with us, SWIPES landed them $23 million in contract sales in two years; the first year yielded $13 million and the second year $10 million.

From the inside, that innovation was a part of their success, but their business strategy was also a huge factor. Because they had a solution that started in R&D and worked with the government to take it through testing, they were able to help shape the future contract. SWIPES is now part of a large Program of Record (POR)—one of those military programs that go on for twenty or thirty years with a consistent stream of revenue.

Just as Matthew Boling's record-breaking 100 meters didn't come out of nowhere, neither did EFB's $23 million contract. Just as Boling put in the work with training and turned in consistent race day performances in the run-up to setting the world record, EFB put in the work. They plugged into an existing system to take their product through a development process within the Federal Procurement Arena.

As Jeff Bezos said in a talk to the Economic Club of Washington, "All 'overnight' successes take 10 years."[8] People often portray the government as slow-moving and backward-thinking. But as EFB's story shows, with the right concept, connection to the right people, and a good process, it can be a fantastic partner on your route to success. I have coached early-stage developers of air platforms, ground vehicles, radar, shelters, renewable energy, and even weapons systems through the same process as EFB—from sourcing and securing early-stage funding from the federal government to landing much bigger contracts.

 YOUR FUNDING OPPORTUNITY

The US government is one of the world's biggest spenders, with annual budgets in the trillions. It is one of the biggest venture capitalists, investing in earlier stage research and development with longer timescales and horizons than commercial investors, and it buys everything from toilet paper to space station parts. Whatever your technology, my system will guide you in taking advantage of this opportunity. If you

---

8   CNBC, 2018.

are an innovator, this book and the solutions offered apply especially to you.

There are incredible opportunities for innovators. If you are looking for an investment in your early-stage off-the-wall technical solution, the government is one of your best bets. As you will learn in **Part One**, while everyone thinks most innovation comes from the private sector, a staggering amount of "private sector innovation" was initially funded by and licensed from good old Uncle Sam.

The problem is most innovators in a position to benefit from government funding don't realize it's available. Even if they do, they think it's a maze of red tape and bureaucracy to get it. They don't know where to start or how to go about it.

Often, they don't even realize the government is actively trying to embrace innovation, and that whole budgets exist to support the research and development of innovative solutions to emerging problems. They certainly don't realize people like me with a passion for innovation and vast experience in the Federal Procurement Arena exist, or that there are programs designed to support them through the procurement cycle.

This book will show you how all those assumptions are limiting your opportunities in playing the game successfully!

As an innovator, you need to be intentional about building your federal and contracting business, and not just close your eyes and hope for the best. You need to know where to obtain initial funding from the federal government for research and how to keep those dollars coming so you can continue development and provide tested innovative solutions to the government and the world.

What you need is a playbook. One that will:
- Help you discover funding grants or contract opportunities for your innovation
- Evaluate your readiness to chase down those grants and contracts
- Show you where to enter the maze, and how to read the signs
- Help you navigate the language to successfully land a grant or contract
- Show you how to monitor and measure your performance
- Give you POWER PLAYs to maximize your return for effort

Lucky for you, I'm going to give you all those things.

 **MY TRACK RECORD**

I have been working in federal procurement since 2007, and I have seen a lot of innovative companies try to break into federal government supply. I have seen the gamut of success and failure, and over the years, I've noticed the attitudes and aptitudes that make the difference.

I kind of fell into the procurement field and developed a reputation for coaching innovators to the "Inside Track" of the government supply chain after coming from a different kind of track and field background. What started on the basketball court ended with full track and field scholarships to my two

Division 1 dream schools: the University of North Carolina at Chapel Hill and Georgetown University.

I am a three-time All American. I set a world record in my late teens. I may not have been the fastest teenager in history, but from February 2, 1999, to January 31, 2004, at 1:11.69, I was the fastest female teenager in history over 500 meters.

However, I sustained a severe injury late in my college career that made me question my Olympic goals. Despite my injury, one of my college coaches, Coach Helmer—who is now the head coach at the University of Indiana—agreed to train me. Since I set the record after "dedicating" less than a year to running track, he was confident that, with a few races under my belt, I would make an Olympic team. And with his support, I ran times that would have qualified for the Olympic trials. But I decided not to enter the trials because my Achilles became a recurring problem.

But my love of sports and athletics led me into my dream career. Most track and field athletes take jobs at bars or as teachers to supplement their income because sponsorship deals are rarely enough to live on. None of those appealed to me. I applied for a job with the Department of Defense (DoD) at the National Defense University, which "Educates joint warfighters in critical thinking and the creative application of military power to inform national strategy and globally integrated operations, under conditions of disruptive change, in order to conduct war."[9]

---

9   National Defence University, 2020.

The job itself seemed interesting enough, BUT before I started, I worried it could be somewhat mundane. As an athlete, taking a desk job was a big negative. However, because NDU is on Fort McNair, which is a historic military installation, working out was baked into the culture. My boss gave me time to complete physical training because I still had one foot on the track and one eye on the Olympics. So, having a somewhat enjoyable job that would allow me to train was a golden ticket. Tony Spinosa—a former military officer and the assistant head strength coach for the Washington Redskins—worked at the fitness center at NDU and later became the director. Tony was always excited to have a break from his regular clients and, as he said, work with a "real athlete."

Being afforded the opportunity to travel overseas with general officers on the government's dime was a bonus. During my time at the NDU, I authored papers for capstone leadership to support a congressionally mandated course.[10] I wrote and created supporting materials including country books that provided background information on different countries for course participants. This led to an invitation to travel overseas with general officers and engage with US and foreign ambassadors and military leaders around the world, including then–Chairman of the Joint Chiefs of Staff General Richard Meyers, General Peter Pace, and Newt Gingrich, who was the regular keynote speaker during the final week of the course.

In 2007, I interviewed with a Christian-based defense contracting company. The work combined my prior experience

---

10   Goldwater-Nichols Department of Defence Reorganization Act of 1986.

with the Department of Defense (DoD) along with the Christian management style and principles I very much desired. The defense contracting company had a contract to perform work at the Joint Improvised Explosive Device Defeat Organization (JIEDDO). We were the military's "internal" skunkworks in the joint environment—on steroids.

JOINT IED DEFEAT ORGANIZATION

There is a pervasive idea that the federal government and the military are not good investors. Because they fund early-stage technology and research that sometimes doesn't pan out, and because there are so many separate forces and branches, some suggest they spend money in silos, each department chasing its own agenda and unaware what other organizations are pursuing.

One of the best things about JEIDDO—which has since morphed into combat support group JIDO (Joint Improvised-Threat Defeat Organization)—was that it was a joint organization. We basically had representatives with skills focused on defeating Improvised Explosive Devices (IEDs) from all the US services, and some from allied nations. We shared information about each other's solutions, so we knew what each service had and what they were working on. We also shared reports and data on how effective these innovative solutions were. The most successful were transitioned in an integrated way to Programs of Record to help the military and partner agencies long term. JIEDDO also had $4 billion in what is known as colorless money.

We focused on developing and implementing disruptive, breakthrough, incremental, or sustaining solutions, with a focus on specific military problems. We had personnel from all disciplines, including innovators, operators (users), security, and acquisition professionals from all four services and communities under one roof. We had scientists and engineers from our National Laboratories, and trainers and testers from the various military innovation centers on staff. We had close relationships with all the innovation, testing, and engineering centers across the nation, including university academics. We were the "Bell Labs" of the twenty-first century.

As Walter Isaacson, a professor at Tulane University, points out: "the rational exuberance of the American economy has been propelled by the combination of three innovations: the computer, the microchip, and the internet. The research and development that produced each came from a triangular alliance of government, academia, and private business."[11] Early computers were built at the University of Pennsylvania and Harvard using military funding and commercialized by Univac and IBM. Bell Labs invested in transistors, which were funded by the government for use in for the space and weapons programs before Fairchild and Intel developed small silicon chips for mass production. DARPA conceived the internet, but it took university research and private contractors such as BBN to bring it to fruition.

---

11   Isaacson, 2019.

Isaacson says, "This tripartite machine of government working with universities and private corporations was not merely a random array with each group pursuing its own aims. Instead, during and after World War II, the three groups had been purposely fused together into an innovation triangle."

Bell Labs, as Isaacson explains, had a symbiotic relationship with the federal government in the twentieth century. They received considerable funding to conduct research or to build solutions to our nation's biggest challenges. The breadth and scope of the items invented or innovated upon at Bell Labs are remarkable. Cellular, microwave, and even satellite communications technologies were rooted in discoveries and the development of ideas at Bell Labs. The federal government provided the challenges, basic research, and—in some cases—funding.

In much the same way, with the right combination of personnel, problems, and resources at JEIDDO, we were discovering, developing, and quickly fielding innovative solutions to solve our nation's and military's biggest challenges and save lives. Our mission directive was "to focus (i.e., lead, advocate, and coordinate) all DoD actions in support of the Combatant Commanders' (CCDRs') and their respective Joint Task Forces' efforts to defeat IEDs as weapons of strategic influence."[12] We had all the critical elements under one roof that allowed us to go from a theory or concept to a prototype, and then to market or field quickly and efficiently, all with federal dollars.

---

12 RAND Corporation, 2013.

We had the technology, business, funding, and market completely aligned.

Unfortunately, during my work with scientists, businesses, and programs since then, I have learned JIEDDO and REF are outliers. They are shining examples, yes, but unicorns created for a specific purpose. They established a new and blossoming field called "rapid acquisitions."

These days, every service has some sort of rapid-acquisition, innovation cell that allows them to short-circuit the lengthy procurement cycle for time-sensitive, novel solutions to urgent problems. However, they are smaller and typically centered around military problems.

 NAVIGATING THE MAZE

In the civilian sector, and even within some parts of DoD, the US public innovation system is much more disparate and discrete. For example, Small Business Innovation Research (SBIR) and Small Business Technology Transfer (STTR) recipients may get Phase I and Phase II dollars but find it difficult to obtain Phase III funding. Scientists, engineers, and inventors in the private sector find it difficult to navigate. They find it all but impossible, depending on their goal, to go all the way from theory or a feasibility study through prototype development to a fully field-tested or commercialized solution because they simply don't understand the arena.

The federal government is an exceptional source of funding for early-stage innovation and technology development, but you can only access it if you understand the rules of the game, navigate the environment, and implement best practices. Further, understanding government organizations are mission-focused—and that their funding is aligned with that mission—is critical.

Unfortunately, I've found some of our "best" innovators don't fully understand the playing field. They are typically good at solving technological problems and coming up with innovative solutions, but they lack the people or organizational skills to navigate the Federal Procurement Arena.

They're like mathletes trying out for the Olympics. They're like a sprinter in the blocks, full of great ideas and nervous energy. They are trying to break into government contracting with an innovation they know is impactful but haven't got a clue how to get it noticed. As you will see later, the reason is that they're entered in a much longer race, and the more experienced runners are lined up on a completely different starting line. When the starting gun sounds, they're left playing catch-up and wondering what happened.

As a result, we have lots of innovation that could be fueling our economy sitting on the bleachers in prototype form. Innovative ideas may never make it to the federal government or the commercial marketplace because the system stymies them.

This is a problem for so many reasons. As you will soon see, so many of the innovations we use today, and who have made a tremendous impact on humanity, were funded at some point in part by the government. Indeed, to continue to "spur" innovation, we need entrepreneurs, thinkers, and tinkerers to successfully navigate this space so we can solve some of our most difficult challenges.

That is the goal of this book: to help innovators like you impact humankind and change the world.

THE FEDERAL CONTRACTING PLAYBOOK

In *The Federal Contracting Playbook*, I want to take you on a journey to **The Inside Track** of federal government contracting. I want to show you how to navigate the **Federal Procurement Arena** confidently so you can access the funding and support you need to bring your innovative solutions to maturity and to market. I want to show you how to hook into the latest contracting and funding vehicles designed to make it easier for innovators like you to do what you do best— innovate. And I want to help you achieve peak performance in your innovation business.

It can be a dry subject if you don't happen to be in love with developing and funding innovation like me. There can be a lot of red tape involved, and a lot of procedures and processes to follow—not to mention the alphabet soup of agency names to get familiar with.

So, I want to make the process—not easy, as some would have you believe, since there's a lot of work involved. But simple. Or at least simpl*er*.

I'm going to give you a playbook. And to make navigation easier, we will use a series of icons to signpost the content along the way:

Zones............ Knowledge to FOCUS On

Skills.............. Abilities to DEVELOP

Tools.............. Resources to USE

Power Plays.... Tips to BOOST Results

Notes............. Important INFORMATION

Exercises........ Activities to DO

Research........ Sources to EXPLORE

Spotlight........ Examples to LEARN From

Characters..... People You Will MEET

Hurdles......... Potential Obstacles to AVOID

This book will walk you through deciding if the **Federal Procurement Arena** is the right place for you. As I hope you can already tell, this is NOT intended to be an academic or legalese piece of writing. It is not aimed at acquisitions professionals or lawyers. RATHER, it is intended to be accessible for everyone. As such, I wrote it in a conversational style. It cannot hope to cover every nuance or aspect of the subject in such a condensed format, so I have tried to give you the information you need in the order you need it to get started. Some complicated subjects have necessarily been glossed over and pared down to the bare minimum, following the principle, "A little inaccuracy sometimes saves a lot of explanation."[13]

In **Part One**, "**On Your Marks**," you'll get ready to start working with the federal government. You will learn about **The Federal Procurement Arena**, the roles and disciplines you'll come across within it, and the players you need in your team.

I'll introduce you to the **Inside Track Framework**, the **Six Zones of Innovation Excellence** and the **Six Skills for Winning** you need to focus on for federal contracting success.

You will learn about the **Inside Track Tools**, designed to coach you using sports analogies that make the subject more accessible. You'll start learning **Playing the Game** and enter **The Strategy Zone**, where you will learn **Planning Your Attack**.

In **Part Two**, "**Get Set**," you'll practice **Building Your Team**, with your three relay teams for innovation, operation, and marketing. Then you will enter **The Teaming Zone**. There, you'll look at joining or forming a winning squad.

Then you will learn **Listening For Opportunities** and set up your **Business Strength Training Center**, where you will set

---

13   Munro, 1930.

up your **Business Capture Machine** with **Relationship Reps, Questioning Sets, Intelligence Scoops**, and **Requirement Relays** in a way that help you wire the requirements to your solution.

Then you'll enter **The Intelligence Zone** and **The Technology Zone** and identify your **Goldilocks Innovation Area**.

In **Part Three**, "**Go!**", we will focus on **Playing to Win** and help you find your values, lay the groundwork, and define your **Proposal Set Pieces**.

You'll practice **Delivering Value** and learn how to price for profit without pricing yourself out of the market.

Then you'll move into **The Pitching Zone**. There you'll learn about the proposal process and set up your **Pitch Perfection Program**, to get your batting averages up without swinging wildly at contracts you can never hit.

Finally, we'll talk about **The Performance Zone**. You'll learn how to manage your contract once it's awarded using your **Program Management Practice**, to ensure your past performance works for and not against you, and to get you playing in **The Big Leagues**.

Figure 1 shows how the zones, skills and tools of **the Inside Track Framework** fit together in the **Federal Procurement Arena**.

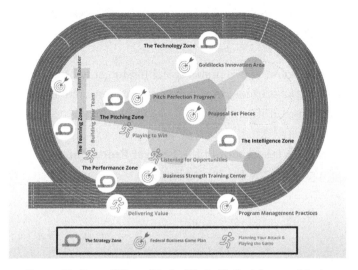

Figure 1: *The Zones, Skills, and Tools of The Inside Track framework in the Federal Procurement Arena.*

And if any or all that sounds daunting right now, don't worry. We're breaking a dense, dry subject down into (hopefully) fun-sized chunks. We called this a *play*book and a *game* plan for a reason!

SUCCESS NOT GUARANTEED

I can't promise you funding, business expansion, or the chance to see your work take on national or international relevance after reading this book, as I don't know you or what you'll do with the information in it. No coach can promise an athlete a shot at the Olympics without knowing if the athlete will buckle down and do the work.

What I can tell you is that—IF you apply it—the information in this playbook has the potential to bring you all those things.

I hope you apply it because I really want to see what you bring to the game.

At this point, you're probably itching to get to the starting blocks and start looking for government contracts and funding opportunities.

First, let's take a tour of the **Federal Procurement Arena**, and get a feel for the other players in the game.

PART ONE:

ON YOUR MARKS

Learn about The Federal Procurement Arena, and how The Inside Track Framework helps Innovators like you Play the Game. Then enter The Strategy Zone and Plan Your Attack.

1

THE FEDERAL PROCUREMENT ARENA

———

"I'd never want to work with the government," Marjorie told me when I explained I worked in procurement.

We were at a small business accelerator networking event, full of start-up owners looking for funding for innovation.

"Really? Why ever not?" I asked, feigning surprise. I'd heard it all before but wanted to hear her reasons.

"There's just so much paperwork," she said. "And so many hoops to jump through. Besides, I've heard stories about people who spent years getting set up to work with the government only to have them pull the funding within months."

Of course, I knew by the way she looked at me—that curious combination of challenge and hope—that what she really wanted to hear was that the stories she'd heard were exaggerated, the horror stories isolated examples of bad luck or poor judgment. She wanted to hear that the same thing wouldn't happen to her.

Marjorie was far from alone. I regularly talk to people who tell me how they would never want to work with the federal government because there's too much bureaucracy. There's a pervasive preconception that it's like running an obstacle course, complete with dirty tactics from the competition and water cannons manned by malicious race officials. They imagine the entire system is set up to prevent them from succeeding.

What they fail to realize is that the big players they aspire to emulate or work for all serve the federal government. They're all competitors in the **Federal Procurement Arena**, a massive competition run by benevolent supporter Uncle Sam.

 INTRODUCING THE FEDERAL PROCUREMENT ARENA

Imagine the Federal Procurement landscape as a sporting event held by Uncle Sam. Competitors can enter events on the **Contracting Track, The Field of Grants**, or the **"Other Transactions" Sidetrack**. We'll use this track analogy throughout the book to explain how the system works and fill in the details. For now, just imagine the running track represents the contract bidding process, the field the grants application process, and the "Other Transactions Sidetrack" the alternative and simplified programs available to Federal Procurement Professionals. It might look something like Figure 2.

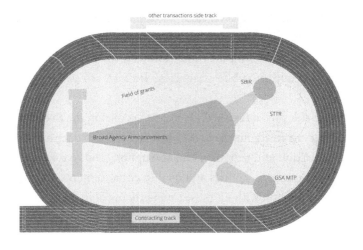

Figure 2: Contracting Track, Field of Grants, and "Other Transactions" Sidetrack

Although the government does also make purchases using credit cards ($6 billion last year alone), we won't be focusing on credit card spending much in this book. It's rarely used for research and development or for the kind of early-stage technological innovation we're talking about here.

Uncle Sam, by the way, goes out of his way to ensure **The Federal Procurement Arena** is fair. All those rules and hoops, form filling, and reams of procurement regulations are all there to make sure the playing field is as open and level as possible. The government has been required to formally advertise requests for proposals prior to awarding contracts since 1809.[14] In 1861 the requirement for all purchases to be made "by open purchases, or by previously advertising for proposals" (2 Stat. 536 (1809))[15] was refined to state that "all purchases and con-

---

14   Manuel, 2011.
15   Ibid.

tracts for supplies and services... except for personal services... shall be made by advertising a sufficient time previously for proposals respecting the same" unless immediate delivery is required due to "public exigencies." (*12 Stat. 220 (1861)*)[16]

Those rules were revisited several times during the twentieth century in an attempt to strike a balance between open and fair competition and nepotism and corruption. The goal was also to maximize the savings and quality enhancements afforded by competition without those savings being obliterated by the sheer size and complexity of the Federal Procurement apparatus.

Current Federal Acquisition Regulations require agencies to "obtain full and open competition... in a manner that is consistent with the need to efficiently fulfill the Government's requirements."[17]

Unlike private market procurement, the government is committed to working with anyone who meets the requirements, and to evaluating tenders on an equitable basis.

Private commerce is the obstacle course. Non-governmental business owners have more latitude. They can decide with whom they will and will not do business, and thus can award solely to friends and long-time business partners. They don't have to let others into the game.

Often, when we talk about cutting-edge entrepreneurs and innovators, we don't realize they're licensing their innovations from the government via US national laboratories or

---

16   Ibid.
17   Federal Acquisitions Regulations, 2020.

innovation centers, or that they are receiving federal grant money to develop them. It's not cheating. And it's NOT unethical. More importantly, opportunities like that are available to you too, IF you know where to look and how to take advantage of them.

 WARM-UP EXERCISE

Go to usaspending.gov/[18] and explore the sheer size of the **Federal Procurement Arena**. Look at the spending explorer to see spending broken down by budget, agency, or the types of products and services purchased (object class).

Figure 3 shows an image of 2019 spending broken down by state, to give you some idea of what to expect on the site.

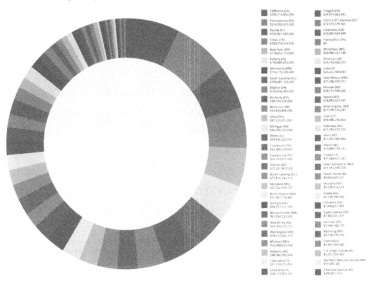

Figure 3: Spending by state in 2019.[19]

---

18   USA Spending, 2020.

19   Figures from USA Spending, 2020.

BIG BUSINESS WORKS WITH THE GOVERNMENT

Some of our biggest companies do a lot of work with the federal government, whether it's shipping things or sourcing things we don't have. They have huge government accounts. It's a trillion-dollar marketplace.

 BOEING

Think Boeing. According to *The Washington Post*, "For Boeing's 102-year history, dating to the start of the First World War, the company and the country have relied upon one another, together creating hundreds of thousands of jobs, outfitting the United States with top military aircraft and supplying planes worldwide to allow the growth of passenger air travel and to boost U.S. exports."[20]

Boeing has been engaging with the DoD (Army) since 1920, when they built experimental armored planes for the US Army and sold off sea planes designed for the US Navy.[21] Today, defense orders and dollars are a huge part of their operations. Two Boeing VC-25As serve as Air Force One. Indeed, Boeing and the US government are so intertwined that when Jim Mattis resigned the post in December 2018, President Trump brought in Patrick M. Shanahan, a former Boeing executive, as acting defense secretary.

Good Jobs First's subsidy tracker[22] shows that Boeing received over $35 million in federal grants in 2018 alone;

---

20   O'Connell and Lamothe, 2019.
21   Boeing, 2020.
22   Good Jobs First, 2019.

a sizable chunk of their $101.1 billion revenue the same year. Fox Business reported, "The company increased its commercial plane deliveries in the year by 6 percent to 806, totaling $60.7 [b]illion in sales. Revenue at Boeing's federal defense contracting business grew 13 percent to $23.1 billion. Among the major U.S. contracts, it won last year was a $9.2 billion order to replace the Air Force's training jets."[23]

Of the top ten millennials' preferred employers in a YPulse survey, if we remove "my own company," "US Government," "school/university," and "hospital," we're left with six big name brands:[24]

- Google
- Apple
- Amazon
- Microsoft
- Disney
- Nike

 GOOGLE

Of these, Google's algorithm was originally funded by the National Science Foundation (NSF). Without funding from the federal government, there would be no Google. More recently, Google's parent company, Alphabet, acquired Keyhole, Inc., the CIA-funded software now known as Google Earth.

---

23   Williams, 2019. The original article misquotes this figure as $60.7 million in sales.
24   YPulse, 2018.

APPLE

Apple has a website especially for government procurement.[25] While older generations know Apple as the company that lost the battle of the PC to Microsoft, we're now most familiar with them as the inventors of the iPod, iPhone, and iPad.[26] But did you know much of the technology inside the iPod was sourced from government-funded research? The dynamic random-access memory (DRAM) cache and microprocessor were both created using Defense Advanced Research Projects Agency (DARPA) dollars. DARPA and the Department of Defense (DoD) jointly funded development of the micro hard drive. The DoD, together with the National Institutes for Health (NIH) and NSF, funded research that led to the LCD screen. The DoE funded development of the lithium-ion batteries, and the Army Research Office the signal compression.[27]

AMAZON

Then there's Amazon. They have a significant presence in the federal market, and it isn't doing what you might think. Amazon started out as a retailer of books and then of other products, but it's their Amazon Web Services (AWS) cloud storage solutions that have seen the federal government become one of their largest customers. Amazon offers the AWS Contract Center for federal, state, education, and other international institutions, and AWS GovCloud for institutions with "sensitive data and regulated workloads" to store "sensitive Controlled Unclassified Information (CUI)."[28] [29]

---

25   Apple Inc. 2020.
26   Shontell, 2010.
27   Mazzucato and Semieniuk, 2017.
28   Amazon Web Services, 2020.
29   Amazon Web Services (Govcloud), 2020.

⊏⊩⊱ MICROSOFT

Amazon isn't the only major player getting in on cloud services for government contracts. Despite Amazon's head start in this area, a recent Joint Enterprise Defense Infrastructure (JEDI) contract for cloud services was awarded to Microsoft in November 2019, after complaints that the initial contract had been tailored to benefit Amazon over other competitors. CNBC's Squawk Alley co-anchor Jon Fortt reported, "The JEDI contract is worth up to $10 billion over 10 years, but just as valuable as the money is it's also worth bragging rights and street cred."[30]

Microsoft has a comprehensive suite of services it offers to governments, but both Microsoft and its subsidiary, Vexelcorp, have been the recipients of numerous government subsidies, awards, and grants.[31] [32]

Indeed, many businesses in Silicon Valley would not exist today if it weren't for the federal government. Indeed, Silicon Valley sprang from the military research conducted in that area before silicon was discovered, and the term "Silicon Valley" was coined. The federal government recently funded that whole area due to the need for better semiconductors. In *Why Silicon Valley's "Self-Made" Millionaires are Really "Government-Made" Millionaires*, Adrain Rehn says, "In fact, Santa Clara County, which encompasses part of Silicon Valley, had the highest per-worker number of defense contract dollars of any U.S. county in 1992."[33]

---

30 Fortt, 2019.
31 Microsoft, 2020.
32 Good Jobs First, 2019.
33 Rehn, 2014.

However, you don't have to be in high-tech innovation to receive government grants. Even Disney Worldwide Services, Inc., received a government grant for the purchase of land and construction of a building in the T-5 Data Center Park in Cleveland County, North Carolina, in 2011.

Additionally, Nike Tennessee received a $1.15 million grant to fast-track infrastructure development from the Department of Economic and Community Development in 2013.

Again, these companies aren't doing something wrong, they're simply taking advantage of the opportunities open to them.

This book will show you how you can set up your innovation business to serve the federal government. It will show you how to take advantage of the existing machinery that will help you source early-stage funding and keep the dollars coming throughout development to maturity and beyond. This chapter focuses on the size of the market, the type of opportunities it presents, and the businesses best placed to seize them. Hopefully, by the end of it, you'll be excited by the possibilities, and eager to get started on your **Federal Business Game Plan**—your personal route to innovation success in the **Federal Procurement Arena**.

First, let's look at the numbers that make the **Federal Procurement Arena** the world's largest competition.

THE WORLD'S LARGEST COMPETITION

Why should you even get involved with the US federal government? What's so great about serving "Uncle Sam" in a contracting capacity, as an innovator or otherwise?

According to the CIA Factbook, the US federal government is the largest government budget anywhere in the world—bigger than China and Japan combined—when taking social benefit expenditures into account.[34] It is also the world's largest marketplace, and the world's largest customer.

USASpending.gov shows that in 2019, the US federal government spent only $602.5 billion of its $6.9 trillion overall spend on personnel and benefits. The remainder went to grants and fixed charges ($4.6 trillion), contractual services and supplies ($9.26 billion), acquisitions of assets ($234.3 billion), and other or unreported sources.[35] That means it spent over $6 trillion with non-government entities.

The government spends this money in two main ways, and two lesser known ones. It gives out grants, which account for almost 60 percent of the spending, and awards contracts, for almost the other 40 percent. The remainder is spent on credit cards or in transactions made using "Other Transaction Authority," which basically means with non-traditional contractors, sidestepping the Federal Acquisitions Regulations (FAR) rules, and using "a form of contract... that is not a procurement contract, grant, or cooperative agreement."[36]

---

34 Central Intelligence Agency, 2019.

35 United States government, 2020.

36 Nash, 2013, supra note 1, at 414.

If you live anywhere in the United States, the federal government is spending money in your area. It spends billions of dollars across states and across localities. Which means wherever you are in the United States, there's a federal contracting **Playing Field** near you.

Some companies mentioned in this chapter, like Google, utilized government funding to develop an idea, initial product, or concept. Others, like Apple, developed a solution that leveraged government technology, did their own internal development, and are currently selling high-tech services back to the government. Some simply went after contracts or grants, like Disney and Nike. But whether they owe their origins to government-funded research or just serve the federal machine, all these big companies have benefited from working with the US government one way or another.

None of this takes anything away from the marketing and development achieved by those companies, or the vision they had to take those technologies and bring them to a commercial market. It's just to say, if you're an entrepreneur with a desire to innovate, you may be able to find your break using federal government support and funding. Uncle Sam, it turns out, can be quite a benevolent supporter.

UNCLE SAM, YOUR MOST BENEVOLENT SUPPORTER

When you think about venture capitalism, you probably think of "business angels," or more likely sharks, as portrayed in the TV show *Shark Tank*. The options for new businesses seem to be bootstrapping and doing everything on a budget in-house or handing over a sizable chunk of equity to an investor in the hopes of receiving their mentorship while getting the business off the ground.

Commercial investors or venture capitalists want to be able to see they can get a return on investment after five years. However, with early-stage tech development, it often takes fifteen to twenty years before you're able to realize a functional product. We're increasingly conditioned to think about "breakthrough" innovation in terms of software development, the release of a new app, or a creative business model. The appetite for such extended investment timescales before realizing profits is almost vanishingly small.

On the other hand, think about developing new lifesaving drugs. It takes a long time, and shortcuts are potentially disastrous. For example, when we think about the HIV/ AIDS epidemic in the 1980s, the disease was always a relatively quick death sentence. Only after nearly thirty years of research has the pharmaceutical industry been able to extend life exponentially for people with the disease. There were no quick fixes. It took years to develop a cocktail that prolonged life.

Amid the coronavirus pandemic, the public paid a lot of attention to how the government was spending its money in search of treatments and cures for the COVID-19. One *Forbes* headline declared "$20 Million On An Unproven Malaria Drug, $650 Million On A Coronavirus Cure: How Trump's Government Has Spent Over $3 Billion Fighting COVID-19." The article went on to state that "over 2,800 separate orders have been recorded as being spent on COVID-19 aid," including "$25 million on big data cruncher Palantir" and "a $20 million trial testing the efficacy of antimalarial hydroxychloroquine," a controversial treatment for the virus. Other awards included a $464 million deal with Johnson and Johnson for a potential vaccine, and a further $30 million to Protein Science for clinical trials into a vaccine candidate.[37]

It's the federal government doing that investing to reach viable product stage, or to find cures. And while the media may be critical about *how* the money is spent, there's no question—at least with such and obvious and urgent threat—that it's the government's job to fund that research and development. With the notable exception of pharmaceuticals, early-stage basic and applied research in the United States that allows for innovation simply wouldn't happen if it were not for the federal government.

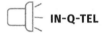 **IN-Q-TEL**

The federal government doesn't have external pressure to turn a profit, so it's a worthy resource to explore. For one thing, if your solution fits within certain technology vectors, such as software, infrastructure, or modern materials, you may be able to get venture funding from an unlikely source: the CIA (or its business arm, In-Q-Tel).

The US Army also has a venture funding entity, OnPoint Technologies, set up to fund high-risk, high-reward technology R&D on a commercial basis on its behalf. There's a growing case for setting up government-sponsored venture

_____

37   Brewster, 2020.

funding firms to serve other agencies. So, even if your solution doesn't fit into the technological innovation niche, you may still be able to attract more traditional forms of government funding.

While information about these entities isn't easily forthcoming, and many companies who have worked with them prefer to remain tight-lipped about it, several have commented openly on their working relationship with In-Q-Tel. In response to a Crunch Base survey, Cloud security company Evident.io said, "While we work closely with our commercial customers to ensure that we have prioritized their needs, it is more challenging to get that level of interaction with some government agencies because of the nature of the programs. In-Q-Tel helps to bridge that gap."[38]

In the same survey, Craig Weich of Sila Nanotechnologies said, "We have a work program as part of the In-Q-Tel investment, as is typically the case. Through In-Q-Tel, we've deepened existing relationships and formed new ones in the Defense and Intelligence Community."[39] Todd Mostak, CEO of MapD, a big data company, echoed the sentiment. Mostak went on to explain that In-Q-Tel doesn't just provide the links to the intelligence community; it takes a hands-on approach to working with its investments. "They have always taken a very collaborative approach to working with MapD," he says, "and there is a high degree of synergy around the shared goal of accelerating federal adoption of GPU-powered analytics."[40]

---

38 Cherney, 2017.
39 Ibid.
40 Ibid.

And you don't have to be working in the fields of security, data, detection, or space technology to find funding with these organizations. Look at a Venture Capital list of "12 Early- And Mid-Stage Startups Backed By The CIA, Pentagon, And US Army." Alongside Fuel3D, which received $11 million to develop a handheld 3D scanner for 3D modeling applications, and Tribogenics, which received $8.7 million to develop portable X-ray machines, you will find Skincential Sciences, the recipient of $300,000 to develop its Clearista Refining Pen, "which delivers focused exfoliation to smooth a range of raised and/or pigmented surface imperfections; bumps, discolorations and rough spots on the skin's surface."[41]

Many people think that idea-generating institutions, including most state-level laboratories and universities, are funded by private entities, but they're mainly funded by federal government contracts or grants lasting between one and five years. If not for that funding, many of these institutions wouldn't exist or survive. In fact, according to a recent Policy Forum study entitled *Government-funded research increasingly fuels innovation*, this governmental support "ultimately leads to jobs, industrial competitiveness, and entrepreneurial success."[42]

Congressman Aaron Schock, representative of the 18th District of Illinois and a member of the House Ways and Means Committee, believes that STEM subjects (science, technology, engineering, and math) along with arts are all "critical

---

41   CB Insights, 2016.
42   Fleming et. al, 2019.

components to a thriving American economy." Global competition, he argues, "requires a consistent commitment to support research and development within these disciplines."[43]

Work done by NASA and other science-based agencies, he says, "strengthens the ability for U.S.-based private sector companies to develop practical innovations, create new industries and jobs, and grow the economy.

"Products, such as the internet, MRIs, GPS, cell phones, and fiber optics, are examples of federal research being applied to achieve economic growth," he explains, adding, "This symbiotic relationship has been estimated by the National Research Council to generate nearly $500 billion in revenue at 30 well-known technology companies...

"That is why federal investments are vital. I've always believed that the best way for government to contribute to a thriving economy is to foster an environment where private industry can prosper. Federal basic research provides innovative companies the raw material to build the next great product right here in America, and the role of both is essential."

POWER PLAY: If you're an entrepreneur or a start-up, it's worth your time to work out how you can serve the federal government. There is so much untapped potential here, and we're going to shed some light on how you can make this work for your business. Even if you don't actually have a business yet, and you're still just thinking

---

43   Schock, 2015.

about how to get funding for your innovation or technology, I want you to start thinking in terms of your fledgling innovation business. The sooner you start thinking about your idea as a business, the better. Even during the development process, you need to think in terms of innovation business. That way, when your technology approaches maturation, you will be able to pivot and deliver your product to market. In the meantime, I will be giving you tips on how you can shape requirements so you can receive a larger contract, which can help you develop a fully-fledged business.

Yes, there's a bit of a process to go through, but we're going to walk through that. Don't let a bit of paperwork get between you and getting your early-stage innovation funded with a solid, stable revenue stream down the line.

Now let's look at the way the federal government spends money, so you can start thinking about which of these routes makes most sense to you.

THE FIELD OF GRANTS

Federal grants are often overlooked, yet they increase a fledgling business's chances of success. The federal government is a powerful seed funder that invests in innovative ideas at the earliest, riskiest stages. Many programs don't dilute the business owner's control over their intellectual property (IP). However, there are certain solicitations that are written so the government retains IP rights. This is often done in a military or classified setting. So, if you're working in a classified area, you may need to consider whether you're prepared to cede those rights in exchange for funding.

The federal government, surprisingly, spends more on grants than it does in contracts. In fact, it awards over $500 billion in grants annually. A lot of that is awarded at the state level to state governments, universities, and other local institutions, with much of it focused on research and development. There are also grants for business development and economic stimulation, some designed to support underperforming geographic locales or those affected by economic downturns. Some are targeted to specific subsets of the population, such as women in business, veterans, and other recognized disadvantaged groups. Yet others are "set aside" for non-profits.

Although the government advertises its upcoming needs using a system that we call Broad Area Announcements (BAAs), federal grants are not only available for people responding to those requests. A BAA is "a notice from the government that requests scientific or research proposals from private firms concerning certain areas of interest to the government. The proposals submitted by the private firms may lead to contracts."[44] Grants may be announced through agency sites, or on program specific sites. Grants.gov advises:

"To sort through the federal grant programs, the authoritative source is the Catalog of Federal Domestic Assistance (CFDA). This catalog lists all the available funding programs to all levels of government, nonprofit organizations, for-profit businesses, and other eligible entities. Search Grants

---

44   AcqNotes, 2018.

within Grants.gov allows you to search, filter, and apply for specific opportunities to receive funding from one of these programs."[45]

In some cases, the government uses existing contracts, such as a multi-vendor Indefinite Delivery, Indefinite Quantity (IDIQ) programs, enabling it to share requirements only with people and businesses that have already passed minimum requirements to serve their purposes.

BAAs are flexible and allow the government to award procurement contracts, grants, cooperative agreements, or other transactions to some agencies. They are general in nature. According to DARPA guidelines:

> *If the Government's need is for the development of a specific system or hardware solution, proposals must be requested by a solicitation type other than BAA or RA (e.g., Request for Proposals). Further, a BAA will not be used if the Government's need is for supplies or services (e.g. SETA support), even though research and development (R&D) funding may be used and the project may be in support of R&D.*

> *DARPA may award procurement contracts, grants, cooperative agreements, or other transactions (including Other Transactions for Prototype, Other Transactions for Research, and Technology Investment Agreements) as a result of proposals submitted in response to a BAA.*

---

45   Grants.gov, 2019.

...The term "RA" refers to "BAA-like" solicitations that may result in the award of any instrument but a procurement contract. RAs generally follow a similar structure to BAAs.[46]

It isn't always the size of the grant or contract that leads to long-term success, either. The initial government funding amount may be relatively small but provide just enough for a start-up or bootstrapping company to survive long enough to generate proof of concept, which later provides the basis for commercial success. Otherwise, the initiative may come from the government agencies with the requirement, and because there is a grant or challenge, we often get ideas that never would have made it to the marketplace without the grant.

For example, software algorithm solutions are not expensive. The initial grant for Data Warehousing and Decision Support awarded to Google co-founder Sergey Brin was one of fifteen small grants sharing a three-to-four-million-dollar budget annually from 1993 to 1999.[47] Typically, with government grants and even with certain contracts, innovators can retain the Intellectual Property (IP) rights to their innovation, so they get to develop solutions for "free" to help the government. The impact of those early investments is MASSIVE in the case of companies like Google.

Go ahead and spend a few minutes searching the Grants.gov database, and make a note of anything that looks interesting. There are even apps for Android and Apple phones, and an online applications system.

---

46   DARPA, 2016.
47   Ullman, 1997.

THE FEDERAL CONTRACTING TRACK

I talk a lot about the technology side of federal funding and spending because that's where I got my start, and where a lot of my personal experience and passion is. It's also an area with the potential to have the most social and economic impact in the long term, particularly when you consider the impacts many of the government-funded technologies have on everyday society. Think about the inventions that came about because of the NASA Space Program, from memory foam to cochlear implants, insulin pumps to water filters.[48]

However, you don't have to be working in technology—or on the forefront of research—to serve the federal government. As Table 1 shows, according to a 2018 Open the Books oversight report, the federal government spent the following in one month alone:[49]

Table 1: Federal Spending in one month

Spending Category	Spending Amount
Miscellaneous Spending	$48.6 million
Guns, Ammunitions, and Bombs	$818.1 million
Furniture	$490.6 million
Food	$402.2 million
Transportation	$295.4 million
Public Relations and Marketing	$462 million
Clothing	$13.1 million
Workout and Recreation Equipment	$9.8 million
iPads & iPhones	$7.7 million
Hygiene	$4.2 million
Musical Equipment	$1.7 million
Alcoholic Beverages	$308,994

---

48   Human Paragon, 2017.
49   Andrzejewski and Smith, 2019.

Figure 4 shows the ten years of government spending up until 2018.

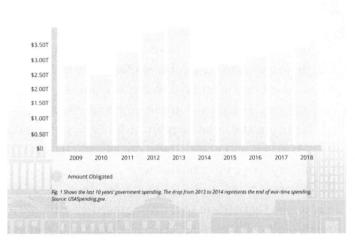

Figure 4: *The last 10 years' government spending. The drop from 2013 to 2014 represents the end of war-time spending.*[50]

 THE "OTHER TRANSACTIONS" SIDETRACK

While most federal contracts are assigned under the Federal Acquisitions Regulations (FAR), some government agencies and departments have the authority to complete "other transactions" using Other Transaction Authority (OTA).

OTA basically allows the government to purchase from "nontraditional" contractors using non-standard contracting agreements. Generally, that includes those who have never contracted with the government before or have not had an active contract within the last year.

---

50   Figures from USASpending.gov

While this means the FAR rules do not apply, OTAs are still subject to a raft of complicated rules, and guidelines on using them even for government officers is scant. Until recently, this led to procurement officers tending to be reluctant to use them.

They're also limited to purchases under set thresholds, which differ from agency to agency. The military services, for example, each have the authority to execute OTAs up to $500 million. You can see a breakdown of limitations by agency at aida.mitre.org/ota/.[51] But there are no limits on the number of OTAs an agency or department can enter, or the cumulative amount they can spend that way.

In 2019, the Department of Defense alone was expected to spend over $7 billion using OTAs, according to Bloomberg Government.[52] Plus, the government uses OTAs almost exclusively for research and development and prototyping.

According to Defense News, in recent years, OTA spending had increased while small business innovation research contracts have decreased to the point where OTAs account for "10 percent of the Defense Department's research, development, test and evaluation spending."[53]

As the GovWin article "Other Transaction Authority (OTA) Trends, Points of Interest, and Entry Points" explains, OTAs can result from BAAs, from agency announcements on federal procurement websites, from the Defense Innovation Unit

---

51   Aida.mitre.org, 2020.
52   Cornillie, 2019.
53   Mehta, 2020.

(DIU) using Commercial Solution Opening (CSO) procedures, through partnership intermediary agreements with the various 'WERX' organizations, through multi-year open solicitations for prototypes, SBIRs and STTRs, through middle-tier acquisitions (aka Rapid Prototyping/Rapid Fielding), or through consortia and consortium management funds, in which smaller businesses work together or through one central administrator who acts as an intermediary to the government.[54]

Use of OTAs has increased in recent years as procurement officers become more familiar with them. The emphasis is to bring technology into the government, and to enable smaller non-traditional contractors to take part without the administrative burden of more structured contracts and grants programs.

While OTAs may be unsuitable for many, they're highly advantageous for the people they're intended to target: small companies focused on research, development, and early-stage tech innovation.

DING, DING, DING! Houston, we have a winner.

There is also The Defense Commercial Solutions Opening (CSO) Pilot Program, which allows the Department of Defense to fund basic and applied research, to acquire components for operational systems development, to obtain innovative solutions to close capability gaps, or make technological advances. While these ARE subject to FAR regulations, they are designed to make it easier for the government

---

54   Mihalisko, 2018.

to buy from small, innovative businesses. For a complete visual breakdown of federal acquisitions options and strategies, see the Defense Acquisition University's Contracting Cone at aaf.dau.edu/aaf/contracting-cone/.[55]

Those are some exceptionally large numbers. By the end of this book, hopefully you will see how you can be able to get some small piece of this.

Soon, you will enter **The Strategy Zone**, and start thinking about how your business might fit into the **Federal Procurement Arena**. But first, let me introduce you to **The Inside Track Framework.**

---

55   Aaf.dau.edu, 2020.

2

THE INSIDE TRACK FRAMEWORK

Now that we've looked at the **Federal Procurement Arena** and established the massive opportunity it represents for businesses, innovators, and entrepreneurs, the question is: how do you even begin to take advantage of that?

When most businesses start working with the federal government, they initially feel lost. They've signed up to play on the team, but then they realize they're just a substitute. Like backup runners in a relay team, they're listed on the schedule, but they won't get a chance to run in the race unless the more established players are unable to perform.

Sometimes it takes a couple of years for a business to find a formula that works for them. Sometimes it never happens, and they're permanently sidelined—technically eligible to play, but just not up to scratch.

My **Inside Track Framework** is designed to make sure that doesn't happen to you. It does that by breaking down the **Federal Procurement Arena** into **Six Zones of Innovation Excellence**—six areas of focus that make the difference between a so-so competitor and one that wins federal innovation dollars regularly. We also teach you **Six Skills for Winning** that you need to develop and practice to shine in the **Federal Procurement Arena**, and introduce our **Inside Track Tools**, designed to help you compete effectively.

First, let's look at the **Six Zones of Innovation Excellence**.

SIX ZONES OF INNOVATION EXCELLENCE

We talk about zones rather than steps because you won't be working through them one by one. You won't complete one zone before moving on to the next; life is not that tidy.

You may find you're working in multiple zones simultaneously. You may circle back to zones several times while working on others, and so on. But if you try to jump straight to the later zones without tackling the earlier ones first, you're setting yourself up to fail.

We will be covering each of these zones in more detail in their own chapters, but it will help to have a clear overview of the entire program before you begin.

 **THE STRATEGY ZONE**

The Strategy Zone is where you draw up your ideas and create your personalized route to winning your first (or next) government contract: your **Federal Business Game Plan**.

If you don't know what you want to achieve, you're unlikely to achieve anything of value. A goal alone is not enough. A goal that isn't broken down into action steps and milestones remains a pipe dream.

Before you leap into competition, you need a game plan. You need to know, at a high level, what you need to put in place to achieve your goals, in what order things need to happen, and the major obstacles you are likely to face.

The good news is, you've already started thinking about your game plan in **The Federal Procurement Arena**. In **The Strategy Zone**, you will nail it.

 **THE TEAMING ZONE**

The **Teaming Zone** will ensure you have all the right players on your squad to complete your **Federal Business Game Plan**. I see a lot of lone-star-syndrome contractors in the innovation and tech sectors. That's where we find a phenomenal molecular biologist or physicist with a PhD, but who has poor interpersonal, organizational, and business skills. The problem is, they think their brilliance in their specialties translates into the ability to do all the other things that need to be done to deliver a government contract or run a business.

That's like a runner refusing to listen to or even hire a coach or trainer, or to be part of an athletics club team, because they think they know it all and want all the glory for themselves. How many gold medalists, in any discipline, do you know who got to the top of their game without any help from anyone? It just doesn't happen.

In the same way, you're highly unlikely to land any kind of government grant or contract without having to build a team around you. The **Federal Procurement Arena** is quite distinct. You might respond to a solicitation about molecular biology, but there will be nuances in the requirement. These requirements might mean that you also need other types of expertise to deliver and build a comprehensive solution. There may be other considerations, such as cost versus performance. It's not just about having the knowledge about how the "science" works, you also need to make it into a functional solution for the specific environment the government is operating in. Further, you also need to have a conduit for the government to reach you. This constitutes the contracting/business function, which often requires a different skill set.

You also need to be able to augment your staff and be able to bring in specialists to help you with specific technical aspects, or to help with writing your pitches, or delivering milestones to a schedule. It's not always the smartest person in the room who is the best suited to everything. The most successful people in the space are the ones who do the best job, not only of building their immediate team, but of building the entire ecosystem of people they can tap into.

The **Teaming Zone** will help you identify the players you need on your **Team Roster**, so you can start networking early.

 **THE INTELLIGENCE ZONE**

In **The Intelligence Zone**, we'll be looking at business intelligence, and the importance of having a systematic approach to business capture.

We're not talking here about your core business that's particular to your company. It is understood that you need to ensure you're the best at what you do, know your unique value proposition, and fill any knowledge or capability gaps in your team.

What we're talking about here are the connections and relationships you need to cultivate, and the "interpersonal muscles" you need to build. We'll also focus on the communications network you need to tap into to strengthen your position within the **Federal Procurement Arena**.

While creating a **Business Strength Training System** may sound daunting, we're really talking about building your network, drawing on the ecosystem you started to build in **The Teaming Zone**, and having conversations where you listen to your buyer's problems and work out how you can help solve them. It's about being close enough so when they talk about their frustrations, you're available to help them think through an issue and codify the solution.

For brilliant scientists and problem solvers, this can come as somewhat of a shock. If you're the type who thinks, "Why

didn't they just tell me what they want, and I'll solve it?",
you'll be left wondering why they picked someone else. The
realization that you must talk to people, sometimes for two
years or more, to land the contract and get paid, can be har-
rowing. That's why you need a team in place to do all that
"people" stuff for you.

When I was working with a DoD program under the
office of small business programs, we had access to a
bunch of business procurement experts, which was great.
What wasn't so great was that those experts didn't have much
experience on the federal side, and so a lot of what they were
teaching didn't apply. Nevertheless, some of the core principles they espouse hold true in the **Federal Procurement
Arena**; it's just how you apply them that varies. You need a
process for capturing business, and that need exists whether
you're servicing the federal government, commercial businesses, or consumers.

The Intelligence Zone will ensure you have the information
coming in and the interpersonal skills on your team to be the
most valuable player (MVP), otherwise known as achieving
trusted advisor status in the government contracting world.

THE TECHNOLOGY ZONE

In **The Technology Zone**, we're talking about innovation. You must remember you're always in competition with the entire market. You need a system and process
to ensure you are current, innovative, and future-focused.
You need to stay, if not ahead of the game, at least in touch
with the game—so you don't end up trying to sell buggy

whips when everyone's in flying cars. But you also need to ensure there's a need for your solution, and that you're not trying to sell spaceships to cavemen. You need to find the **Goldilocks Innovation Area.**

At one end of the scale, we have "too old" innovation. Don't get me wrong, when it comes to federal government supply, there's a place for same old, same old. I'm not sure how much innovation I want with my toilet rolls or tissue paper supplies, and the government buys those. When we're talking about existing, everyday products or commodities, though, the government already has contracts with major suppliers at rock-bottom prices. They're just going to keep renewing those and driving the price down. Unless the supplier goes out of business, or unless you find a way to disrupt the supply chain with a radically new business model, there isn't much of an opening.

At the other end of the scale, we often see brilliant inventors with pointless inventions. They get so wrapped up with what they're doing, and what they're trying to make, that they fail to keep track of what's going on around them. They fail to check if there's a problem that needs their solution before they dive down the rabbit hole. They're so enthusiastic about their idea, they just assume everyone will want it. The federal government does not buy innovation for innovation's sake; they buy innovative solutions to intractable problems.

The sweet spot of new procurement is in solving intractable problems. When the government procurement community opens its doors to new business, it's usually for innovative solutions. There are sections of the government that don't have the in-house capability to have a budget for highly specialized technical solutions, scientists, and engineers. But they do have the advantage of being able to go out into the marketplace and hire the latest and greatest through procurement. The government may not have the ability or need to hire a scientist on a long-term employment basis. But if they have a need to know or to try out the latest solutions in an area, they can contract in, or give a grant to work on something. If, a year down the line, a newer, better solution becomes available, they can terminate for convenience and go after that solution instead.

In **The Technology Zone**, you will make sure you're creating the technology the government wants, needs, and has a way to buy, so you don't disappear down the rabbit hole.

 **THE PITCHING ZONE**

It may seem strange that **The Pitching Zone** is the fifth of our **Six Zones of Excellence**. But federal procurement is a complex, lengthy process. The federal sales cycle is typically eighteen months to two years. By the time a requirement is posted, it's more than half-met. Hopefully, you'll understand why you need to focus on the other zones first. When you get to this zone, and you're starting to submit proposals, you need to understand the **Federal Procurement Arena** extensively. You need to know how to pitch and price your products and services. You need a **Pitch Perfection Program**.

I have seen people submit proposals for the best technical solution to a problem but with no regard for the budget. I remember being part of a test with the Ministry of

Defense in the UK for a radar solution. The product met and exceeded requirements, but it cost over 300 percent of the allocated budget. We didn't end up procuring the solution, even though it was the best-performing, because they priced themselves out of the market. Even though the detection was much better, it was simply too expensive.

There may be times when a solution costs more than expected, and the government might have to "find money." To do that, they may need to borrow it from another program or cut back elsewhere because the agency's budget has already been set based on current and projected bills two years in advance. However, that's mostly for one-off solutions. If a solution must scale, to outfit the military for example, that's not going to be feasible. There may occasionally be room in a budget to stretch to more expensive prototypes or one-off solutions, where you are the only one possible supplier. But even then, you can't write your own checks.

Yes, the federal government has a trillion-dollar budget.

No, they can't give it all to you.

In the above example, the second-best performing solution came in under-budget and was awarded the contract. The best technical solution lost out on a contract because they weren't taking into consideration the reality of the situation. They weren't listening to what we were saying with respect to our problem, required solution, and budgetary constraints.

While pitching and practicalities aren't all about budget—you must get the technicalities right first—there's no denying that pricing is one of the hardest parts new contractors struggle to get right. Fortunately, **The Pitching Zone** will ensure that **Your Pitch Perfection Program** covers all the bases so you don't waste time and money entering proposals that can never win. It will also teach you how to listen to your audience and ensure your pitch solves their problems, based on the intelligence you gathered in **The Intelligence Zone**.

 THE PERFORMANCE ZONE

Our final Zone of Innovation Excellence, **The Performance Zone**, is all about what to do AFTER you land a contract. Program management is vitally important to the federal government, and that's why you need a **Program Management Practice**.

Let's say you win an award. You do everything right. You're on the customer's site, creating the products, delivering the service. That's where a lot of companies get sloppy. That baffles me.

The government has entrusted you with a contract; they're trusting you to manage that contract and to help them serve and protect the nation. They want you to do well. They want you to give progress reports, deliverables, regular updates. I have seen a lot of companies struggle with this. Failing to deliver is like practicing hard, waking up early doing your morning runs, weightlifting, and then giving a half-butt effort at the big dance.

Think about it: you spent two years building relationships, listening to problems, and devising solutions. You put so much time and effort into pitching your business, and had people lobbying on your behalf. You have a four-year contract. It's your tryout. Don't you want to land the part, and become part of the government supply squad? Don't you want to build your innovative technology and land a contract to sell massive quantities of that technology to the government?

Even if you picked up this book because you had a "Lucky Strike" and landed your first government contract or grant with no strategy, didn't build your team, had no business capture plan, no long-term vision to build a government contracting career or business, and priced using a dartboard, your first contract will go a long way in determining whether you land a second.

That's what **The Performance Zone** is all about; ensuring you land the second contract and stay off the benches.

If the **Six Zones of Innovation Excellence** give you the disciplines and structures to strategize your **Federal Business Game Plan**, the **Six Skills for Winning** give you the skills to execute it. Let's look at those now.

SIX SKILLS FOR WINNING

Besides the **Six Zones of Innovation Excellence**, **The Inside Track Framework** consists of **Six Skills for Winning**. These equate roughly to the Six Zones, but they are not an exact match. We present the Skills and Zones in sequence, but as you will see, it's not a one-skill-one-zone process.

The **Strategy Zone** is all about having a plan and **Playing the Game**, is the most essential skill in formulating your plan, but you will also need it in the other zones, especially **The Pitching Zone**.

You will learn skills **Planning Your Attack** and **Building Your Team** before you enter **The Teaming Zone**, and you will have learned all **Six Skills for Winning** before you enter The **Pitching Zone** and **The Performance Zone**.

This makes perfect sense when you consider you wouldn't enter a competition arena without practicing first. At the same time, we don't want to learn all **Six Skills for Winning** before we enter the first zone, or you'll risk practicing forever and never actually stepping into the ring to compete.

So, let's look at the **Six Skills for Winning.**

 **PLAYING THE GAME**

Just as you wouldn't head out onto the race track dressed for a game of football, you need to make sure your business is kitted out for **The Federal Contracting Track**, **The Field of Grants**, or the **"Other Transactions" Sidetrack** before you step into **The Federal Procurement Arena**. By ensuring you have a sound understanding of the rules of the game, you give yourself the best chance to compete.

Playing the Game will give you the practical tools and resources you need to get registered and comply with the Federal Acquisitions Regulations.

PLANNING YOUR ATTACK

In **Planning Your Attack**, we look at WHAT you set as your targets in **The Strategy Zone** and give you the practical tools and the set-play routes to HOW you're going to achieve that. You'll look at the tactics other businesses have used and consider whether any of them apply to you. You will learn about the **Procurement Leagues** and **Open Playing Fields** and identify any "Set Asides" or **"Power-Ups"** you can take advantage of to increase your chances of winning a federal contract. Then you will complete your **Federal Business Game Plan**.

 BUILDING YOUR TEAM

Building Your Team is all about dealing with people. Where **The Teaming Zone** will show you WHO you need to have on your team, **Building Your Team** will give you the skills you need to make alliances with other businesses within the **Federal Procurement Arena**. You will learn about **Buyers on the Inside Track**, **Trackside Officials**, and the external and internal **Relay Teams** for which you need to create **Team Rosters**. You'll start making connections, building relationships, and carving your niche, as well as start to really develop your team identity and reputation.

 LISTENING FOR OPPORTUNITIES

With a clear idea of who your customers are, you'll start listening for buyer signals. These will help you learn to read the state of play and anticipate future developments.

You'll learn to meet buyers on their home ground and speak their language.

Where **The Intelligence Zone** will tell you WHERE to look for information, **Listening for Opportunities** will give you the questions to ask, the "codes" to government procurement language, and practical tips for extracting information from data.

PLAYING TO WIN

Having learned to fit in, we'll start looking at how you stand out, stay future-focused, and develop innovative solutions, in order to ensure you stay relevant and ahead of the game.

Where **The Pitching Zone** teaches you the mechanics of completing a pitch that meets requirements and technical specs, **Playing to Win** shows you HOW to seal the deal.

Here you'll focus on distinguishing yourself from the pack and avoiding the trap of complacency. You'll start to develop your **Proposal Set Pieces** and **Win Themes**—the words, phrases, and themes you will use throughout your business capture activities to cement your unique value proposition in the buyer's mind.

DELIVERING VALUE

In **Delivering Value**, we'll look at how you measure performance, and bake delivering value into your **Federal Business Game Plan**. That way, you can ensure that once you get your big break, you don't drop the ball in front of the selector.

Instead, you will build a strong past performance record that powers your future efforts.

 ## THE INSIDE TRACK TOOLS

As you work through each of the **Six Zones for Excellence** and the **Six Skills for Winning**, you will be introduced to several **Inside Track Tools**. These tools, when combined, will create your **Federal Contracting Playbook**.

 ### FEDERAL BUSINESS GAME PLAN

This is your eye-in-the-sky overview of your business goals and activities. It's the one-page summary of your strategy and how you plan to achieve your goals.

 ### TEAM ROSTER

Your **Team Roster** will map out your team players internally and your external alliances onto a series of **Relay Teams**. It will show your major clients, competitors and collaborators, and highlight areas where you need to build connections.

 ### BUSINESS STRENGTH TRAINING SYSTEM

Your **Business Strength Training System** will be your Operations Manual for Business Capture activities, or sales and marketing in non–Federal Procurement Arena language. This is where you'll keep track of all the diverse sources of information and manage your client relationships. You will learn Welcoming Warm-Ups, Relationship Reps, Questioning Sets, and Intelligence Scoops, along with TAFE Analysis.

GOLDILOCKS INNOVATION AREA

Your **Goldilocks Innovation Area** will highlight the problems you're working to solve, the Technology Readiness Levels you're working at and toward, and map those levels to potential sources of funding or clients. Its purpose is to keep you focused on where you can achieve the most good.

 PITCH PERFECTION PROGRAM

Your **Pitch Perfection Program** consists of checklists and instructions to ensure your pitches are both technically correct and winnable. It will walk you through the steps from making a Request for Proposal to entering your (hopefully) winning bid.

 PROPOSAL SET-PIECES

Your **Proposal Set-Pieces** are the words and phrases you will use in your proposals and business capture activities to ensure you stay on brand and embed your preferred language in both your business culture and your communications with federal clients and representatives.

 PROGRAM MANAGEMENT PRACTICE

Your **Program Management Practice** will show you what to measure and report after you win the contract to ensure you over-deliver and garner great past-performance feedback from your federal clients.

POWER-UPS

Power-Ups are "Set-Asides" and other regulatory conditions that might favor your business if you meet certain requirements. Throughout the book we will highlight these Power-Ups and tell you how to make use of them if they apply to you.

 POWER PLAYS

POWER PLAYs are things you can do to make your efforts more effective, get ahead of the competition, or boost your results in some way. You will find these throughout the book. They're easy to spot because they're set apart in boxes like this:

 **POWER PLAY:** *Use as many POWER PLAYs as you can for maximum effect.*

Just as a great coach gives you the knowledge, the skills, and the tools to compete in your discipline, **The Inside Track Framework** is designed to give you the knowledge (**The Six Zones of Innovation Excellence**), the Skills (**The Six Skills for Winning**), and the Tools (**The Inside Track Tools**) to take your business from where you are now to landing and delivering your first or next government contract in **The Federal Procurement Arena**.

I've done my best to make it entertaining and to keep it light, and even used elements of game theory to create a system that walks you through a dense, dry subject with at least a modicum of fun.

It comes with just one warning: reading this book alone will not land you a government contract. You MUST DO THE WORK along the way.

I really hope you will put it to use because I know from experience that the information here can make a dramatic difference to your federal contracting business.

With that in mind, it's time to start learning **Playing the Game**.

3

PLAYING THE GAME

———

Are you excited to start building your **Skills for Winning?** Good. We're going to start with the basics in **Playing the Game**. Here, we're going to cover:

1. Understanding the Federal Procurement Arena
2. Getting Registered to be Eligible
3. Finding Your Way Around the System Online
4. Starting Your Potential Buyers List
5. Understanding the Rules of Engagement

Knowing these three things before you enter **The Strategy Zone** will ensure you don't do anything to jeopardize your fledgling federal contracting career before it gets off the ground. Learning these topics will also help you make the most of your time and effort from the outset. Everything you do will be focused on honing your **Federal Business Game Plan** into a winning one.

 UNDERSTANDING THE FEDERAL PROCUREMENT ARENA

To develop a winning **Federal Business Game Plan**, you must first understand the **Federal Procurement Arena**, and the rules that apply to it. Many of you may not have experience dealing with federal buyers, though you may have plenty of experience working in commercial, academic, or industrial fields. These different spaces require different strategies, so you need to know the federal space inside and out.

The first thing you need to understand about the **Federal Procurement Arena** is that it's a highly regulated, scrutinized, and charged space. It's lucrative, and because there's a significant amount of money up for grabs, there are some big players chasing that prize. But because it's also money spent in the public interest, there are myriad rules that must be followed to ensure there's no corruption. A lot of spectators with vested interests keep an eye on proceedings and raise red flags if they detect even a hint of impropriety. At first glance, it can seem like the **Major League** teams—the prime contractors who deal with multi-billion-dollar contracts and coordinate large programs filled by smaller businesses—have the game sewn up so tightly that there's no opening for a new player. But the game is designed to allow players of all shapes and sizes to participate; you just need to learn the rules and know how to follow them.

GETTING REGISTERED TO BE ELIGIBLE

The General Services Administration (GSA) website, somewhat blithely, assures you all you have to do to start supplying the US government is find a suitable contract, set up your company to be eligible to bid, and tender an offer.[56] To do those things you're going to need to prepare in several ways:

- Head over to the Dun and Bradstreet Request Service at fedgov.dnb.com/webform/ to request your free DUNS number.
- Make sure you have your business registration details to hand, including your Individual Tax Identification Number (ITIN) or Employer Identification Number (IEN).
- Find Standard Identification Codes (SIC) that apply to your business at osha.gov/pls/imis/sicsearch.html.
- Check support.outreachsystems.com/resources/tables/pscs/ for Federal Supply Codes and Product Service Codes that may apply to your business.
- Go to sam.gov/SAM/ and register in SAMS.

POWER PLAY: *Go to sba.gov/federal-contracting/ contracting-assistance-programs/ and see if you qualify for any of the current Contracting Assistance Programs. At the time of writing this book, these are Women-owned, Service-Disabled-Veteran-Owned, small disadvantaged businesses, and HUB Zones—economically underperforming locations. You want to enter as much information as you can in your SAMS account. It's easy to forget SAMS is not just a resource for vendors looking for contracts; it's also a database of suppliers for buyers in search of that elusive product or service. You want to make it easier for government representatives to find you!*

---

56 General Services Administration, 2019.

FINDING YOUR WAY AROUND THE SYSTEM ONLINE

At the time of writing, the FedBizOps website (fbo.gov) has recently been transferred to beta.sam.gov, designed to be a single central hub site for managing federal awards. The transfer began in November 2019 and was completed in early 2020. However, it's not the website address that matters; it's your understanding of what the website represents that matters.

Far too many would-be contractors imagine the SAMS site—the place where federal business opportunities are announced—to be the starting gate. They imagine it's where the government agency announces its needs to a level playing field of eager bidders. A Request for Proposal (RFP) invitation to tender on SAMS is more like the start of the last leg in a relay race. The government agency probably put it out with a solution in mind.

If you look at Requests For Information (RFIs) or Sources Sought announcements, there's a chance the person putting out the request doesn't really know what the solution would be. In that case, you may be able to be part of the process of shaping the RFP. You should use SAMS as part of your original research to identify potential buyers, and at the end of the process to enter your proposals, but there's a lot of invisible work that goes on between those two stages.

STARTING YOUR POTENTIAL BUYERS LIST

The first thing you're going to do is start building a list of potential government buyers. If you already have leads and contacts, you might be tempted to skip this step. I would urge you to do it anyway because you want to get a feel for the whole **Federal Procurement Arena** rather than focus on a single opportunity, in case that opportunity falls through.

This step is even more important when you are dealing with early-stage technology and innovation. Remember, the government generally conducts its market research by looking at known products and solutions. As an innovator, you need to be vigilant about creating a list of potential buyers and getting your solution(s) in front of them. Acquisitions professionals will NOT plan or write a solicitation for a solution of which they are unaware. How could they? It just doesn't work like that. So, this step is CRUCIAL for innovators.

1. Start broad and work toward being more specific.
2. Go to https://beta.sam.gov/ and familiarize yourself with the search interface.
3. Change the search criteria from "All award data" to "Contract Opportunities" and type "BAA" into the search bar.
4. Scan the Broad Agency Announcements for areas of interest where your solution may apply or where you may be able to innovate. For example, in 2020, some of the Army Research Laboratory's BAAs included "Highly Stable High Fidelity Trapped Ion Systems," and "Development of Quantum Algorithms."[57] On the other hand, the Navy's BAA sought Long Range Research on topics including high-frequency radar, advanced computational electromagnetics, and materials performance, processing, and modelling, among others.[58]

---

57 U.S. Army Combat Capabilities Development Command, 2020.
58 U.S. Navy Office of Naval Research, 2020.

The important thing is, at this point, these government entities likely haven't decided on a solution; they're looking for good ideas. So, you should be monitoring BAAs constantly because they really are the starting gun. A lot of the time, there will be twelve or fifteen different areas that tell you the agency has a gap and is looking for potential solutions. It will also set out the eligibility requirements, the procedures to follow, and the regulations and budgetary codes that apply. Often you can respond to a BAA with a white paper. If your paper has merit, you will be invited to submit a full proposal, and if you get the proposal right, the agency can do a small procurement to fund your idea. From there, you may be able to progress to traditional acquisitions and set out a full-scale contract to pursue your solution.

5. Clear the filters again, and then scroll down, and switch to "Advanced" under Federal Organizations. Enter the first agency on your list and browse their current entries. Repeat the process for every agency on your list.

6. Clear the search filters and try a few searches using keywords that relate to your business. Make a list of the agencies and departments putting out requests in your area.

You now have the beginnings of your potential buyers list: a list of agencies with Broad Area Announcements, Open Contracts, Requests for Information, etc., that you might be able to bid on. This list includes Federal Procurement Agencies with both the budget and need for your solution, or a solution you might be able to devise.

POWER PLAY: Go to each agency's website and search for their current BAA there. *Read the BAAs and open requests and start to get a feel for how that agency frames requests, what their procedures and timelines are, and what they are likely to be looking for. You're not ready to jump in the ring yet; you're just watching the game to see how it's played.*

Now that you have your list of potential buyers, you might be tempted to rush into approaching them. Don't. You need to understand a few things about the Rules of Engagement first.

UNDERSTANDING THE RULES OF ENGAGEMENT

Marketing to the government is quite different from marketing to commercial customers; you can't wine, dine, and entertain them. Since they are not allowed to accept gifts outside very stringent guidelines, if you try to give them anything, you're putting both their career and your federal contracting business in jeopardy. They'll simply avoid you.

If you go to lunch, it should be a place where your government contact can pay. Remember that government salaries tend to be lower than those in the private sector, so avoid meeting at overly expensive venues. If you pay for a meal, government employees will normally offer to pay for their portion of the food. You should not refuse, and should record the payment. When they visit you at your facility and you offer them food, supply a donation jar so they can contribute a symbolic amount of money—otherwise they might have to do a considerable amount of paperwork.

If you offer one government employee a discount, you must give the same discount to other government employees as well. You can offer free training to government personnel if it is a "widely attended gathering."[59]

Interacting with the government and building customer relationships is different from relationship management in other environments. Remember government employees cannot take gifts, and that even the appearance of impropriety will damage their careers.

Now that you are set up to bid for contracts on the SAMS system, have a list of target agencies, and understand the basic Rules of Engagement, you're ready to enter **The Strategy Zone**.

---

59   National Institutes of Health, 2017.

4

THE STRATEGY ZONE

In **The Strategy Zone**, you're going to start outlining your **Federal Business Game Plan**. You'll answer a few questions and use the answers to work out where you fit in the **Federal Procurement Arena** and what you want to achieve. First, you'll answer a few questions honestly about why you want to get into federal contracting and what you hope to achieve. Then you'll think about the sort of person you are and the work you're best suited to, before focusing on the types of opportunities that may be open to you.

First, let's talk about why you want to serve the government in the **Federal Procurement Arena**.

 YOUR GOVERNMENT SERVICE OBJECTIVE

As the Cheshire Cat famously says, "If you don't know where you want to go, then it doesn't matter which path you take."[60]

---

60 Carroll, 1865.

Without a clear idea of what you're trying to accomplish, your chances of landing a government contract or attracting funding are minuscule. You need to be clear from the outset about what you want to achieve.

What do you want to achieve as a government contractor long-term? Is it all about you and your business, or are you interested in having a wider impact?

IN IT FOR THE MONEY

I worked for a company that provided support services to the federal government. Essentially, it provided acquisitions, technical, and operations personnel, and supplied the people who understood the tech space, innovation, and federal acquisitions. The government went from needing a few people for these purposes to needing to stand up an entire organization overnight. As a result, the business became a hundred-million-dollar company overnight with the stroke of a pen on a contract.

Many government contractor businesses turn over more than $1 million per annum.[61] A 2012 American Express Open report found:

Although women and minority contractors take different routes to achieve procurement success, both are more likely to own larger firms versus their non-contracting peers: 42% of women and 41% of minority business owners have business revenues in excess of $1 million, coming in just under the

---

61   Overfelt, 2014.

average among all small business contractors (47%). This far exceeds the 5% of all small businesses that have achieved that level of business success [according to U.S. Census Bureau's 2007 Survey of Business Owners].[62]

As Mike Armour of Startups After 50 explains:

According to IRS records, about 23 million sole proprietorships file income tax returns each year. Roughly five percent of these businesses are structured as single-member limited liability companies. The rest are purely sole proprietorships. They have no encompassing legal structure to limit their liability.

In this universe of 23 million businesses, fewer than 11% have annual receipts of $100,000 or more. And that's gross revenue, not net income. For most sole proprietors, therefore, owning a business is hardly a fast track to fabulous wealth.[63]

I'm not saying winning a federal contract is going to make you rich. But the statistics suggest it's not going to hurt your chances of making a good living. And there's no shame in wanting to get something out of the deal yourself.

 STIMULATE THE ECONOMY

Winning a federal contract doesn't just impact the business owner, or even just a single business. If you win a federal contract, yes, money's going to flow into your company. You're

---

62   American Express Open, 2012.

63   Armour, 2009.

going to do well. But this has a larger impact on the community in three separate ways:

- First, where one business wins a federal contract, others in the locality often follow suit when they realize how lucrative it can be. As more companies get involved, more entrepreneurs get involved, more moms and dads get involved, and more new companies are formed. Money flows into the community, as the contractors spend and subcontract work.
- Second, as the businesses win grants and contracts, they expand and need more labor. Jobs are saved, created, or expanded, and more people receive better wages.
- Finally, as federal contracting businesses grow, their revenues and profits go up. Other businesses in the area must compete and standards rise across the board. The local economy becomes more competitive.

Virginia is a prime example of a local economy stimulated by federal contracting. Virginia is located next to the federal government in Washington DC, and Northern Virginia has done exceptionally well in figuring out how to win federal contracts and working within the federal procurement landscape. Virginia gets the largest amount of federal contracting dollars of all the states. Perhaps this is not surprising for the state the houses the Pentagon, and where 12 percent of the state economy comes from the Department of Defense. However, as Scott Cohn reporting on CNBC's Top States for Business report 2019 explains,

Virginia's success involves much more than the military. The state offers the best workforce in the country, reveals our 2019

study. Nearly 38% of adults have a bachelor's degree or higher, according to the U.S. Census Bureau, placing Virginia in the top 10 for educational attainment. And per the U.S. Bureau of Labor Statistics, Virginia has the nation's fourth highest concentration of crucial science, technology, engineering and math (STEM) employees, making up 9% of the workforce in 2018. All of this in a right-to-work state with a minimal union presence — something companies prize.[64]

Virginia's population is small, yet several Northern Virginia counties are the richest counties in the nation. There's a lesson to learn there.

 HELP SOLVE INTRACTABLE PROBLEMS

We talked in **The Federal Procurement Arena** about some of the innovation and technology government research has funded over the years. Is your biggest desire to be a part of that progress?

- What big problems can you help solve?
- Who are you helping?
- How will that benefit you?

Allow yourself to think big here for a moment. Imagine there's no limit.

---

64 Cohn, 2019.

 SET YOUR GOVERNMENT SERVICE OBJECTIVE

Fill in the blanks in Figure 5 before you move on.

I want to ....

for ....

and get .... while doing it.

Figure 5: Your Government Service Objective

Now that you know what your long-term objective is, let's think about the short term and the next step you can take toward that goal.

YOUR QUICK-WIN GOAL

Long-term goals and lofty ideals are fine, but they can be demotivating at times. That's because with a huge long-term goal, it takes big strides to see yourself moving closer to achieving it. The smaller steps sometimes don't feel as though they're moving the needle.

One effective way to overcome that is to take a leaf out of Terry Fox's book. During his Marathon of Hope run across

Canada in 1980, Fox ran 3,339 miles in 143 days with an artificial leg.

When asked, "When you're running, what do you think about?" he famously replied, "I only think about the next mile."[65]

Ask yourself:

- What's your "next mile?"
- What's the next major step you can take to move toward that?
- What can you do to earn a quick win?
  - Do you need to do some initial research?
  - Do you need to identify funding sources and potential buyers?
  - Do you need to set up your business to be eligible to supply the government?
  - Do you need to win your first government contract?
  - Do you need to pivot your existing product or service to better serve the government, or to win more clients?
  - Do you need to level up your game to win bigger contracts and increase your win rate?

Determining your goal will shape the way you approach seeking government funding and the route you choose.

 NAME YOUR QUICK-WIN GOAL

Before you move on, consider what one thing you can do in the next week, month, or quarter to get a quick win, and write it down in Figure 6.

---

65   MacIntyre, 2017.

I can ....

....

....

....

.... to get a quick win goal.

Figure 6: Your Quick Win Goal.

Now that you know what your quick win is, let's look at how you're going to move toward that win.

 YOUR INNOVATION DISCIPLINE

All innovators are not created equal. And thank heavens for that, because it takes a whole bunch of people to bring a bright idea to life.

Simon Hill, founder of the innovation management software company Wazoku, identified thirteen innovator archetypes.[66] I adapted my **Innovation Disciplines** from those archetypes and other sources to cover the most important roles in the government innovation game.

---

66 Hill, 2016.

As you will see in **The Teaming Zone**, depending on where you are in the game, you will need to assemble a team of players from different Innovation Disciplines to join your squad.

But first, you need to know what your **Innovation Discipline** is. If you are a visionary, you might be most suited to go after grants or organizations looking for ideas to solve complicated solutions. Visionaries are NOT always looking to turn their ideas into a big booming business, and many scientists fall into this category. Knowing that will help you determine the best way to approach the public sector and which organizations to approach.

As you read about the **Innovation Disciplines**, consider which most closely describes you.

 FACILITATOR

You make something possible. You develop or teach methods or processes or equip others with the necessary tools to create innovative ideas. You provide a critical sounding board to help keep solutions on track without stifling innovative thought.

 VISIONARY

You are a "big picture" thinker. You imagine how things could be and come up with imaginative solutions to intractable problems. You can pull inspiration from a range of sources and put them together in new ways, but you pass your ideas on to others to bring them to fruition.

RESEARCHER

You are a subject matter expert. You take a visionary idea and do the background work to bring depth and substance to it. You run the numbers, check facts, and spot trends and patterns. Where most people see only obstacles or flights of fancy, you see the outline of a solution that you can turn into a working model.

CREATOR

You love to take a theoretical idea and turn it into a physical reality. You are the natural practitioner of innovation. A tinkerer at heart, you will try multiple configurations until you get something to work.

DESTRUCTOR

You love to tweak, test, poke, and push something until it breaks so you can rebuild it better. You will never be happy with the current version of anything and are always looking for ways to improve.

REFINER

You like to take a working prototype and iron out the bugs. You don't want to tear the thing apart and start again; you want to perfect what's in front of you through small tweaks and changes. You want to get the solution into the hands of the end user and see how well it works.

CHAMPION

You may not be an innovator yourself, but you are passionate about innovation and progress. Unlike the Facilitator, who plays a supporting role and provides the environment for innovation to happen, you take the result out into the world to share it. You may be entrepreneurial or simply believe in a specific solution so strongly that you will put yourself on the line to get it out there.

CHOOSE YOUR INNOVATION DISCIPLINE

Which of the above best describes you? _____

This is your **Innovation Discipline**. That will help you understand where you best fit on a team. It will also help you distill the right federal opportunities. For example, if you are a Visionary, you may do well with opportunities at some of our engineering centers or laboratories. They are sometimes looking for solutions to problems they haven't been able to find solutions for in the existing commercial market.

Knowing your personal **Innovation Discipline** is only half the equation, though. You also need to know your **Technology Team Sport** so you can find opportunities that will suit your personality in your field of interest.

YOUR TECHNOLOGY TEAM SPORT

Knowing your **Technology Team Sport** from the outset will save you countless hours wasted trying to attract the wrong type of funding or trying to sell to the wrong type of government buyers. If you're playing baseball, you don't want to invite basketball and football talent scouts to come watch you play.

Before you start looking for government clients or customers, consider where your solution fits into the **Federal Procurement Arena** and how that affects your business. This is a three-part process; you need to understand the **Technology Position**, **Developmental Stage**, and **Business Model** that makes sense for your business.

First, let's consider the type of technology you're looking to create, develop, or implement. This will affect the way you engage with the government.

TECHNOLOGY POSITION

Your **Technology Position** is all about how your solution interacts with other solutions. Does it stand alone, does it support or enhance another complete solution, or is it inextricably interlinked with another product?

- **Enabling Technology**: Enabling technology cannot stand alone. It is a complementary part of a larger solution. It is typically applied to perform a function or work in combination with component technologies and to add value to the technology it supports. Examples of solutions that fall within this category include missile guidance protocols, data analysis algorithms, product training or manuals, or after-market consumables that extend or enhance the performance of existing machinery.
- **A Component Technology**: A component is part of a system that performs a specific purpose. The difference between an enabling and a component technology solution

is that a component solution is typically sold to the major supplier and bundled as part of the main solution, rather than being sold as an aftermarket extra. Examples of component technologies include microchips, electronic boards, and screens through to valves, gauges and sensors, and myriad other things. If there's a part that consistently fails in a design, there's an opportunity to improve on it.

- **An Integrated Technology**: An integrated technology solution is a product designed to perform a specific set of functions or satisfy a specific set of needs. It may need consumables, or fit into a larger system, but it is whole or complete as sold. Examples include laboratory equipment, weapons systems, CCTV equipment, and computers.

Knowing where your solution fits into the landscape is vital to identifying and approaching the right buyers. There's no point trying to sell your valve or sensor directly to the government if they only buy integrated solutions; you would need to sell to the manufacturer instead, or to a **Major League Player** (or a prime vendor) who the government relies on to handle supply logistics for a specific product line. On the other hand, if your enabling technology is an aftermarket addition, you may be able to sell directly.

 IDENTIFY YOUR TECHNOLOGY POSITION

My **Technology Position** Is _____

By knowing your technology position, you also know who your target end users and buyers are as a group. However, you also need to know how close you are to the market. You need to think about your product development stage.

 **DEVELOPMENT STAGE**

It's easy to think that if you don't have a mature, fully functional, tested product, you don't have customers. But when we're talking about early-stage innovation, you just have different customers. Your research, prototypes, data, etc. are your product at this point, not the technology you're developing. You can sell Intellectual Property (IP) rights to your technology for others to develop or patent your innovations and license the IP rights that way.

 **WESTINGHOUSE**

Westinghouse offers an excellent example of the use of Intellectual Property rights and patents to start a business, or to keep one afloat, along with a cautionary tale about engaging in patent wars.

George Westinghouse was an early pioneer of alternating current (AC) electricity. After inventing the air brake and using that to found the Westinghouse Electric Company in Pittsburgh in 1886, Westinghouse found himself the center of a smear campaign by Thomas Edison, champion of the then-prevalent Direct Current (DC) electrical system and founder of General Electric Company. As Funding Universe explains, between 1886 and 1896 both companies "spent small fortunes accumulating patents, with the result that neither company could market new products without fear of patent infringement litigation."[67]

---

67   Funding Universe, 2020.

Westinghouse was ousted from the company in 1910 after a stock crash made it impossible for the company to raise the $14 million necessary to pay its debts. The company went into receivership, and the receivers appointed a new board of directors, who pivoted the company into wireless communications and started accumulating patents in that area. In 1920, "Westinghouse and GE carved up the exclusive right to manufacture radio receivers between them, with RCA as the selling organization."[68] Rather than going out of business, Westinghouse became a broadcasting pioneer.

Westinghouse survived the Depression of the 1930s selling household appliances, and in 1941 pivoted into military service for the first time as a radar contractor. According to Funding Universe:

Westinghouse radar had provided a warning signal of the advance of Japanese planes on Pearl Harbor, but it was assumed that the planes were American. During the war years, Westinghouse grew at a frenetic pace and its defense business became so large that CEO A. W. Robertson hired banker Gwilym Price in 1943 just to handle financial negotiations on military contracts.[69]

Westinghouse has also spun off other companies through patent sales. These sales have helped Westinghouse stay focused and generated operating revenues while enabling other businesses like Wescam to get off to a flying start.

---

68 Ibid.
69 Ibid.

 **WESCAM**

In 1957, Westinghouse Canada Inc. engineers began developing a stabilized camera system for surveillance applications. In 1960, the completed product WESSCAM—Westinghouse Steered Stabilized Camera Mount—was delivered to the Canadian Defense Research Establishment.

In 1974, John "Nox" Leavitt, the lead engineer on the project, bought lab equipment and patents from Westinghouse and founded Istec Limited, Isolation Stabilization Technologies. WESCAM's website explains:

The company, in Hamilton, had 17 employees and generated approximately $1 million in revenue. It experienced substantial expansion through internal growth and strategic acquisitions. This brought complementary technologies, broad intellectual capability and increased market share to the company. In 1994 Istec changed its name to Wescam and in 1995 Wescam went Public on the Toronto Stock Exchange under the leadership of Mark Chamberlain, a well-known, and respected Hamilton businessman.[70]

Today, L3 Wescam supplies industry-leading, multi-spectral and multi-sensor imaging and targeting sensor systems. It has thousands of systems deployed to military, national security, and law enforcement customers in over eighty countries worldwide.

---

70 WESCAM, 2020.

Is your product or service ready to go now, or is it still in development?

- **Ideation stage:** You are simply interested in solving hard problems or looking for funding for a theoretical or applied research study that someone else can build on.
- **Early Development stage:** You need early R&D dollars or early-stage investment without giving up equity. You want to take your breadboard prototype to a working prototype.
- **Late Development Stage:** You are looking to develop your working prototype into a full-fledged solution, with government dollars that can be used for government-only purposes.
- **Mature:** Your product or service is mature and ready to go. You may be looking to adapt an existing product or service for one or multiple government purposes.

 IDENTIFY YOUR DEVELOPMENT STAGE

Which of the above most applies to you? _____

Also, consider whether you plan to take a single solution from beginning to end, or to specialize in a certain stage of technology development. Some companies specialize in data modelling or data analysis for innovators, and others in producing early or late stage prototypes. Still others take advantage of government funding throughout the entire process. That might look like funding for a white paper, followed by R&D funding for an initial prototype, then a small procurement for testing, then more RDT&E development, and finally larger procurements.

Once you know the **Technology Position** and **Development Stage** of your **Technology Team Sport**, you need to think about how you're going to make money from it.

 **BUSINESS MODEL**

Although your **Business Model** technically also includes operating procedures, goals, and mission objectives, at base, it's about how you raise money. While there are many varied business models, these break down into selling products (whether as a manufacturer, wholesale or retail), providing services (whether on a subscription, hourly or result-based basis) and a combination of the two (as in Software as a Service.)

You need to know whether you're planning to sell a product, a service, or a hybridized product/service.

- Are you going to deliver a physical product and have no further involvement in how it's used?
- Are you going to do something for the government and effectively sell them the outcome?
- Will you patent technology and license IP rights?
- Or will you be doing two or more of these things?

IDENTIFY YOUR BUSINESS MODEL

My business model is: _____

The combination of your **Technology Position, Development Stage**, and **Business Model** will give you your **Technology Team Sport**. Circle the word that best fits your **Technology Team Sport** from each list.

IDENTIFY YOUR TECHNOLOGY TEAM SPORT

Complete your **Technology Team Sport** in Figure 7 by selecting the appropriate item from each list and combing them.

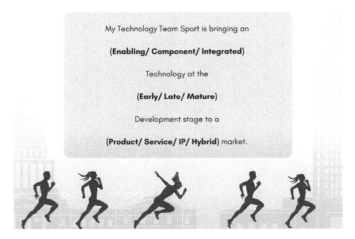

My Technology Team Sport is bringing an

(Enabling/ Component/ Integrated)

Technology at the

(Early/ Late/ Mature)

Development stage to a

(Product/ Service/ IP/ Hybrid) market.

Figure 7: Your Technology Team Sport.

Now that you know what you're going to do and who you're going to sell to at the broadest level, you need to think realistically about the opportunities open to you and how you're going to compete with the existing players in the arena. It's time to start **Planning Your Attack**.

5

PLANNING YOUR ATTACK

In **The Strategy Zone**, you looked at WHAT you hope to achieve in your Federal Contracting Business. In this chapter, we're going to focus on **Planning Your Attack** and think about HOW you're going to achieve that at the bird's eye level. By the end of this chapter, you will have completed your one-page **Federal Business Game Plan**, which will inform your decisions and actions throughout the rest of the book. First, you need to pick a Procurement League.

 PROCUREMENT LEAGUE

When we talk about **Procurement Leagues**, we're talking about who you will be competing against, and the size of contracts you will be competing for. Now, while I want to encourage you to go after federal funding because it's there, and because the government and the country needs to invest in the best, I don't want to paint a picture of easy money and riches for all.

To keep things simple, we're going to break Procurement Leagues down into three camps: **The Little Leagues, The Big Leagues,** and **The Major Leagues.** Let's consider each in turn.

 **THE LITTLE LEAGUES**

The Little Leagues are for you if you are still in the process of setting up your business, or if you're still trying to land your first government contract.

Little League activities might be covered by:
- General Services Administration (GSA) Micro Purchases Threshold (MPT), which is under $10,000 except for DoD, which is $5,000.[71]
- GSA Simplified Acquisition Threshold (SAT) currently set at $250,000.[72]
- Small Business Innovation Research (SBIR) and Small Business Technology Transfer (STTR) schemes, which "fund a diverse portfolio of startups and small businesses across technology areas and markets to stimulate technological innovation, meet Federal research and development (R&D) needs, and increase commercialization to transition R&D into impact."[73]
- Other Transaction Authority and credit card purchases.

Any US citizen or international company with a US-based company/entity can sell to the US government. We do buy from other entities in certain situations, but those are

---

71 Koses, 2018.
72 Ibid.
73 SBIR, 2020.

beyond the scope of this book. Almost anybody can sell to the federal government so long as they are registered and in good standing.

 You should have registered on SAMS.gov and be eligible to bid for contracts by now.

If not, go back to **Playing the Game**, and follow the instructions there.

Now that you're registered, let's talk numbers.

According to the census bureau, there are around 28 million businesses in the USA today. Of these, around 136,000 have registered to work with the federal government. If these figures are correct, then less than one percent of businesses in the US are eligible to work with the federal government.

That means less than one percent of potential players are even in **The Little Leagues**. You have an exceptionally good chance of winning a federal government contract just by doing the paperwork to make yourself eligible.

 **THE BIG LEAGUES**

Between **The Little Leagues** and **The Major Leagues** in baseball, there used to be the Big 8 and leagues for fifteen to eighteen-year-olds. Although **The Big Leagues** were decommissioned in 2016, when it comes to Federal Procurement Leagues, they're alive and well.

For our purposes, **The Big Leagues** are for you if you already have one government contract and you're looking to find additional contracts. Often, these contracts will be awarded through Small Business categories such as the North American Industry Classification System (NAICS) $30M Small Business Size Standard and the new Small Business Runway Extension Act of 2018, which revised how Small Business status is calculated, and extended the annual averaging from three to five years.

As well as being eligible, you need a product or service that the government wants, needs, can buy, and has a mechanism through which to buy. Let's look at each of those in turn, briefly.

- **Interest:** Shocking news for *Field of Dreams* fans; if you build it, they will NOT come UNLESS what you build is what they want. If the government has no interest in buying whatever you're trying to sell, you're not going to make a sale.
- **Identified Need:** If the government has an identified need, they will also have a budget allocated to buy your product or service somewhere. In the commercial sector, you can take funds from one budget area and buy something for another budget area. In the federal government, the money must be assigned to the right bucket to buy the right kind of things. If the budget exists, the need exists.
- **Budget:** It's worth bearing in mind, however, that sometimes government agencies will have a need or a desire to purchase something, BUT the budget hasn't yet been allocated due to the time lag between submitting and approving budgets. Sometimes things change and needs arise that budgets haven't accounted for. So, sometimes

innovators must be creative and look at funding from a different angle. But don't worry, we'll cover that in **The Technology Zone.**

- **Buying Authority**: The person you're targeting needs to be the one with the authority to buy. Within the federal government, specific offices and specific people have the authority to buy on behalf of the government. You need to make sure you're dealing with somebody who has that authority, otherwise your sale will fall through.

- **Procurement Vehicle**: Finally, the contract vehicle or GSA Multiple Award Schedules to buy whatever you're trying to sell must exist. The government cannot just go out and buy things from you. Even if your buyer can use a credit card or Other Transaction Authority, they have rules and procedures to follow. That's why you need to be registered and eligible first, and then track down the best contract opportunity for your business.

Even if your product or service falls under credit card and OTA limits, you don't want to limit your federal customer base to only those agencies or departments who have those buying options and are comfortable with them by failing to register.

You may also go directly to **The Big Leagues** if you're bidding on a single-vendor contract over the simple procurement thresholds of your target department or agency (usually around $10,000 for a single purchase). That means you must submit a complete proposal and the buyer can't use a credit card to make a purchase from you.

 **THE MAJOR LEAGUES**

If you're reading this book, you're not likely to be bidding for contracts in **The Major Leagues** right away. In **The Major Leagues**, there will be no Small Business Set-Asides. You'll be competing outside the NAICS $30M Size Standard, with no allowances for socioeconomic disadvantage and in full competition. If you're hoping to bid for a $100-million-plus contract right out of the dug-out, you're setting yourself up for a strike out. Sure, you might be that unicorn that has an early lucky strike. But the chances are much higher you'll be betting on a fixed game you cannot win.

Of the 136,000 companies registered, only around 10,000 of them are actively and aggressively working with the federal government. These are the experts. The serious competitors. These are the companies pursuing contracts and grants regularly, who have figured out how to work with the federal government world. They're **The Major Leagues**. And if you go up against them without the proper training, they will eat you for breakfast.

 PICK YOUR PROCUREMENT LEAGUE

Based on what you now know, whether you have an existing contract, and the size and type of contract/grant you hope to pursue, choose the **Procurement League** you think makes most sense for you right now. Of course, you might change this later.

Now that we know the **Procurement League** you'll be playing in, let's think about the **Playing Field** you'll be playing on.

OPEN PLAYING FIELDS

If your **Procurement League** is the size and type of contract/grant you'll be bidding for, the **Playing Field** is the industry or subject matter area you're focusing on.

A quick look at USASpending.gov shows that in 2019, the four biggest budget spending areas were:

- Medicare (16.8 percent)
- Social Security (15.8 percent)
- National Defense (15.3 percent)
- Health (10.5 percent)

The biggest spenders by agency were:

- Department of Health and Human Services (26.1 percent)
- Social Security Administration (16.7 percent)
- Department of Defense (15.7 percent)
- Department of the Treasury (15.5 percent)

Now for the downside.

The current administration is investing less in early-stage R&D, continuing a downward trend in investment in innovation—at least on the surface. Differences in reporting and what counts as R&D, and huge investment from pharmaceutical companies in basic research, have skewed the figures in recent years.

But if we categorize OTAs as R&D and consider the $7 billion in 2019 in OTAs, you will see that if you look deeper there is a still lot of R&D spending occurring. And, of course, this will skyrocket in 2020 in the health arena as we collectively scramble to develop effective treatments, cures, and vaccines for coronavirus, and produce the attendant medical equipment and Personal Protective Equipment (PPE). However, there are still four big **Open Playing Fields** of Federal Procurement for Innovators.

 THE BIG FOUR OPEN PLAYING FIELDS

Does your solution fit into any of the following "**Open Playing Fields?**"

- **Defense**: Defense remains the largest focus of federal research and innovation, although there's a shift away from basic and applied research toward development within the DoD.
- **Intelligence**, and military applications in pursuit of National Security remain our biggest expenditure, at all levels of technology maturation.
- **Health and Life Sciences**: There's a shift toward health in the civilian sector, and as the population ages, spending on medical care only looks set to increase.
- **Energy**: Regardless of where you stand on the climate change debate, it's hard to make a case against energy innovation and research with dwindling resources and a burgeoning world population.

We're seeing a fundamental shift toward investment in life sciences research, but defense, intelligence, and military applications in pursuit of National Security remain our biggest expenditure.[74] While Congress is assigning less money to R&D, there are still opportunities. The

---

74   National Science Board, 2018.

government is always looking for solutions to specific challenges or ideas. If you can meet their needs, the budget still exists.

Does your solution fit one of the **Open Playing Fields?** If your solution doesn't immediately fit into one of the big four **Open Playing Fields**, you might still be able to find a smaller opening by solving an intractable problem in another area.

 MAKE YOUR OWN OPEN FIELD

As a country, what we really need is more innovative ideas to enter the pipeline, and that requires more innovators—which is good for you. The government funds one of the best ideas currently available. If the current "best option" is a poor fit or only a partial solution, even ideas that ultimately don't deliver value can gain funding for a while. This is good for you! It means if you can provide a better solution than the existing best-but-still-poor fit, you can steal a base or two before your competition knows what's hit them.

If federal agencies or Congress aren't seeing value, they cut funding. They will only follow a promising idea down the rabbit hole for so long before deciding to cut their losses and try something else. That means there is a growing need to ensure people with promising ideas can successfully navigate the space. With less money to go around, we need to help people be more intentional and find the right buyer faster. This is also good for you because it means there are organizations being set up across the country to help you match your products and services to government buyers.

Competition is proof of demand. No business truly has no competition. If there's no competition, there's no problem to solve, and few businesses can serve all their clients' or customers' needs. If there's a market and an existing supplier, there's a way in.

POWER PLAY: Make Your Own Playing Field.
If you're not playing on one of the Big Open Playing Fields, here are some ways to open up a space for yourself:

- Find an intractable problem with a partial solution
- Design a better solution
- Find the right buyer at the right agency
- Get your solution in front of them

Yes, competition may be a bit stiffer than in previous decades. Yes, you may need to adopt a more professional and systematic approach to funding than your forebears. But the situation is far from bleak.

The surest way to convince Congress and federal agencies to invest more in R&D—or in any area—is to deliver success. The more success stories we can show, the more the government will want to invest.

What is YOUR **Open Playing Field**? If not one of the Big Four, how will you open your own? In your quest to open those playing fields to you, you may have one or more "**Power-Ups**" available to you.

 ## "SET-ASIDE" POWER-UPS

While the government is supposed to do its best to provide a level playing field, there's a constant struggle between maintaining the status quo and encouraging inexperienced players. As we've seen, government contracts are lucrative; the existing incumbents don't want to give them up. Why would they?

From time to time the rules of the game change. The government creates programs to support special interest groups.

Sometimes those changes make it easier for new suppliers to break in. Sometimes they make it harder. So, the **Power-Ups** available to you will always be changing.

Here's the thing: if you fit into a group that currently receives set asides or favorable treatment—use them. Sports teams compete in leagues, and competitions are graduated to enable competitors of all ages, experience, and ability levels to get a fair chance. You wouldn't pit a five-year-old against a teenager or expect Paralympians and Olympians to run the same race. If you're still in **The Little Leagues**, not taking advantage of **Power-Ups** available to you is like playing golf against the world number one seed without taking advantage of the handicap difference to level the game.

Do any of the following describe you?

 **SMALL BUSINESSES**

The government works with the Small Business Administration (SBA) to encourage the procurement sector to buy through small to medium enterprises (SMEs) because of their ability to galvanize the economy. If you own or work for an SME with a transformative or innovative product, service, or approach, they might be interested.

By the way, what is included under the definition of "small business" might surprise you. The treasury uses the moving average of your last five years' receipts, compared to industry averages, or the number of employees, to determine eligibility for SME status. As an example, according to the US Treasury Department:

"If you were selling Computer Programming Services under NAICS code 541511 your average annual receipts over the past three years would have to be below $21.0 million to qualify as a small business concern... a mining firm is considered 'small' if it has fewer than 500 employees."[75] [76]

You can find the full list of NAICS and their associated dollar and employee size standards at naics.com/sba-size-standards/. [77]

---

75 As of January 2020. Prior to that, averages were calculated using a three-year moving average. The new rule was introduced with a 2-year grace period, allowing businesses to elect to calculate averages using either the three- or five-year timeframe between 2020 and 2022.

76 US Department of the Treasury, 2020.

77 NAICS Association, 2019.

The Small Business Set-Aside is called the 8(a) Program. To qualify, your business must:

- Be a small business. Use the size standards tool to see if you qualify.[78]
- Not already have participated in the 8(a) programs.
- Be at least 51 percent owned and controlled by economically and socially disadvantaged US citizens as defined by *Title 13 Part 124 of the Code of Federal Regulations.*[79]
- Have owners whose personal net worth is less than $250,000.
- Owners' average adjusted gross income for three years must be less than $250,000.
- Owners must have less than $4 million in assets.
- Owners must manage day-to-day operations and make long-term decisions.
- Principals must demonstrate good character.
- The business must show potential for success and be able to perform successfully on contracts.

 DISADVANTAGED SMALL BUSINESS

Currently, there are programs for Woman-Owned Small Businesses (WOSB) and Veteran-Owned Small Businesses (VOSB), with extra help for Service-Disabled Veteran Owned Small Business (DSVOSB) and Economically Disadvantaged Woman-Owned Small Business (EDWOSB). Particularly with Veteran-Owned businesses, certification for eligibility for these programs differs between agencies, but if you are eligible, take full advantage.

---

78 Small Business Administration, "Size Standards Tool," 2020.
79 U.S. Government, 2020.

It's also worth considering that while not disadvantaged programs, Alaskan Native Corporations, Indian-Owned, and Native Hawaiian–Owned Organization concerns do have different limits and ceilings on sole source work than other 8a companies. Consider this factor when deciding how to structure a business or a teaming agreement.

 **HUB ZONES**

Do you have an existing business in a designated HUB-Zone—a historically underutilized business zone in the US eligible for stimulus grants? If your business isn't already in a HUBZone area, can you start up or move your business to one?

To qualify for the HUBZone program, your business must:
- Be a small business. Use the size standards tool to see if you qualify.
- Be at least 51 percent owned and controlled by U.S. citizens, a Community Development Corporation, an agricultural cooperative, a Native Hawaiian organization, or an Indian tribe as outlined at *Title 13 Part 126 Subpart B of the Code of Federal Regulations.*
- Have its principal office located in a HUBZone.[80]
- Have at least 35 percent of its employees live in a HUBZone.

---

80 Small Business Administration, 2019.

ALASKAN NATIVE CORPORATIONS (ANC)

Can your business be designated as an ANC? Congress has given ANCs contracting advantages other businesses do not have.

 POWER PLAY: *Use the SBA's Certify website to find out whether there are any current set-aside programs that you qualify for, and if you qualify, how to get certified.*[81]

 NON-PROFITS

If you're a non-profit and you have proven regional programs, innovative programs, or a transformative approach in mind, you should consider federal contracts and especially grants. The federal government may give you a grant to help you build on your past success.

The chances are good if you're reading this that you fall into the small business category. But even if none of the **Power-Ups** apply to you, don't worry. I have plenty of **POWER PLAY**s throughout the book that will help you navigate the **Federal Procurement Arena**.

YOUR FEDERAL BUSINESS GAME PLAN

Your **Federal Business Game Plan** is the basis for everything you do to win business or funding from the US

---

81 Small Business Administration, "Is There an SBA Contracting Program for Me?" 2020.

government. It's your high-level overview of what you're trying to achieve, and the broad strokes of what you're going to do. Your **Federal Business Game Plan** is the glue that holds everything together and the lens that focuses action in the right direction. Without it, your business capture effort is meaningless.

If you don't have a strategy for playing the game, getting in front of the customer will only get you so far. Without a solid strategy, you could do directionless intelligence gathering and competitive research for hours without achieving results that will lead to business capture success. It would be like practicing shooting hoops and dribbling for hours without ever taking a run-up against another player. You might find the right teams, join the right clusters, and even come up with amazing solutions, but if you don't nail the game plan, you'll be forever benched, unable to land the contract that will get you your big break.

If you're not in early-stage R&D or your solution doesn't fit the BAA requirements, you still need to find a way to enter the process earlier than the Request for Proposals on SAMS. Just because there isn't a formal request for information out doesn't necessarily mean there's no need for your solution.

A lot of good companies, especially if they are already working for the government, constantly pulse the end user to find out where their gaps and complaints are. In the military, this might mean soldiers in-theatre. I have seen companies that hire former military representatives to talk to soldiers in units or pre-deploying units about their problems. Sometimes they get excellent feedback and start creating solutions to address the needs of those solders. Sometimes they keep in touch with soldiers or units to learn about problems as they are happening real time. That allows them to work with soldiers to formulate a requirement for a technical solution and offer solutions, tailoring them to a specific, identified need.

In health, it might be physicians and other healthcare professionals, and in other areas it might be administrators, police officers, or other auditors.

We will talk more about this in **The Teaming Zone**, and in **Listening for Opportunities**, but spend some time thinking about whose problems you're trying to solve, and how you can reach those people. You need to find out what the end user's gaps and constraints are—in commercial terminology, their pain points.

Then use that information to either suggest a solution, have the end users submit a requirement to procurement, or push for a Broad Area Announcement (BAA), a Small Business Innovation Research (SBIR), a Small Business Technology Transfer (STTR), or any other suitable vehicle or program to be put out for that solution area.

This process is about talking to your customer community and having them codify their needs and post what their problem is so that you can address it. On the civilian side, that means constantly cultivating relationships with government personnel, and constantly gathering information about what their gaps are, what their ceiling is, etc.

I've seen people who have developed strong relationships with the logistics community. Every acquisition professional who manages Materiel Solutions for the government learns that Operations & Maintenance (O&M) is 65 to 70 percent of the solutions lifecycle cost. When we're talking about 70 percent of a billion-dollar program, that's a lot of money.

If you can develop a solution that cuts the cost of the planned lifecycle sustainment, that is an incredible opportunity. And if you're getting information from the logisticians and technicians who are responsible for maintaining the equipment, you find out where there are errors, where things are breaking, and where you can potentially provide a solution and capture a lot of business. By understanding the logistician's problems, you can understand the system better and provide a better solution.

Now that you're starting to get an idea of who your customers might be, it's time to look at your business model in more depth. There are three factors to consider before engaging with the federal customer. Asking and answering these questions will help you engage the right person who can lead you to succvess.

TECHNOLOGY POSITION:

- Is your Primary **Technology Position** (Enabling/Component/Product) the only option?
- Could you adapt or pivot your technology to produce a range of enabling and component options, for example?
- Do you plan to take a specific product through multiple Development Stages, or will you focus on a specific developmental stage?

BUSINESS MODEL

We need to look not just at what you're selling, but at who you're selling to in a little more detail.

- Is your primary option, product, service, or IP licensing the only option, or can you provide a hybrid?
- How do you plan to monetize your solution?
  - Are you looking at one-off major purchases, or smaller recurring transactions?
  - Can you license or sell Intellectual Property rights (IP) in your technology or solution?
  - Can you look at subscription or scheduled fulfillment options?
- How can you increase transaction values?
- How can you increase transaction frequency per customer?
- How can you find more customers?
- How do you plan to supply your product or service?
  - Will the government be the end user, or will the government license a service from you that is used by the public?
  - Will you develop and manufacture in-house and deliver to the supply chain?
  - Will you form a new company to deliver to the supply chain?
  - Will you license the IP rights to a technology to another entity already in the supply chain?
  - Will you sell to another entity already in the supply chain?
- How will you fund development?
  - Is federal funding your only hope, or part of a larger funding plan?

- Do you have existing internal or external funding sources?
- How do all the available funding sources align with the various stages of the technology maturation process?
- Once your solution is hardened, do you have a defined approach to market penetration?

 PLAYING FIELD

Consider the procurement channels open to you:
- Which agencies have historically purchased solutions like yours?
- Which agencies have BAAs with areas of interest that match your business?
- Which agencies have budgets assigned for your solution?
- Can you make sales to state or other governments?
- Can you sell direct-to-market in the private sector?

Now think about your markets and end users:
- Will you be selling to the DoD?
- Will you be selling to other federal agencies?
- Will you be selling to state and local organizations?
- Will you be selling to commercial markets?

 ## DEFINING YOUR FEDERAL BUSINESS GAME PLAN

Using your answers to the previous questions, you can draw out your **Federal Business Game Plan** on the template shown in Figure 8. A blank template is also in the **Resources** section at the end of the book.

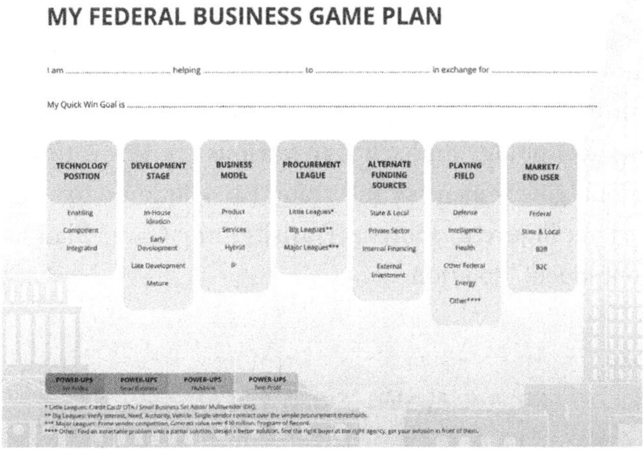

MY FEDERAL BUSINESS GAME PLAN

I am .... helping .... to .... in exchange for ....

My Quick Win Goal is ....

Figure 8: Your Federal Business Game Plan. See Resources for blank template.

Circle the PRIMARY response in each column and draw connecting lines to create your Primary Game Plan.

Figure 9 shows a game plan for developing an enabling technology using federal funding:

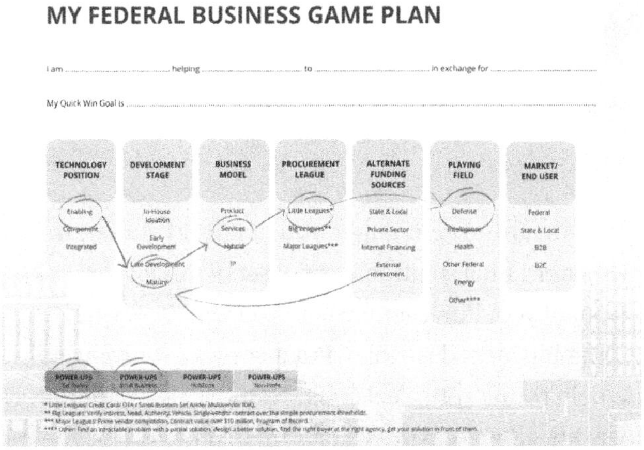

MY FEDERAL BUSINESS GAME PLAN

I am .... helping .... to .... in exchange for ....

My Quick Win Goal is ....

Figure 9: An Example primary Game Plan.

Then circle secondary and tertiary options in different colors

For example, if you've developed an "enabling" technology using federal dollars, BUT you're also looking to then scale that technology and sell it to various entities within the federal government, or integrate that solution into a larger system, Figure 10 shows a Transitioning Game Plan for a "component" solution:

MY FEDERAL BUSINESS GAME PLAN

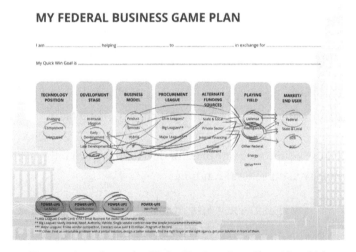

Figure 10: A sample completed Federal Business Game Plan with multiple routes to market.

It's important to remember your **Federal Business Game Plan** is not a final solution. It's not set in stone. Always keep it in front of you. Pin it somewhere you will see it when you are making business decisions. Put a copy in your journal. Use it to help frame your decisions. You will also want to review it periodically, to ensure it stays up to date. When you move from one **Development Stage** to another, or you move from one **Procurement League** to another, update your **Federal Business Game Plan** accordingly.

That's the end of **Part One.** You are now **Ready** to start your federal contracting career, in that you're registered and eligible to play the game, and you have a **Federal Business Game Plan.** In **Part Two, Get Set,** we're going to make sure your business is set up properly to bid on and win government business by focusing on your team and your business systems, particularly your intelligence gathering and forward planning.

PART TWO:

GET SET

Build Your Teams, Create Your Business Systems,
and Identify Opportunities

6

BUILDING YOUR TEAM

Remember how we imagined the **Federal Procurement Arena** as sporting event? The federal buyers run on the **Inside Track**, with the **Major League** players in the lane next to them. Existing **Big League** business clusters and established contractors run in the middle lanes, and you, as a **Little League** new vendor, are in the outer lane.

At the track side are **Trackside Officials**, support teams of trainers and coaches—the facilitators who help businesses identify opportunities and improve their operating procedures to perform better—and the race officials, who ensure everyone follows the rules.

In **Building Your Team**, we're going to look at the **Buyers on the Inside Track, Trackside Officials**, and your Internal and External **Relay Teams**. You will start to work out, based on your **Federal Business Game Plan**, who you need on your **Team Roster**—a list of key players and positions you need to fill both internally and externally.

Then, in **The Teaming Zone**, we will look at the **Major League** and **Big League** players between you and the **Inside Track.**

Let's start by looking at the **Inside Track**, your buyers.

 ## BUYERS ON THE INSIDE TRACK

These are the people you need to reach and to convince. There are several types of customers involved in the procurement process. Understanding who they are brings you one step closer to understanding what drives different government players, how to build relationships and influence them, and what they would like to see in your offer.

It might seem strange to think about government buyers as part of your team. It might help if you think in terms of *you* being on *their* team instead. Either way, the procurement process is a team effort, and you need to know who is on the team with whom you will be collaborating. The following sections break down each role and member so you can put together the best team possible.

 ### SOURCE SELECTION AUTHORITIES

In the government sector, source selection is the process of choosing the proposal that offers the best value.[82] Source Selection Authorities may consist of a single person, or there may be a team assigned to the role. Acquisitions are organized using a **Source Selection Plan (SSP),** which describes

---

82   GSA, 15.302, 2019.

organizational, evaluation and selection procedures and criteria. You could think of this as the government's Procurement Game Plan.

- **Contracting Officer (CO/KO)/Procuring Contract Officer (PCO)**—The Contracting Officer is normally the Source Selection Authority. The contracting officer acronym is CO in the civilian agencies, and KO in the military, so as not to be confused with another CO, the commanding officer. It's their job to establish a team including technical, legal, and other specialists to approve selections, oversee the selection process and ensure it's fair, act as the focal point for enquiries during the bid process, and award contracts.

- **Contracting Specialist (CS)/Technical Point of Contact (TPOC)**—A Contracting Officer is often assigned a contracting specialist, or Technical Point of Contact, who might be your immediate interface and whose name is on the Request for Proposal (RFP) as the addressee or TPOC. Sometimes the contracting officer and contracting specialists are the same person. In R&D and RDT&E settings you will often see and interface with a true TPOC. They are sometimes engineers, physicists, or technical advisors who are government employees.

- **Source Selection Advisory Council (SSAC)**—For acquisitions with estimated values over $100 million (**Big and Major Leagues**), there will be a Source Selection Advisory Council, consisting of senior government personnel. They advise during the source selection process and prepare a comparative analysis of the SSEB's evaluation results.

- **Source Selection Evaluation Board (SSEB)**—For larger procurements, a PCO may be appointed to oversee a selection committee, variously called an SSEB or an SST.

This team will include government personnel. Where necessary non-government advisors will be brought in, but they are not allowed to vote on the outcome. This group will review all proposals and select a recommendation. The SSA will either accept the recommendation (which is done in most cases) or veto it.[83]

- **Source Selection Team (SST)**—A Source Selection Team may be a smaller unit tasked with selection for a specific acquisition.

When you're playing in the **Little and Big Leagues**, and even more so when you're dealing with early-stage tech development, your SSA may be your TPOC. They may well be scientists and engineers as well. They may be well-versed in the technology and know the specs they are working to and the criteria the solution must meet. They may take a much more hands-on approach to source selection, and talk to you about the technology, performance issues, and potential solutions. They may also only purchase in small quantities (often one to use, one for spare, and a redundancy backup). When you develop your technology to a position where you are looking at fielding an entire army, navy, or the federal government, you will be dealing with different players.

Outside the RD&E environment generally, and in **The Major Leagues**, SSAs care about making the right decision and how their choice reflects on the agency and its professional performance. They care about following the rules and might not know the technical details of the contract. Their biggest concern is to avoid failed bidders raising a protest. They will

---

83   GSA, 7.503(c)(12)(ii), FAR 37.203, and FAR 37.204, 2019.

want to keep their relationship with you as official as possible to avoid even the impression of impropriety, but they also hold the purse strings and control the buying press. Their approach will be more hands-off.

POWER PLAY: *Work out the **Innovation Discipline** of your SSA players, and tailor how you talk to them accordingly. Talk specs and performance with the TPOC, and efficiency and value with the non-technical SSA.*

CHAMPIONS

Champions are people inside the customer organization who want your solution. They may be able to coach you on how to navigate through the process. An effective champion must respect you and be respected by the other buying influencers in the organization. You should actively work on developing at champions in the customer organization.

Many personnel in procurement offices and R&D centers rely heavily on the opinions of their internal technical staff. Program Managers or Contracting Officers in these environments depend heavily on their scientists, engineers and subject matter experts when making decisions about new and emerging technical solutions. Getting them to champion your technology is key. You want the Program Manager or Contracting Officer's Technical Representative championing your solution because they are usually extremely helpful in getting the right intelligence. And you want the Contracting Officer championing your cause because they're the decision makers. If you cannot reach members of the SSA, talk to the representative from the Office of Small & Disadvantaged Business Utilization (OSDBU).[84]

END USERS

End users are your customer's customers. They benefit from your work, and your customer is interested in providing the best solution possible for their benefit. For example, on a large centralization effort of IT support for the Department of Energy, IT managers are the end users of the services. They must be happy with the solution or they will complain to the either the program manager or contracting officer, which is never a good thing.

There are tiers of end users as well. For examples, while developing and selling a portable detection system for use in the field, you might deal with:

- **PhD Scientist**—working in ideation or early development, these users are mostly focused on wanting the best and most current technology, regardless of cost. They typically have limited buying power, however, restricted to three of an item: one to use, one for spare, and one as a backup for redundancy.
- **Warfighter ground units**—the intended field users. These are the people who will use the mature product in the field. While they also want up-to-date technology, they're typically more concerned with the effectiveness and convenience of the product. They want to know how

---

84   United States Department of Commerce, 2011.

it handles, how easy it is to carry and use, and how sensitive it is to damage.

- **Warfighter Command**—Like the scientists, commanders want the best technology, and like ground units, they want it to be effective, robust, and practical. But they are also aware of the need to equip larger numbers and may share the program manager's budgetary concerns.

Whoever your end users are, there are those who experience the program's services firsthand, and those who might be a tier or two below them. You must take all their needs into consideration. The ultimate end user for most DoD programs is the warfighter. For civilian agencies, it will be the population the agency services.

End user representatives could be part of the SSEB. You need to speak to their concerns as well as those of the CO and PM. End users usually want more than the government has money for. The PM and the CO will usually be more in tune with the available budget.

 PROGRAM MANAGERS

Program or project managers (PMs) oversee the use of your proposed solution at the agency or program level. They come from the program management organization or are the Contracting Officer's Technical Representative (COTR) from the contracting organization. They oversee proper program execution for quality performance, on-schedule delivery, and budgetary constraints. Program Managers and COTRs are your BUYERS. These are the decision-makers and the people you need to build relationships with.

The CO's priority is following the rules, while the PM or COTR's priority is getting the project done properly. PMs usually personally care about fulfilling the pressing need and how the proposed solution will affect their work and lives. They often create and drive the requirements on the end users' behalf. They want the work done well. They know their performance depends on your success with the project. They have a lot of influence on the process because they are the ones who live with the project and its results.

 SPONSORS

Sponsors work at the highest level within the government to lobby for budgets to meet agency requirements. They could include personnel from organizations high in the chain of command such as the Office of the Secretary of Defense (OSD), and government oversight authorities such as Congressmen and staffers with various committees in the House and Senate.

Because they are vocally and visibly advocating for large, highly visible programs, they need to ensure the programs they sponsor are executed well. Ensuring your solution fits the sponsors' requirements is extremely important. They may be difficult to access, but if you can solve their problems, having a sponsor advocate with your solution in mind can increase your chances of success.

Those are the major players in the government procurement team; the people you need to access and impress with your solution. Now let's look at the people on the sidelines, whose job it is to make sure the process runs smoothly one way or another.

TRACKSIDE OFFICIALS

It's easy to feel overwhelmed as a small business attempting to land a government contract. You can feel a bit like an out-of-shape couch potato going up against an Olympic gold medalist. However, there are people who work in and around the **Federal Procurement Arena** who are not directly involved with the procurement process, but whose job it is to make sure it runs smoothly.

COACHES

Coaches are often public servants whose role is to support small business in their government contracting business capture endeavors. Everyone can get help with getting started as a government contractor. The usa.gov website has a whole sub site devoted to just that.[85] As well as the online Government Contracting Classroom, over 300 Procurement Technical Assistance Centers (PTACs) exist nationwide, where you can access one-on-one counselling as well as help with form filling and other technical aspects of the contracting process.

Other sources of coaching may include:
- **Procurement Center Representatives (PRCs)**—These are Small Business Administration (SBA) staff who work within other federal agencies to advocate for small businesses.

---

85   United States Government, 2020.

- **Office of Small and Disadvantaged Business Utilization (OSDBU) or Office of Small Business Programs (OSBP)**—This office can offer help for small businesses to identify contracting opportunities.
- **Agency Small Business Offices**—Branches of the military and the DoD have small business offices who will be able to help you identify opportunities within their BAAs and procurement programs.

 REFEREES

As well as people who may coach you to a win, there are people in the **Federal Procurement Arena** whose job is to ensure everyone follows the rules. Fortunately for you, that usually means making sure the little guy gets a fair shot. There are two main types of referees you need to be aware of.

- **Commercial Market Representatives**—Commercial Market Representatives (CMRs) are Small Business Administration staff responsible for monitoring prime contracts. Their job is to ensure larger businesses comply with subcontracting goals.
- **Technical Experts**—Technical experts, often referred to as Systems Engineering and Technical Assistance (SETA) contractors, serve as the government's technical eyes and ears. Often, if they are not direct government employees, they don't have voting power during a proposal evaluation. However, they check if the solution is viable and can screen out technically inadequate solutions.

Referees could also be contractors hired for the purpose of helping the government, or they could be borrowed from the national laboratories, think tanks, or test and evaluation organizations. They are the gatekeepers who check the technical accuracy of your proposal and vet the solutions on offer. They might deem your solution unacceptable and thus preclude you from winning, and they also consider if you are compliant with the technical specifications.

> **POWER PLAY: Don't wait to get started on creating your Team Roster.** Draw up a complete list of every office or position that has an impact on your business capture efforts and identify the key players. Find a champion, coaches, and referees who you can ask for support.

Now that you've looked at this from the government side, let's look at **Your External Team Roster**.

YOUR EXTERNAL TEAM ROSTER

Now that you know how the game works, and you have your **Federal Business Game Plan** mapped out, you need to start thinking about the team players you will need on your **Team Roster**, both internally and externally. We'll work from the broadest strokes and slowly get more granular.

We're going to start by building **Your External Team Roster**. This is a list of key players in external positions who can be considered teammates because they come with problems that need to be solved and access to funding. Building this list can be broken down into three major steps. First, you will map **The Buyer Arena**, then create cluster maps to help you visualize data and identify target customers. Only then will you create your list of key players, knowing you're focusing on the right players on the field.

 MAP THE BUYER ARENA

Using your research from **Chapter 3, Playing the Game**, start building a "Buyer Map," a visual representation of all the agencies and departments within the federal government that might buy from you.

Your buyer map will probably be more useful if it looks more like a mind map than a geographical one. Answer the following questions, and start mapping the relationships between your contacts, agencies, and the problems you solve.

- Who else might encounter the same problems, given their mission and what they are trying to achieve?
- How does procurement work at that agency?
- Who has the budget to procure your solution?
- How far ahead do they forecast?
- Who do they listen to?

The answers to these questions will help you start developing your contact database, but it will also help you start thinking in terms of the timelines and deadlines you need to work toward when dealing with federal buyers.

Another approach you can take is to look at the tactical side.

- What technology has the buyer already procured?
- What are their mission sets?
- What equipment do they already have?
- Who else is buying those technologies?

Especially if you are selling a component or enabling technology, you might not sell directly to the government. There usually will be a **Major League Player**—a prime vendor—who oversees the larger system of systems.

If you can provide something that is cheaper, faster, better, or more reliable, and the switch doesn't call for inordinate re-engineering to insert your solution into a future iteration of the solution, you could land a sale. That's a way into the **Federal Procurement Arena** that doesn't call for dealing directly with federal buyers.

Another possibility, if your component is more reliable or extends the shelf life of a solution, would be to approach the sustainment community with an aftermarket solution. They might be interested, especially if significant cost savings are involved.

Start investigating the procurement processes at these prime vendors.
- Who makes the decisions?
- What are their criteria?
- How can you get on their radar?
- Do they have a small business point of contact (POC)?

You can tie into certain communities to get your product into the federal program in ways other than a direct, single-company contract. But you must do some deep thinking about how and where you can fit into those gaps, and with whom you can partner.
- Consider whether you're selling a product, a component, a part, or a piece of a larger solution.

- Think about what it fits into. Even an integrated solution fits into a larger picture.
- What is the problem you're trying to solve?
- Where is the problem or solution typically encountered?

Now, armed with a deeper understanding of the **Buyer Arena**, you can start looking at the other players within the arena, and how you might fit in.

 CREATE YOUR CLUSTER MAP

You need to have a way to see the layout of the **Federal Procurement Arena** as it relates to your specific solution. And with so many agencies, buyers, contractors, and end users, it can start to get a little confusing, to say the least. You need a visual tool.

Cluster maps typically mine large datasets to create a visual representation of a specific industry, to show concentrations of economic activity and competition. When it comes to building a cluster map, you can start with resources like clustermapping.us, which helps to visualize data on different industries and includes data about R&D spending.[86]

You can also pull data from USASpending.gov, using the advanced search option and searching "All United States" by agency, product code, etc., to get a clearer idea of how much the government is spending in your industry and which agencies are buying.[87]

---

86 Cluster Mapping US, 2020.
87 USA Spending, 2020.

Let's say, for instance, you're working on space vehicle technology. You'll quickly see from this USA Spending map in Figure 11 that most of the spending is concentrated in Texas:

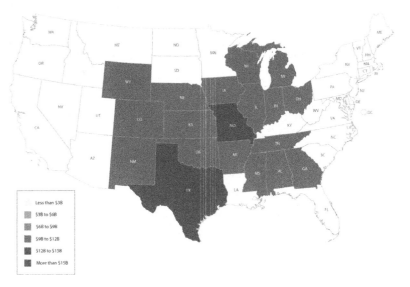

Figure 11: USASpending.gov cluster map of Space Vehicle Manufacture spending.

Zooming into Texas in Congressional District view as in Figure 12 will also show that most of this spending is concentrated in Fort Worth, Dallas.

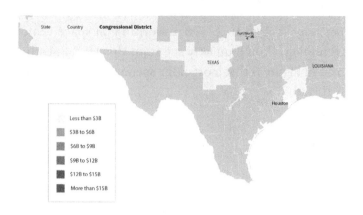

Figure 12: USASpending.gov cluster map of Space Vehicle Manufacture spending zoomed into Texas.

Switching to Table view will then give you a list of all the contracts and recipients. You can even look at the contracts for more detailed information and combine that with information on SAMS about those contracts. You can also add the major players, offices, and sites to your map and color code them for quick, meaningful viewing.

Figure 13 shows the locations of some national laboratories and engineering centers. Note the locations of any that may be of interest to you and add them to your cluster map.

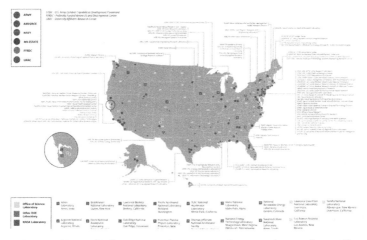

Figure 13: National Laboratories and Engineering Centers in the United States.[88]

🏆 **POWER PLAY:** *Build your own cluster map. Add the agencies, vendors, businesses, and other major players who have a bearing on your Federal Business Game Plan. Add potential buyers in one color, potential partners in another, and competition in another. You might want to represent bigger players with bigger symbols, or darker shades, to make it easier to spot where there might be openings.*

IDENTIFY KEY PLAYERS

Obviously, I can't give just one source to help you identify the names and contact details of the people you will need to reach out to and start building relationships. Whom you

---

88   Adapted from Office of Science, 2020 and Office of the Under Secretary of Defense, Research and Engineering, 2020.

approach and how will depend on where you are, what you're hoping to achieve, and who your federal customers are. However, if you followed the steps so far, you will have a list of agencies and departments who are potential buyers. You will also have a list of existing government contractors in your arena, and the details of government spending to date. With a bit of digging and cross referencing, starting in the **Resources** section at the end of this book, you should be able to start a contacts list.

Start collecting the names and contact details of end users, contracting officers, technical officers, and program officers at the agencies of interest to you.

With your Cluster Map and your **Federal Business Game Plan** in hand, start making a list of **Key Players** you need to cultivate relationships with. Don't just include procurement officers and buyers; start thinking about influencers, champions, and lobbyists who will fight your corner. Don't forget about the end users who will advocate for your solution.

 SOURCE SELECTION AUTHORITIES:

Find out who is the SSA for your target customer.
- Is it a single contracting officer, or an evaluation board?
- Are there any contracting specialists?
- How can you open lines of communication with these buyers?

Add them to your contacts list software.

Program Sponsor: Find out who the program sponsor is and add them to your contacts list. If you don't know who the program sponsor is, you can find out from several places.

- The most cost-effective place to find contacts will be bata. sam.gov, which will give you the contracting officer's names, the agency website, and details of small business specialists from the Office of Small and Disadvantaged Business Utilization (OSDBU.)
- Among paid sources, GovWin IQ has a huge database of up-to-date government contacts, and you can also get the congressional sponsor information.[89]
- Carroll Publishing, now going by the name of Gov-Search, offers organizational charts and contact information as well.[90]

Once you have identified the program sponsor, do everything you can to learn their priorities, and how you can meet them. Then see how you can get your solution in front of them.

Champions: Make sure you have champions within your target agency.

Program Manager: Make sure you have a relationship with the PM on the government side in addition to the contracting personnel. They could be either your biggest advocate of your biggest obstacle.

End Users: Consider your end users, and which of them influences the SSEB. Add them to your list, either individually

---

89   USA Spending, 2020.
90   GovSearch LLC., 2020.

or as a group. Run focus groups to find out what the end users really want and see if there is any way you can make your solution solve their major problems without taking it over budget.

Support Teams: See how many of the following groups of people you can identify; you never know when they might be able to help you, and you need to start building relationships with them, too.

- Coaches
- Referees
- Commercial Market representatives
- Technical Experts

Add the key players you identified to your list and start thinking about how you might reach out to them.

This is not, of course, a one-and-done exercise. Your cluster map will quickly become useless if you don't keep it up to date. But we will talk about that in **Chapter 11, Playing to Win.**

 POWER PLAY:
Earning MVP / Trusted Advisor Status

Government repressentatices universally despise sales-people, so your goal is not to sell yourself and your company; your goal is to become their trusted advisor and Most Valuable Player (MVP). Yes, selling to the government is different compared to dealing with commercial or industrial sales. There are more rules, procedures, and paperwork. But if you remember you are still dealing with people, it's not so complicated.

Government officials have their own culture and language, but all the universal rules for building relationships apply, with some interesting twists.

When you build a relationship with government representatives, you need to take a multidimensional approach. You need to build as many relationships as possible. Your main government contact could leave after you invested all your time and efforts into building a relationship. This was a common narrative when I worked with the DoD Office of Small Business Programs (OSBP) and the SBIR / STTR programs. Small businesses won an initial grant via SBIR, and the Technical Point of Contact (TPOC) they originally worked with left before there was a large need for their solution. The companies were at a dead end with their product. The last thing you want is to be stuck with no contact, and no way in.

You also need to create a contact plan using phone calls, visits, and email. Through this process, you will learn about the customer's pressures, key concerns, hot-button issues, and needs.

*You will need to give them help—they might need you to consult for them on preparing the statement of work; or to find out about state-of-the-art technology, or different options to solve challenging problems on their projects. You will have to practice **Listening for Opportunities**.*

We dive deep into the relationship-building side of culti-vating government contacts later. For now, always remem-ber that to succeed with the government, you need to work at becoming a MVP or trusted advisor. That means:

- *You have to be honest, and ethical, and avoid even the appearance of impropriety.*
- *You must show you care about them and the project more than your company.*
- *You must understand how this government servant's mission impacts the country.*
- *You must show you are there to help and solve their problems.*

Above all, recognize they are human. This includes remembering birthdays, family members, and what makes them laugh. While you can't give them lavish gifts, a simple message of well wishes is always acceptable and welcome.

Now that you know who your main buyers and contacts might be, and an idea of the audience groups you need to speak to, you can focus on making sure you have the best internal team to interface with them effectively.

YOUR INTERNAL TEAM ROSTER

In football, you have over twenty specialized positions; yet only eleven players on the field at a time. You have an offen-sive platoon, a defensive platoon, and a specialized platoon. Looking at your **Federal Business Game Plan**, you should see that you need different people and personalities to deal with the technology, business, and market aspects of your chosen route. We will refer to these as your **Innovation Relay Team**, your **Operations Relay Team**, and your **Business Capture Relay Team**.

You may have some players whose positions overlap two or all three teams. Also, within teams, players have specific roles or positions. In our football example, you don't expect your center to touch down, you expect him to pass to the quarterback, who will in turn pass to a running back or wide receiver. Similarly, you can't expect one person to deal with every aspect of the technology; the person who is conducting a study or doing early-stage research is often not the best suited for actually building and developing a solution.

You need to work out, based on where your solution is now and where you need it to be, which roles you need to fill to harden the technology.

In football, you don't expect your defensive line to do the job of your cornerbacks, or your jammers and gunner to be interchangeable; some positions call for lithe, fast runners, and others for bulk and strength.

Similarly, you probably want different people in charge of operations and logistics, finance, and marketing.

You need to know which roles to fill operationally, and who will be responsible for distinct aspects of Business Capture Management.

When you're training for a relay and handing off to different teammates who have different strengths, you go through one zone, and you do it over and over. Some teammates are power sprinters and take off super-fast. They accelerate for the first fifteen to twenty meters and decelerate near the end because they are power sprinters, but they have so much top speed that they are able to carry it through to the end. Others have better end speed. They start off slower but accelerate through the zone. Some are faster on the curve while others are faster on the straight. Some are better at closing. You find out which athletes are better at what and then have them practice together to nail the relay.

In the same way, your relay teams need to be set up to handle a process or business cycle from end to end with smooth transitions, and you need to find the best people for the job at each stage of the process. In the case of federal contracting, you will team up with companies that add value or have strengths in areas you don't. You need to ensure you have multiple skill sets to create a winning team. Even when you think of a winning NCAA track and field team, you don't win a championship with only distance runners. You have a variety of sprinters, pole vaulters, hurdlers, and so on who all make significant contributions to helping the team win.

Figure 14 below shows an image of a standard 400-meter track. As you can see, it has a whole host of markings. The average person would look at a track and only see the lanes. They have no idea there are rules that determine where things are marked or that many of those markings are required for race times to be official. In athletics, you need to have at least one person who understands what all of the markings mean if you are to participate in track successfully. In the same way, as an innovator you need to make sure you have all your positions covered in federal contracting to build your business.

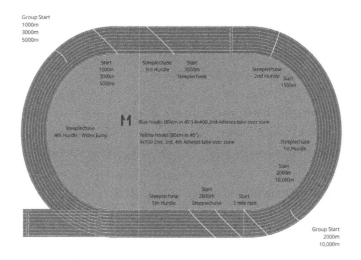

Figure 14: Athletics track with relay markings.

 YOUR BUSINESS CAPTURE RELAY TEAM

Imagine the business capture process as a relay race. It's vital that you enter the race at the earliest possible moment, and that you assign someone (or a team of people) to do the work for each leg of the race.

You need:
- A team to deal with personal interactions
- A team for intelligence gathering
- A team to deal with proposal writing
- A team to deal with contract management

Your business capture management team might consist of:

- A figurehead, who goes out and meets the sponsors and champions
- Researchers who conduct focus groups with users and end users
- Your bid writing team, which we will talk more about in **The Pitching Zone**
- Program managers, who interface directly with PCOs and PMs on the government side

Imagine the **Business Capture Race** as a relay, as shown below. As you can see in Figure 15, the race begins over in the bottom right corner, and completes a full lap before reaching the finish line. You don't want to be the team trying to fit all that activity into the bottom left corner.

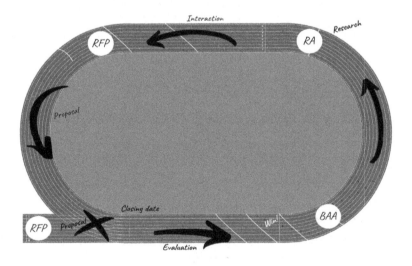

Figure 15: *The Proposal Process visualized as a relay race.*

You need to identify the right people to reach out to, not start spamming every government office and official whose remit vaguely matches your solution. You may need to get someone who understands the ecosystem to help you make those early connections. In the early days, you'll have to do some legwork, and some digging for an admin's contact details. It's hands-on work, and you must do a lot of networking, especially on the military side.

This is where soft skills such as communication, networking, and teamwork come into their own. You need to make human connections. There's no getting away from it; someone must go and find out the customers' names and build relationships with them. If that's not you, you'll need to team up with someone with those skills. There's no substitute for face-to-face interaction.

A lot of people getting started don't understand this—particularly in the military community, because it's a tight-knit community and that's the way they operate. It's very much an old boys' network. People who went to West Point together, who served together, or who were on the same joint task force or joint operation, bond. They work with the same group of people on and off throughout their military careers, and it creates an insular community—especially when so much of what they experience is classified and they can't talk about it with non-military personnel without the proper clearance.

Of course, these guys all know each other, and they have these linkages, and contacts they've built up over a twenty-five or thirty-year career. These guys lived on base together and went to war together, and when they get promoted to these acquisitions assignments they work together and talk to each other. The smart companies understand that old boys' network.

As an example, if you're supplying custom military solutions, there's a good chance your end user customers are operating outside contiguous United States (OCONUS). You might need to talk with the unit directly as part of your research. But the number you must call then is an unmanned, or marginally staffed, office in the US. You may be calling some administrative support officer and not the unit itself. If you don't know that, you have a problem because you have no way to reach the people with whom you need to speak.

You need someone on your team who knows their way around that network, and who can reach the end user. The smart companies hire someone from that community as a consultant, to do those handshakes, and to talk about their technology to the end user. Because a lot of this information, especially on the DoD side, is classified.

If you're in the research phases of development, and you're looking for grants and funding, you need to understand which agencies have funding available for which development phases. If you are at technology level five, and an agency or department only has finding through to level five, it will do you no good to continue applying for funding from that agency. You need a roadmap of funding from where you are now to where you need to be.

POWER PLAY: Draw your business capture activity onto a relay map

Start to assign activity to team players. See what gaps you need to fill, and where you may need specialist advice.

YOUR INNOVATION RELAY TEAM

Your innovation team may consist of researchers and buyers in charge of sourcing existing products and raw materials, and packaging for your solution. Or it may consist of a full-fledged technology development plan from basic research through to a mature product.

What I love about track and field is that there is something for everyone. The same is true for innovators and federal contractors. Remember back in **Chapter Four, The Strategy Zone**, we talked about the Innovation Disciplines, and the diverse types of innovators? The facilitators, visionaries, researchers, creators, destructors, refiners, and champions. We also talked about your technology's development stage, from ideation through development to maturity.

Now, we need to talk a little bit more about the technology development process. There are a lot of ways to talk about technology readiness. We'll cover them in more detail in **Chapter 10, The Technology Zone**.

For now, it's enough to know that NASA and the DoD define nine **Technology Readiness Levels (TRLs),** which take any new technology from basic research (levels 1-2) through feasibility research (levels 2-4), technology development (levels 3-5), technology demonstration (levels 5-6), systems development (levels 6-8), to systems test, launch, and operations (levels 8-9).

You will need innovators from different **Innovation Disciplines** at various stages of development. And if you're starting at level 5 and planning to take a product to market, you will have a different entry and exit point than someone taking a technology from level 3 to level 6, for example. Just as in a race, the entry or starting point is different, depending on the race you want to run or the race you are BEST at. Figure 16 shows how you might identify your innovation personnel needs for a complete produce development cycle from TRL1 through to TRL9.

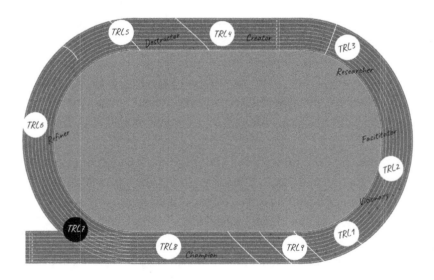

Figure 16: The Technology Readiness Levels Relay Race.

YOUR OPERATIONS RELAY TEAM

Consider your business model and the roles you might need to fill associated with that model.

- Will you need an Intellectual Property (IP) lawyer?
- Will you need a grant writer?
- Will you need production managers and operatives?
- What kinds of liaisons and service specialists will you need?
- What about accountants and quality assurance specialists?

You will also need to consider how you price your product or services, including:

- Cost of service/product
- Cost of overhead
- Cost of G&A
- Profit margins
- Discounts or volume discounts
- Pricing to get into the market

This might mean adding people to your team who can help you work these things out.

I can't give you as much help with this one because this is what makes your business unique; it's the actual work that you do. On the upside, that should mean you already have an intimate knowledge of who does what and when.

> **POWER PLAY:** *Make a list of the roles you will need to fill at each stage of the process and map out who they will receive work from and hand it off to. Understanding your internal workflow and processes at this stage will not only help avoid bottlenecks and knowledge gaps, it will help every team member understand how and where they fit in, and how vital their role is.*

 COMPLETE YOUR TEAM ROSTERS

If you haven't already, complete **Team Rosters** for your **Business Capture, Innovation,** and **Operations Relay Teams.**

Follow your **Federal Business Game Plan** from where you are now to market and list the positions you might need to create or fill at each stage of the journey.

Don't forget to add legal and financial advisors, and other professionals whose services you will need along the way to the list.

Add the positions within the **Federal Procurement Arena** you will interface with. Add your **Buyers in the Inside Track** and **Track Officials.** Show where in the process they are interfaced, and which team members will work with them.

That's how you build your **Team Roster**. You may want to break each leg of the overall race into its own relay and map out who does what and when within teams. You can get as granular with this as you like, but by the end of this exercise, you should have a clear idea of who you need in your team, where they fit in, and where your current gaps are.

So, that's **The Inside Track** and **The Outside Lane**, but what about all those people between you and your buyers? The other **Little League** small businesses, **Big League** larger firms, and **Major League** prime vendors who may be in competition or collaboration with you?

While you may be able to get a small procurement direct from a PCO, you might want to consider teaming up with other small vendors or subcontracting to a prime vendor. Thus, we enter **The Teaming Zone**.

7

THE TEAMING ZONE

———

Teaming is the term we use in the **Federal Procurement Arena** to describe one or more businesses working together to serve a government contract. In teams, there will be a designated prime vendor and subcontractors.

Teaming enables the government to tap into the expertise of multiple companies. How this works depends on how the contract is constructed. Often, there is one prime vendor who assumes responsibility and the risk for completing the contract, and through whom all monies and official communication pass, making it easier for the government to manage the contract.

As well as mitigating the consequences of taking a risk on a small, new business for the government, teaming can help new companies break into **The Federal Procurement Arena**. Teaming can also help agencies meet their small business contracting goals. Depending on the contract, they sometimes require that large companies team up with small ones.

Conversely, small companies often need the resources of large ones to help them fulfil a contract.

Through teaming, you may be able to:
- Pursue contracts that would otherwise be beyond your reach because you can draw on another company's resources to:
  - Fully develop new technical solutions where you may only have a partial solution.
  - Take a solution through testing that you alone may not have the ability to complete.
  - Meet the technical specifications or scope of a requirement that may otherwise be out of your reach.
- Gain access to the client through teammate's past performance or access security clearances by joining an existing incumbent as a subcontractor.
- Lower costs, distribute financial risk, and increase revenue and working capital by pooling resources and sharing the workload.
- Access expertise, experience, and technical skills to further the technical state or research.
- Leverage a teammate's presence in other geographical locations, expand into new technology verticals, and pivot your technology to meet new needs in different markets.
- Reduce the competition: if you are on the same team exclusively with each other, you are not competing with one another for a specific bid.

With all these benefits, why wouldn't you consider teaming?

First, we'll look at how you can use your **Team Roster** to identify teaming opportunities and build your own winning team. Then we'll consider when it makes sense to join an existing winning team. Finally, we'll consider the limits and pitfalls of teaming, so you know how to avoid becoming affiliated with another business and falling foul of Federal Acquisitions Regulations (FAR) rules.

BUILDING A WINNING TEAM

Teaming is a bit like taking part in the NBA draft. The most valuable players get snapped up first, while unknown, untested, or unreliable players may get lucky and fill a spot if a more valuable player is injured, or they may be left out. The key to success is to start the teammate identification process early, making alliances and floating deals. You don't want to find yourself teaming in the eleventh hour with companies that will bring you no closer to winning than bidding by yourself.

SELECTING YOUR DREAM TEAM

Here are a few simple steps you could take to start drawing up your teaming plans.

First, look at your **Team Roster**. Are there big gaps that could be filled by teaming up with another small business, or subcontracting to a larger business?

Look at your **Business Cluster Map** for complimentary businesses you could work with. Make lists of potential teaming partners in each area of your **Federal Contracting Game Plan**. You could even draw up charts with the potential partners, and list pros and cons of each, or assign priorities and score each partner according to your criteria.

Select your own "dream team" with backups should your first teaming strategy fall through.

🏆 **POWER PLAY:** You've already drawn up **Team Rosters** and **Relay Maps** from your perspective. Now draw them up from the perspective of the agency and contract you're targeting. Mark in where you can deliver, and look for companies or existing teams that have a gap in that area, but can deliver where you can't

Make sure you analyze your solution or every area of the work scope, and determine the gaps each teammate has to fill, rather than approximating and guessing. This is how you avoid problems in the future. You don't want to find you are missing a key capability during the proposal.

Start a dialogue with the most competitive companies to get them on your team. Find contact information on their websites and approach them. Ask who oversees teaming for government contracts. You can also use the number provided on SAMS in the interested vendors section or look up their contact information on Bloomberg Government, GovWin IQ, or Hoovers.[91] [92]

Consider how you can make a good case to them for why they should work with you as opposed to going after government contracts on their own or with someone else, and then negotiate their place on your team (or your place on

---

91   Bloomberg Government, 2020.
92   Dun & Bradstreet, 2020.

theirs). Depending on your circumstances, you may have to negotiate with potential teammates, only approaching your second choice if your first falls through.

Remember, all of this takes time. Teaming and deal-making is as much art as science, and while you're trying to convince people to team with you rather than your competition, your competition is doing the same. Think of it like the draft season in sports. Everyone is jostling to fill their own team rosters. Some teams have bigger budgets and can offer more benefits, while others are "scrappier" and offer more opportunities for growth. Companies often start this process a year or more prior to the RFP.

There are a few reasons to wait on committing to a company. The main one is an uncertain government procurement strategy. Not knowing, for example, if the government plans to make it a HUBZone set aside, a small business set aside, or full and open competition. You might want to maintain a dialogue and work as if you were teammates toward the win but have an opt-out clause in case the government shifts strategies. This doesn't make sense just for you, but for your teaming partners as well, since there's no point being committed to bidding on work you can't win together.

As you are in discussion with your potential teammates, you need to decide how you are going to form your team. But before you commit to anything, you need to do your due diligence and qualify your potential teammates.

QUALIFYING TEAMMATES

When you are selecting teammates, make sure you are not just seeking any company with complementary capabilities, but an all-star team member. Ensure they are the right player with the right skills set for your team and the customer. Don't stack your team with only "sprinters" when it is clear the customer also needs stellar distance runners. You want players who have a track record of not only winning races (a.k.a. contracts) but also doing so cleanly—that is to say they have excellent past performance. Avoid joining forces with tracksters who do not race well because you have a good relationship with them. Remember, you can only win by convincing the government your team is superior. Your team must be stacked with the right players who make a major contribution—this is how you win the race.

As you get ready to finalize your teaming decisions, you need to perform due diligence on your candidate teammates to decide whether you want to partner with these companies, and what issues should be addressed in your teaming agreement.

You must thoroughly examine the company by answering such questions as:

- Does this company have reputation with the customer? If so, what is it?
- Does this company have reputation in the industry? If so, what is it?
  - Specifically, does this vendor have a reputation of completing quality work on schedule and within budget?
  - Have they received cure notices or terminations for convenience or fault?

- Does the company have any known organizational conflicts of interest (OCI) or appearance of OCI for this procurement?
- Can you get crucial information on the company's financial state, assets, and liabilities that would assure you this is a solvent and responsible partner?
  - What does Dun & Bradstreet show about this company, and what's in the company's annual reports?
  - Does the company have solid accounting and administrative mechanisms to be part of this contract? For example, some companies might not be approved by the Defense Contract Audit Agency (DCAA).[93] Some contracts may require you to provide earned value management (EVM) reporting.
- Does the company have any past or pending lawsuits against them?
  - Have any of the company's executives been prohibited from doing business with the government?
  - Is the company on the Excluded Parties List System (EPLS), preventing them taking part in federal procurement activities?
- Are all the required licenses, bonding and insurance documentation, clearance, and necessary certifications in order?

Evaluate all teammates early, so you have time to make changes if necessary.

Once you have firmed up your teaming partner strategy, you will enter more formal negotiations to create Teaming Agreements.

---

93 Defence Contract Audit Agency, 2020.

NEGOTIATING TEAMING AGREEMENTS

If you begin a teaming discussion it is strongly recommended that you sign a mutual nondisclosure agreement (NDA). It will protect the proprietary information of both parties and ensure confidentiality that will enable you to work out all the details on teaming for a specific pursuit.

After the NDA, some companies might use a letter of intent to sign a teaming agreement as an interim step, but normally the path is straight from an NDA to a Teaming Agreement. First, however, you need to designate a team captain, or prime vendor.

 ESTABLISHING THE PRIME VENDOR

The first stage of your teaming negotiations usually involves deciding who is going to be the prime vendor and who will be the sub. If you know the government's intended procurement strategy ahead of time, that might determine your teaming strategy, as in the case of a small business set-aside opportunity.

Just because you're an individual innovator or small business, doesn't automatically mean you can't lead the team. After all, in rowing, the coxswain is usually the smallest person on the boat. I have seen a small business identify a fantastic opportunity, structure the early capture effort correctly, and build the relationship with the customer so the customer preferred the small business to win and do the work.

The general rule of thumb is that the company in the best position should be the prime. Once it is decided which business will act as the prime vendor and which will be subcontractors, it's time to write the teaming agreement.

 THE AGREEMENT

When developing a teaming agreement, a small business will have to work hard to protect its interests. If you, as a small business or innovator, decide to work with a larger company, they may have generic teaming form that they will send over. Be careful with this because larger companies may have a different strategy or goal that may conflict with yours. You don't have to accept that "standard" agreement, which will be written in the larger business's favor.

Don't be surprised if the language of the agreement includes some sort of exclusive commitment. Be extremely careful and look closely at the language. There have been instances where primes end up awarding subcontracts to cheaper sources after winning.

It is often favorable for subcontractors to avoid getting locked into exclusive agreements because they may be able to subcontract with another prime.

You want to strike the right balance between obligations and privileges, and make sure you have clarity on what you sign. You need to address many areas proactively and discuss them up front. Here are some things you need to discuss:

Exclusivity: Is the partnership to be exclusive or non-exclusive?

Ideally, you want the teammate to be exclusive with you, meaning they are teaming only with you for this pursuit, and no one else. If the contract is awarded to someone else, can you or your teammate later team with the winning prime because your teaming agreement ends?

Obligation to Team: Does the teaming agreement obligate the prime to award the subcontract to the teammate? Or do negotiations continue after the contract award, meaning the subcontractor could lose the subcontract to someone else after having done all the proposal work?

Does the prime agree in advance to pay the subcontractor for proposal expenses if the government cancels the subcontractor's part of the work or disapproves the subcontract? How will the subcontractor handle the prime's wanting to self-perform the scope, give the subcontractor less qualified positions, or award the subcontract to another, cheaper provider?

Dispute Resolution: How will disputes be resolved? Who will have the final say, and will their decisions be binding?

Capture, proposal, and negotiation pre-award: How is everyone going to do capture and proposal work together? What specific personnel will they each provide? How will they share costs of the capture and proposal effort?

Who will represent the team in negotiations with the government and how will others support these negotiations? In what capacity? Ideally you want people to support your proposal if they are getting work share. Sometimes contractors do not hold up their end, leading to more problems. You will want penalties in place to "incentivize" them to comply, which is harder to enforce with a small company as a prime and the large company not performing.

 Special quid pro quo clauses: Are there any special stipulations about the workshare?

For example, would sharing work on this project by the prime with the teammate be in exchange for workshare on another project that the teammate primes? Do you need to make other stipulations, such as conditions on whether you win this work, and whether they win the work?

 Management Controls: Who will manage the project daily (usually a PM from the prime)? Will team representatives be needed as part of the Program Management Office (PMO) or special team leads to reach for resources? Will there be ways to reach a compromise in daily decisions? How would conflicts be escalated? What is the proper hierarchy when addressing performance issues with a teammate's employee, for example?

 Roles and responsibilities during project execution: Who handles performing what part during the contract? How much expertise, capital, people, facilities, equipment, and other contributions does each teammate need to make for project execution? What specific personnel is each team member required to provide, especially key personnel? Are these personnel dedicated 100 percent of the time, or some other set amount of time, to the project? What are the performance responsibilities for performance quality, cost, and schedule? Are there incentives and disincentives?

Ability to subcontract to the next tier: Can a teammate subcontract part of the work to the next tier of subcontractors?

Insurance, bonding, and indemnification: Will the parties' existing bonding and insurance cover this new pursuit, or will the parties have to buy separate coverage, and who will pay? Will teammates share the costs? Can one party indemnify the other, and what acts and claims can it cover?

POWER PLAY: Once you have your teaming agreements signed, integrate your exclusive teammates into your capture and proposal effort. Add them to your team roster and relay maps. This way, you will use the joint talent of your team to work out how to beat the competition. It will be especially useful to get them to take part in your solution development brainstorming.

 ## THE LIMITS OF TEAMING AGREEMENTS

While a Teaming Agreement, like the NDA, will give you a sense of security in dealing with another business prior to bidding on federal contracts, Teaming Agreements are often hard to enforce because they are nonspecific. You will need to solicit the help of a good lawyer to put together a watertight agreement text for you. However, don't rely on your lawyer to negotiate the terms of the agreement on your behalf. You need to understand every single clause that goes into the agreement yourself and read the documents you sign carefully.

After the contract award, the Subcontracting Agreement replaces the teaming agreement.

Teaming Agreements are useful to include with your proposal as part of the costing materials, even if they are not required.

But what if you're not able to build an all-star team? What if you can only deliver on a small part of the overall contract? Sometimes, it makes more sense to join an existing team. That's fine, but how do you know which team is the right one to join—the winning one?

 JOINING A WINNING TEAM

Depending on the contract size, the program, and a contract officer's goals, smaller contracts could be bundled or executed through large vehicles or multiple award contracts that will require multifaceted solutions.

Most businesses can't execute **Major League** contracts on their own—especially if the contract includes a diverse scope of work. Even if they could perform the work on their own, it would be difficult for them to win the contract because most solicitations require past performance for every single aspect of work.

That means there may be opportunities for you to plug the gaps in a **Major League** business's expertise and join their team. So, let's look at the pros and cons of joining someone else's team, and what you need to be aware of if you decide this is the best route for you.

 SHOULD YOU JOIN A SQUAD?

While joining a winning squad can have multiple benefits, there are also potential drawbacks to consider.

- This environment is circular. Companies you may team with today might be your competitors in the future. Therefore, you may want to limit sharing proprietary and technical data.
- If you form a separate entity, called a joint venture (JV), your company might have extra liabilities. Developing a joint venture may put you over the small business limits.
- When you are a subcontractor, there are many ways a prime contractor could take advantage of you and not deliver on their promise during the proposal stage. They might not pay you in a timely fashion.

Here's our list of teaming pros and cons.

Table 2: Teaming Pros and Cons

PROS	CONS
Teaming agreements in this sector, unlike other teaming arrangements, often only apply to one solicitation or to a specific government program and therefore:	
• Limit the parties' obligations to one another. • Can be tailored to the specific solicitation and provide for a variety of termination provisions. • Allow parties who are unfamiliar with each other and therefore reluctant to joint venture on a "trial" basis.	• Must be renegotiated for each solicitation. • Do not guarantee the prime contractor and the proposed subcontractor will be able to reach an agreement on the terms of a subcontract. • Prime contractor is the only party in direct contact with the government, and therefore bears the entire risk of contract performance.
Joint Venturing is an alternative to teaming, in which a separate company is set up to perform the contract.	
• The new company can be established to cover multiple solicitations and contracts • The separate company can benefit from the combined bonding capacity of its member companies. • Liability can be limited to the new legal entity if the partners form a limited liability partnership • The entity may be able to avoid the high-cost structure of its member companies, which is important if price is a major source selection criterion.	• In a joint venture, each member company may have liability for the obligations of the joint venture. • Management issues or partner disagreements may be difficult to mitigate and may result in delayed decision-making. • Members may be locked into a relationship with one another for a longer period than intended. • The member companies will likely be considered "affiliated" for small business size calculations.[1]

Regardless of the form of the teaming arrangement, contractors should perform the following due diligence on their prospective teaming partners:

- Confirm the proposed teaming partner is not suspended, debarred, or proposed for debarment by checking the Systems for Award Management (SAM) website.
- Consider the proposed teaming partner's past performance history.
- Confirm the proposed teaming partner is in a sound financial position to perform any resulting prime contract or subcontract.
- Confirm the proposed teaming partner does not have an actual or potential organizational conflict of interest that should prevent the team from receiving the contract award.[94]

POWER PLAY: *Make your decisions based on your own priorities and circumstances. Make your own pros and cons list. This will both help you decide if joining a squad is right for you and remind you of the things to look out for during teaming negotiations.*

If you do decide to join a winning team, how do you go about choosing your best option?

---

94 (48 C.F.R. § 9.501).

HOW TO SPOT A WINNING SQUAD

Now that you know the pros and cons of teaming or joining a winning squad, let's look at how you find teammates. If you're wondering why we didn't start with this, it's for the same reason we cover the skills you need before we enter a zone: we don't want you to jump in unprepared.

You can find teammates in multiple places, some of which are listed below. Use a combination of the methods described here to confirm your findings:

- Talk to the federal buyers about their preferred vendors. Ask questions about their strengths and weaknesses.
- Ask your seasoned staff who might know different companies.
- Look up top subcontractors by agency and research them further.
  - Look up spending by contractor for each agency at USAspending.gov or BGov.com.
  - Check past performance at USAspending.gov, BGov. com, or beta.sam.gov.
- Check the interested vendors list at SAMS and GovWin IQ (iq.govwin.com).
- Use the teaming module on GovWin and The Federal Contractor Network (TFCN).[95]
- SBA's Dynamic Small Business Search can help you find small business teammates.[96]
- The SBA SubNet at eweb1.sba.gov/subnet/client/dsp_ Landing.cfm is another place to start looking for subcontracting opportunities.

95 The Federal Contractor Network, 2020.
96 Small Business Administration, 2020.

- Consult the Department of Defense Subcontracting Directory from the Office of Small Business Programs (OSBP) that includes prime contractors with contract information including a guide to marketing to DoD.[97]
- Check whether the company has a GSA schedule at GSA E-Library.[98]

Once you've found your potential teams, run through the "**Qualifying Teammates**" and "**Negotiating Teaming Agreements**" sections above. Be aware that as a subcontractor, it's even more important you get a specialist lawyer to negotiate the agreement on your behalf and ensure every clause before signing.

Whether you're building your own winning team as the prime contractor or subcontracting to someone else's, there are a few issues you need to be aware of in **The Teaming Zone**.

 SIZE MATTERS

Most teaming arrangements take place between large and small businesses, where either one could be the prime depending on the procurement type.

Because size rules can be complex, small business size is a large cause of protest over the award of contracts. Teaming with the wrong partners on a project could leave you open to protest.

The Request for Proposal (RFP)—the document setting out the rules of the application process for a specific

---

97   Office of Small Business Programs, DoD, 2020.
98   GSA Federal Acquisition Service, 2020.

contract—will state a few things you have to pay attention to when teaming.

- It will include a North American Industry Classification System (NAICS) code that will tell you what is considered the small business size for that procurement.
- It will also give the maximum dollar value average gross annual receipts for the past five years to qualify (for most businesses in the services industry), or the maximum number of employees (applicable to manufacturing, telecommunications, and transportation companies).

For example, if the RFP is released under *NAICS 541330, Engineering*, then the small business under the NAICs should have made no more than $16.5 million in average gross receipts for the past five years by the time of proposal submission.

You can find the full list of NAICS and their associated dollar and employee size standards on the NAICS Association website.[99]

🏆 **POWER PLAY**: *Understand the Federal Acquisition Regulations (FAR) regarding small business types and sizes, and how the government views your size. Know any set-asides you can take advantage of, and the thresholds where you would no longer be eligible. Consider how any teaming arrangements would impact your eligibility, or how you might make otherwise ineligible teammates eligible.*

---

99 NAICS Association, 2019.

But business size isn't the only issue to consider. There's also the issue of affiliation, and how that can affect your eligibility to small business status, among other things.

AVOIDING AFFILIATION

In government contracting, there is a concept called affiliation, which essentially means the government can add up the size of all the companies teaming together. Instead of just looking at the size of the small business prime alone, they can treat the team as one bidder. These rules are in place to prevent **Major League players** abusing the **Power-Ups** intended for **Little League players** by taking advantage of socioeconomic categories, creating shell companies for individual contracts or groups of contracts, or to funnel work through shell companies to themselves while maintaining their own socio-economic category standing, and so on.

You may want to avoid being affiliated with another company in the government's eyes for several reasons. It dilutes your brand, and should things go south with the other company, you don't want to be tarred with the same brush. But mostly, you don't want to be affiliated for size purposes because that limits your ability to access the Small Business set aside categories and support programs designed to help innovators like you to compete with big business.

If the government considers companies affiliated for size purposes, it will add teammates' gross receipts numbers (or employee numbers) together. If they do that, the sum might exceed the size standard of the NAICS for that RFP, rendering the proposal invalid. If that happens, all your work will have been for nothing, because your bid will be ineligible and won't even be considered.

Behaviors that can leave you vulnerable to an assessment of affiliation include going after the same bid with the same team repeatedly, using each other's office spaces on a regular basis, or habitually sharing resources, such as a proposal team or laboratory equipment.

You don't have to fear this in your regular teaming arrangements. Even if you tend to pair with the same teammates, Teaming Agreements don't automatically create an affiliation. Just make sure you have a formal Teaming Agreement in place, which helps establish the separate entities, their roles, and responsibilities.

Joint Ventures (JVs) between a large and small business that are not part of the Small Business Administration Mentor-Protege Program, can create an affiliation.[100] So if you're considering teaming with a **Major League player**, consider an SBA approved mentor, so that the affiliations rules won't apply.

To avoid affiliation, a small business joint ventures can win no more than three contracts in two years (with some exceptions). If the JV is ongoing, and is pursuing multiple contracts, it becomes a partnership, not a JV. At that point, the companies will be affiliated for size purposes.

---

100 For a full explanation of the Mentor/Protege program see Small Business Administration, "All Small Mentor-Protégé program," 2020.

You also need to follow the rules specific to each type of small business. You will probably need advice from a government contracts lawyer or a consultant to guide you through them.

 POWER PLAY: *Identify the rules that apply to your business and ensure your teaming agreements respect them.*

As if that wasn't complicated enough, there are also rules about how much of the work a prime vendor must do and how much they can subcontract to other suppliers.

 SUBCONTRACTING LIMITS

In general, the government doesn't approve of pass-through, and I see A LOT of people getting in trouble with this. That's where a prime vendor acts as a conduit to subcontractors only, without doing a significant share of the work themselves. Here is what a government requires small business prime contractors to perform in a teaming arrangement:

- In the services arena (but not construction), the small business prime must perform 50 percent of the cost of the contract incurred for personnel with its own employees.
- In the supplies or product arena, the prime must supply 50 percent of the cost of manufacturing the supplies or products, not including the cost of materials.
- In special trade construction, the prime must be responsible for 25 percent of the cost of the contract with its own employees, again, not including materials.[101]

---

101 (85 FR 11746, 2020)

Recently the SBA has cracked down on companies violating the limits. The government is contemplating a rule change whereby it would create a mentor-protégé program for service-disabled veteran-owned small business (SDVOSBs) and HUBZone companies that has similar benefits to the 8(a) mentor-protégé program, such as an ability to form a JV with a large business without being affiliated for size purposes. It will be exciting if it happens.

 POWER PLAY: *Check your teaming agreements for subcontracting limits and ensure you and all team members stay compliant.*

So, now you know who your buyers are, how and where to get support, which players you need on your team, and how to build or join a super squad without breaking the rules.

With your **Team Roster** complete, and your key players and teaming partners in place, it's time to start business capture activities in earnest and learn **Listening for Opportunities**.

8

LISTENING FOR OPPORTUNITIES

Before we enter **The Intelligence Zone**, we're going to focus on **Listening for Opportunities** and make sure you have the beginnings of your **Business Strength Training System** in place. That way, when you enter **The Intelligence Zone** and start collecting data in earnest, you'll both know what to look for and ask, and what to do with information once you have it to increase your chances of winning your first federal contract.

Many people don't realize that by the time a need has been posted on a government procurement website, the decision is already 70 percent made. It's already too late to start going after that work.

What does that mean?

It means that whatever the requirement, the technical specifications of the solution must be defined before they can be filled. For most medium to large acquisitions—**The Big and Major Leagues**—to set the scope of the requirements, the procurement specialists will have been talking to somebody else for anything from one to two years.

They will have worked with someone to determine what's possible and what needs to be done to solve the requirement. They will have put the solicitation together based on those conversations. The chances of them not going with the provider they're already talking to are slim.

 ## KNOW YOUR AUDIENCES

As a federal innovator, you need to know your audiences, and you need to be talking to them all on their own terms.

- You need to know who your end users are and what their pain points are SO THAT you can talk to them about mission success.
- You need to know who your intermediaries are and what their priorities are SO THAT you can talk to them in terms of efficiency and key performance indicators.
- You need to know who your buyers are SO THAT you can talk to them in terms of value.

Using your **External Team Roster,** consider your audience groups. Start collecting words and phrases you hear repeatedly from each of them and echo those phrases back to them in your conversations.

Have a process of talking to buyers, cultivating relationships, and having those discussions about upcoming requirements and solutions. You want to become a part of that shaping process. If you're hoping to step in at the last stage and swoop off with the contract, you're setting yourself up for disappointment. You need to develop a process for tracking and managing all that internally. By the time it appears on beta. sam.gov, it's too late.

In my personal experience, when I was the one recommending what to purchase or assisting with buying on behalf of the federal government, the best and most successful companies were the ones who were constantly calling me and updating me on their product development even when I didn't have any new contracts to award or requirements, and who asked questions. They were the people who, when a new problem emerged, I would call to discuss workable solutions. I knew them so well, I had them on speed dial. When you need a solution, you're not going to call a complete unknown, you're going to lean on the people you know first because they have helped you solve problems in the past.

 **RAYTHEON AND GENERAL DYNAMICS**

For example, during my time at JIEDDO, a number of business and sales representatives from Raytheon and General Dynamics would "magically" call me or request a meeting about once per month to keep us abreast on their latest technical and product developments. They understood our office was primarily working with air platforms, so they armed us with appropriate materials such as spec sheets which offered critical information such as size, weight, and power (SWaP)

in addition to cost. They were relentless about sending "spec" sheets and information briefs about their products.

They were also strategic. They understood their product offerings were typically expensive and required considerable capital, and therefore made sure they started their campaigns early in the fiscal year. I knew their names, email addresses and phone numbers so well, I didn't need to keep them on speed dial. I still remember some of those email addresses, and I'm familiar with their product ranges to this day.

 OPPORTUNITIES TO ENGAGE

Government procurement differs widely from private enterprise in the length of the procurement cycle. You need to start early. Ideally, you will be working at least a year ahead of the Request for Proposal (RFP). You can do many things in capture as a last-minute crunch, but building relationships is not one of them.

You need to understand the government WANTS industry to approach government customers. The Federal Acquisition Regulation states: "Exchanges of information among all interested parties, from the earliest identification of a requirement through receipt of proposals are encouraged."[102]

The FAR then states that the purpose of exchanging information is to improve the understanding of government requirements, thereby allowing potential offerors to judge whether

---

102 (FAR) Part 15.201

or how they can satisfy the government's requirements. This also enhances the government's ability to obtain quality supplies and services at reasonable prices. It goes on to express the government's desire to further increase efficiency in proposal preparation, proposal evaluation, negotiation, and contract award. The same law encourages one-on-one meetings with potential offerors.

Despite this law, government employees are often worried about breaking procurement integrity rules (FAR 3.104-3). Program personnel, scientists, engineers, other government personal and their support contractors will generally communicate with you freely prior to the development of the Source Selection Plan. However, after that point, throughout the development of the solicitation and contract award, communication will be limited and through the Contracting Officer via formal channels. As a result, you'll want to start as early as possible.

Let's look at how the government deals with interaction throughout the procurement cycle.

- **Pre-RFI**—The government will typically be very communicative as they are trying to collect required information to put together a requisition and or an acquisition package. During the Pre-RFI phase they are heavily involved with conducting market research. Indeed, the RFI might be part of that research.
- **Post-RFI**—However, once the government put out a Request for Information (RFI) or Sources Sought, meeting with you informally would open them up to accusations of favoritism or collusion, and can lead to pre-award protests.

- **Draft RFP**—Government employees won't share what they discuss with you with other bidders, and you should not ask or expect them to divulge the contents of conversations with other bidders or contractors with you. Only in special cases will you be able to talk to the government directly after the draft RFP is created to avoid even the appearance of giving a leg up on the competition. The Contracting Officer will be the point of contact because they want to avoid a protest. All communications will be in writing and made public. Often, they will post a public Q&A response list.
- **Final RFP**—After they issue the final RFP, the government will not meet with you and will not discuss any details of the procurement.

The solicitation often provides information about a question-and-answer period shortly after the solicitation is posted. This leaves little time to thoroughly process the entire RFP depending on the complexity. Remember, all questions and answers are disclosed to the playing field to avoid impropriety.

POWER PLAY: There is always a way to meet with the government in an unofficial setting before the draft RFP or the final RFP are issued. However, this is usually through special relationships that already exist. As you are building any relationship with a customer, you can only go and see the same person so often. You won't succeed in building a relationship if you only allot a couple of months to do it. It takes much, much longer because you need to space visits out over time. Your best bet is to get to the right people early. Also, cultivate relationships with as many people within an office as you can. Employee churn tends to be high, and you don't want to have to constantly start from scratch with a single point of contact.

But first things first, let's take time out to set up the basis for your **Business Strength Training System.**

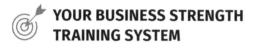 YOUR BUSINESS STRENGTH TRAINING SYSTEM

Why do all kinds of athletes, from sprinters to marathon runners, football players, and even Formula One Drivers include strength training in their workout regimes? Because they know it's not enough to practice their own disciplines. They need to maintain overall fitness, and Strength Training—whether in the form of power lifting, parkour, or Pilates—if they want to perform at their best.

As an innovator, you may want to focus on your core strengths of understanding the technology and science and leave the "people-ing" to others with "softer skills." But if you're working as a small team of innovators, you have to interface and work on creating relationships. It's not enough to listen to your buyers and end users' needs on an ad-hoc basis, go away and tinker, and then expect them to buy your solution. Although you never want to turn down the opportunity to listen to your buyers talk about their needs and issues, as that is free market research, what you really want is a system in place that helps you keep track of your buyer's problems.

You need a tool to help you cultivate the relationships you need to build with all the diverse actors in the procurement process, from end users and program managers to procurement and contract officers, and above. Investigate Customer Relationship Management (CRM) software designed specifically for Business to Government (B2G).

At the time of writing, some of the options include:

Dynamics 365 for Government Contractors (infostrat.com/crm-for-govt-contractors)[103]

Jamis Customer Management Suite (jamis.com/products/jamis-prime-erp/customer-relationship/)[104]

Salesforce Platform for Government (salesforce.com/solutions/industries/government/government-contractors/)[105]

Government Contractors (governmentcontractors.co/crm-marketing-automation/)[106]

You might want to spend some time investigating the options and see which works best for you. Set up the categories to suit your needs and start entering your contacts details into the database. Ensure the database is accessible enough so that

---

103 Information Strategies, Inc, 2019.
104 JAMIS Software Corporation, 2020.
105 Salesforce.com, inc, 2020.
106 Government Contractors, LLC, 2019.

everyone who needs to access it can, but secure enough that there's no unauthorized access.

 TAKE USEFUL NOTES

From your first conversation with any new contact, try to start making notes in your CRM software. Don't just note everything they say; listen to what they are telling you about how you can serve them better. Each of your audience segments has different priorities and uses different language to express their needs. You want to be collecting that data to echo back to them later.

When the ACQUISITIONS community starts talking about things that impact cost, that impact schedule, or that impact performance, you need to listen, because those are the things that impact their grades and are most important for them to be successful. That's their responsibility. When they start talking about programs going over cost or over budget, you need to start drilling down into why that's happening. Those are the kinds of conversations you need to have with the acquisitions professionals. You need to be talking about how or why your solution can help bridge that problem.

When you're talking to the SCIENCE AND TECHNOLOGY crowd and hearing they're struggling to get a solution to work, that there's something wrong with their underlying theory, or that they have performance issues, pay attention. Ask yourself if you have something that can address the issue.

When you're listening to the USER community, listen for issues such as falling behind, having operational challenges, or not being able to make mission. That's when you need to take notes because that's their bottom line.

Start building a picture in your CRM software. Look at the language patterns, about what terms each of your audiences uses most frequently and match your language to theirs in your interactions with them. Don't talk to science geeks about mission success, talk to them about the specs and variances. Don't talk to end users about the specs; talk to them about the user experience. Talk to program managers about capability gaps, and to contracting officers about budgetary constraints.

Flag things for follow up and assign them to the right people. Start making sure information flows throughout your organization smoothly; it's the lifeblood of your business capture activities, and the core action of your **Business Strength Training Center**.

With that in mind—and knowing many innovation and technology-focused professionals are often less than stellar at the soft skills of communication and relationship building—let's give you some basic tools to work with.

POWER PLAY: *Many players in the Federal Procurement Arena, and especially in the innovation space, on both sides of the divide, are very much stuck in their own world.*

From scientists and technical engineers, to soldiers, to Procurement Officers, to every other stakeholder you care to mention, many of the players involved understand their own corner of the game extensively, but are HOPELESSLY lost when it comes to dealing with other people and their perspectives.

Because many of these roles are also high-pressure or detail-oriented, and require specific skill sets, they also attract highly intelligent individuals. Unfortunately, many of them don't relate to people very well.

Therefore, whoever you are dealing with, you need to understand them. You need to learn their coded language and jargon, and know both how to SPEAK to them so they understand you, and how to LISTEN to them, so you don't miss the nuances of what they are telling you.

If you're working in innovation, and particularly in early-stage development in the Little and Big Leagues, you likely will deal with Technical Points of Contact (TPOC), Government Engineers, Government Scientists, Technical Program Managers, etc., who are very different.

As you move into higher technology readiness levels and the procurement side of the house, you will deal with procurement officers with very different concerns.

I've seen SO MANY people fail at this and miss out on millions of dollars in federal funding because they didn't understand who they were talking to and that person's motivations and limits.

MAKE SURE you LISTEN to the language your different audiences use, RECORD their EXACT words, DOUBLE-CHECK you understand their meaning, and ECHO their concerns back to them IN THEIR OWN LANGUAGE at EVERY stage of the cycle.

 ## WELCOMING WARM-UPS

You need to make a good first impression on government personnel. Despite what you might think, that doesn't mean dazzle them with your superior knowledge or technical ability from the outset. There's an old saying: "People don't care how much you know until they know how much you care." That means you must show you care about not just the job at hand, but about your country, and your relationship with them. In other words, you must be likeable.

First, always remember, when you are meeting with a government representative, your purpose is to listen, NOT to show off.

 ## RELATIONSHIP REPS

One of the most important tasks in capturing and winning federal contracts is to get the customer to want to do business with you. People do business with people they know, like, and trust. So, your job is to be visible, friendly, and trustworthy. Create lasting relationships with government customers, and that means routinely touching base with them. Calls, emails or written communication, and face-to-face meetings form the basis of your Relationship Reps. You need to be comfortable reaching out to government employees.

By building relationships with potential buyers, you also open a channel to gather information from customers to gain insights into their requirements. This will help you understand what's important to them and what influences their buying behavior.

 **ATLAS RESEARCH**

During research for this book, I spoke with Young Bang, vice president for growth at Atlas Research, a consulting and applied research firm that serves federal health and social services agencies.

He told me, "I have a rule of six. Meet with the potential client at least six times to build a relationship! The first couple of times should be MOSTLY listening. The third or fourth, maybe follow up with a couple pain points from your first two meetings and discuss them more in depth. The fifth or sixth, offer potential ways to help them with previous pain points. On the sixth and following, refine the 'solution' with the client, get feedback, and refine some more."

Atlas Research LLC has enjoyed massive success as a federal contracting company since their inception in 2008. These principles are obviously working because they grew exponentially.

Following these principles can be particularly difficult for scientists and specialists, who often are the most intelligent people in the room. Learning to listen first, ask questions second, and offer opinions last helps you form a great relationship with the customer. It's also a valuable information-gathering technique.

You should come to your meeting well-prepared having researched as much as possible about the customer and their agency mission. Be prepared to talk about yourself, but only in the context of the customer. Then be prepared to ask open-ended questions about the procurement you are chasing, getting the customer to open and talk. It's much easier to get the government to be open with you early in the procurement cycle.

But what if you're not naturally a people person? Once you've made contact, what do you talk about? How do you build a personal relationship without crossing professional boundaries? You use **Questioning Sets** to gather information.

 QUESTIONING SETS FOR INFORMATION GATHERING

When you're practicing playing a sport, you practice specific actions over and over until they become natural and instinctive to you, an involuntary response to certain conditions. A sprinter will practice getting out of the starting blocks quickly, and use a series of "drills," such as running exaggerated arm movements (big arms) or with no arm movement (no arms), kicking legs as high forward or back as possible, all aimed at training different muscles for different aspects of sprinting.

You're going to practice asking a series of questions in small groups, or "sets," each designed to elicit information from your contacts in certain situations.

SET 1: GREETING THE CONTACT

Practice asking these questions and showing genuine interest in the answers whenever you meet a contact or colleague.

- How have you been?
- How is work treating you?
- Has anything changed since we last spoke?
- Is there anything I can help you with?

 SET 2: DIGGING FOR DISSATISFACTION

If the contact tells you there are no changes and nothing you need to know about, you want to do a bit of prep work, and get to know how things currently work, in preparation for the day something does change.

- Are there any contracts due for renewal?
- Who are the present incumbents? How is that working out? Would you do anything differently next time?
- What's the present contracting vehicle? Is it an existing contract or does the government plan on developing a new contract developing a new contact based upon a requirement?
- Could the way the work is being done be improved in any way?

 SET 3: IDENTIFYING ISSUES

If your contact shows any sign of having issues with the present setup, you want to know how to dive into them professionally.

- Are your customers having issues with existing solutions or technologies?

- Can you describe them?
- How would you fix it?
- Do you have a specific vision or solutions in mind?

 SET 4: SCOPING THE WORK

Once you have found an identified need, you want to focus on the requirement, and the scope of work. You want to ask questions that help frame the requirement and position you as a trusted advisor in the process.
- Can you describe your requirement?
- What is the most important outcome for the project?
- What issues remain unresolved that need to be addressed before putting out a request?

 SET 5: STRATEGIZING

Before you invest too much time investigating a specific opportunity, test the waters to see if there's a possibility of winning work from it. If you're a small business, and you'd be bidding in The Major Leagues, you may not want to invest the energy and, instead, focus on finding an opening in The Little Leagues. Ask these questions to find out where you stand.
- Is there a formal requirement?
- Are there available funds? If not, when do you expect to have funding for this requirement?
- Are you considering a COTS solution? Or are you thinking of developing/creating something from scratch?
- Does the planned funding align with the type of solution you're looking to purchase or develop?

SET 6: TALKING TIME

If the project looks set to go ahead, you want to ask questions about the timeframes and schedules the government is working toward. Remember what we said about funding earlier? They could be talking about developing something they have in a plan for two years from now.

- When would you like the project to begin?
- When do you expect to get the procurement approved?
- Have you defined the key project milestones?
- Is there anything we can do to expedite the process for you?

 SET 7: TALKING MONEY

Of course, at some point, you need to check the budget exists or will exist for the project to go ahead. Asking these questions early on is another way to make sure you don't spend too much time and energy on a project that won't be profitable in the long term.

- What is the budget for this opportunity?
- Has this budget been approved and funded?
- What are the milestones for approval and funding?
- What is the risk that the project will not be funded?

 SET 8: TALKING PERSONNEL

You need to know where work is to be completed, if you need personnel with clearances for government facilities, etc.

- Where will the work be carried out? Onsite or offsite?
- Are there any personnel specific requirements on the contractor side? Do they need specific qualifications or clearances?

Sets two, five, and seven are aimed specifically at the buying audience. But the other question sets can be used with end user and intermediary audiences as well.

POWER PLAY: *Work those questions into the conversation naturally as the opportunities come up; don't turn this into an interrogation. Some of them will apply, and others will not. These are just a few examples of questions to get you started. Starting is the hardest part.*

As you get the hang of it, and especially as your relationship with customers grows, you will come up with more questions to ask that are specific to an opportunity.

Be prepared not to get all this information in one visit. You might not get it all from one person either. You might have to meet with several people in the customer's organization to get full and credible answers.

Remember to update your CRM software with the information you gather after every meeting; your **Business Strength Training Center** is only as good as the data you enter it. But one-on-one conversations and meetings are not the only way to gather intelligence.

INTELLIGENCE SCOOPS

You can gather intelligence from a range of sources on upcoming needs and knowledge gaps. We call this **Intelligence Scooping** because you're drawing in data from various sources to pull in information you will then filter and sort through to inform your business capture activities. **Intelligence Scooping** will enable you to bring something valuable to your customer.

Intelligence Scooping is research and detective work, where you collect little pieces of intel and put together as complete a picture as you can to help you make good decisions. As you learn about the opportunity and gather information you will realize it has multiple dimensions and information sources. You will want to formulate more pointed questions and go back to the same source or find new sources. It is an iterative process.

But what is the best way to prioritize your information gathering? It's usually a good idea to start broad, then get more specific, looking for more detailed information.

 KNOW YOUR HISTORY

Your first task will be to research and understand the history of the requirement or opportunity. There is a reason and a story behind every requirement. Not knowing and understanding the history will often hurt you. You should research to find out how this requirement came about and how it evolved.

Who or what is behind the genesis of the requirement?
- An end user?
- An agency mission?
- A specific person saw a need?
- A program listed the work as an essential element?
- An existing procurement is about to end?

You really need to understand the source.

 KEY EVENTS

Then you will want to work out what key events happened to influence the course of the procurement.

- Were there any problems encountered along the way?
- Have they been resolved?

Knowing your timeline against the political backdrop is vital.

 KEY PEOPLE

Check which contractors and contracting officers have been involved with this opportunity from the start.

- Was this opportunity issued as a contract before?
- Is there a prime vendor you will subcontract to?
- How many people are involved in the decision-making process, and what are their roles?

You need to know who you are up against, and who you must convince.

 KEY ISSUES

Find out if there are specific issues with the site, the nature of the location, suppliers, technology, or any other considerations that would be important in your solution development effort.

- Did any technical or management solution fail or get rejected along the way?
- Are there any areas the customer is sensitive to?
- Are there things you should avoid when dealing with the customer?

As you answer all these generic questions, you will come up with answers that might prompt you to ask more specific questions.

 POWER PLAY: *The goal is to become at least as knowledgeable as your customer is about this opportunity and preferably more so. Knowing more than your customer could help you educate them and capture their interest. Knowing the "story behind the story" helps you shape your solution by taking all the nuances into consideration. You will also quickly achieve trusted advisor status and smooth your way to the Inside Track.*

CONTEXT

Your next step is to find out the origin of every requirement. Don't overlook big stuff. Consider the larger context for the opportunity, the problem in the field in general that could impact this opportunity. For example, if this project is about soldiers in the field, it helps to understand general issues surrounding deployed soldiers with recent repeated deployments.

Research starts with the right questions, and the most important ones you can ask are things like:
- What keeps your customers up at night?
- What are their goals?
- What are the recurring themes and words you keep seeing in all the information that you find?
- Where does the contract you are pursuing fit in all of this?

After you ask these questions, you need to know where to look for answers. The information is out there but you need to know how to search. We'll talk more about that next in **The Intelligence Zone**.

9

THE INTELLIGENCE ZONE

Armed with your **Questioning Sets** and with your **Business Strength Training System** fully loaded with contact details, and the details of any upcoming projects you might be interested in bidding on, it's time to enter **The Intelligence Zone.**

EVERY successful team or coach does some sort of targeted intelligence gathering, obtaining statistics on another team, individual player, or runner to gain a better understanding of the environment, and the competition.

Here, we're going to look at some of the sources you might use for **Intelligence Scooping.** You may be able to think of others, but these should at least get you a healthy start.

INDUSTRY INTELLIGENCE SCOOPS

The government uses industry days, proposal conferences, and site visits as ways to involve the industry and to maintain a dialogue to improve the government's procurement process. This is a fantastic opportunity for you, so you want to be prepared for these events and get the most out of them.

Here are some pointers.

Send the right people—Even in the smallest innovation teams, team leaders are not always the best people to collect the right intelligences and ask technical questions. Most often, you want to send the capture manager and the technical subject matter expert (SME).

Do your homework—You don't want to use the industry day to learn about the opportunity; you want to have done that beforehand. The best use of the industry day is to hear things beyond the most basic data.

Create a list of questions—Especially include specific technical questions you might get direct answers to on the spot, which might otherwise never be answered in the RFP. Just remember your competitors will be listening.

Collect Literature—Try to gather any documents that might be available and request them for reading later

Look around—Who is there from your customer's organization? Write down the customer representatives' names and positions.

Listen—As your customer is speaking, listen for the following information:

- **Priorities:** What do they want to see come from this procurement? Are there goals they are looking to achieve? Specifications they have to meet?
- **Themes:** What are the recurring themes they keep weaving into the points that they make? Pay attention to comments about lessons learned from the past program, quality, and certifications.
- **Language:** Note any buzzwords they are using, such as quality system or performance metrics.

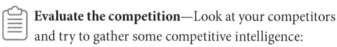 **Evaluate the competition**—Look at your competitors and try to gather some competitive intelligence:

- Glance over the sign-in sheet that gets passed around. Note who is attending from what companies and from which divisions in those companies.
- Request a vendor list from the customer as part of the Q&A session, unless they already said they would post it.
- Who could be your competitor's program manager candidate?

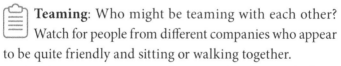 **Teaming:** Who might be teaming with each other? Watch for people from different companies who appear to be quite friendly and sitting or walking together.

- Are there any companies advertising that they are looking for teaming opportunities?

 Site Visits—Look at the site condition and collect as much information as possible about the following:

- Work location
- Equipment (government and contractor furnished)
- Potential challenges posed by the site

Interact—Open days are meant to be an opportunity for you to meet the government personnel involved in the project and get your questions answered. Don't attend just to listen and observe. The more you interact with the Source Selection Authorities, the more they will remember you when it comes time to enter your bids.

- Ask for what you might like to see included in the solicitation and elaborate how it is in the best interest of the customer.
- Make suggestions to the customer during the conference that would be regarded by them as insightful, helpful, and proactive.
- If you have a chance for any one-on-one time after the briefing is over, introduce yourself, socialize your key staff (such as your own PM), and reiterate your key messages.

Follow Up—After the event, while your collection is still fresh, immediately document everything you have found out in your **Business Strength Training Center.** Note the resulting action items and share those with your management and capture team.

Also remember people within your target agency are not your only source of intelligence. You can get information, in many cases, from asking end users.

 ## END USER INTELLIGENCE SCOOPS

When you can talk to and can reach the end users—people who are your customer's customer—you can gain a lot of valuable information:

- How are they experiencing your customer's service and what do they feel about it?
- What are their key concerns and specific problems?
- What do they need for the service or solution to work better?
- What feedback have end users been providing to the customer on the quality of performance, schedule, budget, and risk from the solution that has been offered?

All this information leads to new intelligence, and new intelligence leads to more detailed questions. Sometimes it will take you a lot of digging to work out several layers of end users. For example, there are multiple layers between heads of departments and service administrators, office managers and service providers, and ultimate end users. Each set of users will have its own set of concerns.

Your task is to understand what each set of end users care about. You need to ask probing questions for their preferences and needs. You need to convey that you really want to make a difference and solve their problems. You will then have a chance to show this understanding in your proposal.

 ## RUMOR INTELLIGENCE SCOOPS

Speaking of rumors, sometimes secondhand information can offer added insights about an "emerging" opportunity. It can be extremely valuable if you subscribe to the belief that there is no smoke without fire.

Sometimes you might receive a piece of information that doesn't make sense alone. Make a note of it. As you continue the process, other pieces of data could surface, which might give powerful insights.

You need to consider the source of rumors, though. Rumors can come from competitors, creating misinformation, from disgruntled end users, from other personnel blowing off steam, or from half-heard and misconstrued conversations. You should never act on a rumor alone.

FREE INTELLIGENCE SCOOPS

The government publishes information about who holds contracts and subcontracts for what work and indicates the contract value in the Federal Procurement Data System and other websites such as USAspending.gov.[107]

TARGET AGENCY INFORMATION

Requests for Information—Although Requests for Information (RFIs) from your target agencies may be the starting point for your research, you don't want to rely on them to give you a complete picture. Due to space constraints, only the basic version of the story of what the government needs might make it into the requirement. Unless they have a Systems Engineering and Technical Assistance (SETA) expert from the industry on staff, many agencies may not be able to fully express their complex needs succinctly in a set of requirements.

---

107   Federal Procurement Data Systems, 2020.

Sometimes a well-expressed initial set of requirements will be simplified and changed based on multiple inputs from other stakeholders or budgetary constraints—which can distort the original intent.

You should assume request documents will be limited. They will not be enough for you to write a compelling proposal. Remember, the government will worry about repercussions from violating procurement integrity and will shut the door early on. Unless you start way ahead of the game, you will be operating blind in a silent world. You will often only have bits of information to build a mosaic of a whole picture to compensate for the lack of knowledge.

Even if you have contact with customers, they won't tell you everything—so you will still have to search for information to fill the gaps. In the **Federal Procurement Arena**, the best-informed player often wins.

 INTELLIGENCE ARTIFACTS

Besides Requests for Information and Proposals, your customer probably drops all kinds of interesting intel in unique places to help you win your race. You should find these documents and sift through them to extract the right type of information. Good places to look include:

- **Briefs, presentations, speeches, and papers**: It is possible to obtain some of this information online, or by asking around to see if anyone has saved copies of these.
- **Budgets, annual funding, and availability of funds**: Check the President's Budget, USAspending.gov, The Congressional Budget Office, The Project on Government

Oversight (POGP) FEDspending report, Exhibits 53 and 300, and the Program Objective Memorandum (POM) for each DoD customer. [108] [109] [110] You can also ask the customer directly whether they have the funding and how much they have for the year versus total budgeted for the program. Glean insights from the paid sources such as BGov, GovWin IQ, and Centurion about the program value and spending history.

- **Congressional testimony and statements**: Congressional hearings, Inspector General (IG) and Government Accountability Office (GAO) reports will highlight issues and challenges you may be able to help solve. Bloomberg Government (BGov) offers a compilation of this information for each agency, or you can find it by scouring the customer's website and other web resources.
- **Conference programs**: On the Internet, as part of a conference or a media event, or on a customer's website. If your customer spoke at some conference, you may be able to get a copy of the presentation from the conference organizers.
- **Mission Statements**: We often find these on the customer's website, subscription services, and various other locations. The agency's mission statement will tell you about the agency's priorities and will provide context for how your opportunity fits into this larger mission.
- **Press Releases**: These are available on the customer website (in the press room section) or through an internet search. Press releases usually discuss various contracts

---

108 Congressional Budget Office, 2020.
109 Congressional Budget Office, 2020.
110 Project on Government Oversight, 2020.

and events that might shed some light on the opportunity history.

- **Reports and plans**: Check your customer's website or those of contractors who work at the government site. This information can help shed light on an opportunity's history, accomplishments, problems, needs, strategies, and potentially future opportunities.

On top of these government-specific sources, scour local news outlets, industry magazines, and read the latest books released in your industry.

 ## PAID INTELLIGENCE SCOOPS

Sports leagues are now using paid intelligence and data to understand the players and win the game; you can also do the same with government contracting.

- **Bloomberg Government**: Bloomberg offers news, analysis, and data for people who interact with the government. The site is split into two sections: Government Affairs for those concerned with policy and Government Contracting for those who want to win federal business.
- **Carroll Publishing:** Carroll Publishing offers information for intelligence gathering to obtain detailed agency organizational charts and agency contact information.
- **Centurion Research (now a part of Deltek)**: Information on Centurion for capture purposes is organized by opportunity, with associated information, including pricing, competitors' proposals, past contract information, and task order forecasts.[111]

---

111 Centurion Research, 2020.

- **GovWin IQ (now a part of Deltek)**: Offers past contract information, interested vendors, teammate search, small business directory with contracts, competitor rates, profiles for each agency, organizational charts and agency contacts, market research papers, task orders forecasts, and purchase capture reports.
- **Hoovers**: Hoovers offers information for teaming and competitive analysis, along with a directory of companies that includes summaries, decision makers, contract information, etc.

By the time you've trawled all those sources, you should have a lot of information and a sound knowledge of the agency and competition. However, there are still more places to find intelligence.

 ## ONLINE INTELLIGENCE SCOOPS

There's no substitute for face-to-face interaction to get a feel for the customer's needs, mood, and priorities, and to read the nuances of the internal politics driving the procurement process. But if you're not great at interfacing with people, or if you just want to be thorough and back your hunches with evidence, online searches are invaluable. Start with agency-specific websites, and the sites of your competitors, but also search industry and science journals, interviews, and articles in specialty online magazines.

Searches you might conduct include:
- **Beta.sam.gov and D&B**: You can search both for financial information on your competitors and potential teammates.

- **Defense Budget**: The Office of Under Secretary of Defense (Comptroller) may provide insights regarding what potential agencies and customers could be looking for.[112]
- **President's Budget**: This shows money allocated to each program. Historically, the numbers proposed and those approved by Congress have been close, so you shouldn't discount this resource.
- **USASpending.gov**: This is where you can find a lot of competitive intelligence and historic information on different contracts.
- **For Programmatic Issues**: You could check for relevant GAO findings, articles, and news stories that concern the performance of your customer in managing the incumbent program and your competitors.

Remember to feed all this information back into your **Business Strength Training System**, and ensure the right people have access to it and are updated regularly. Otherwise, all that background work will be a wasted effort.

 INTELLIGENCE, NOT ESPIONAGE

Remember we talked about staying ethical when dealing with government employees? Well, the same goes for **Intelligence Scooping**. It's one thing to want to be aware, and to gain a competitive advantage, but you must take great care not to slip into underhand or illegal techniques that delve into espionage.

---

112 Under Secretary of Defence (Comptroller), 2020.

When seeking information, use this section as guide, not as an exhaustive list.

- If you hire personnel from competitors, do not ask for or accept any company sensitive information or document they may bring with them.
- Don't accept sensitive information about your competition from anyone, including subcontractors, ex-employees, or even potential teammates.
- Don't talk about acquisitions specifics and decisions during the bidding process with federal employees.
- Don't make offers of employment or payment of any kind to federal employees. They can't accept, and you could jeopardize their position in the SSA simply by making the offer.

Phew, that was a real workout. But now you know who your customers are, you're listening to their problems. You have a **Team Roster** and **Relay Teams** in place, and you're gathering data like a demon. You know your target audience inside and out, and you know what their problems are. Now, it's time to enter **The Technology Zone**, where we're going to look at how you systematically work on creating the right solutions for the future and align your development activities with funding sources to discover your **Goldilocks Innovation Area**.

10

THE TECHNOLOGY ZONE

———

Welcome to **The Technology Zone**. In this chapter, we're talking about how to stay current, innovative, and future-focused. We are also discussing how to systematize that forward thinking to minimize the risk of being caught off guard with an obsolete product or solution, and how to identify your business's **Goldilocks Innovation Area**.

How do we do that? We already have our **Business Strength Training Center** set up. We're habitually **Listening for Opportunities**, and we're disseminating the intelligence we gather throughout our organization. We're in touch with the landscape. Now what we need is a way to consider any threats and pivot before our solutions become obsolete.

We also need an innovation pipeline into which we can feed ideas and challenges to come up with innovative solutions. First, let's start with an evaluation of your current position from an innovation viewpoint.

INNOVATION TAFE ANALYSIS

Most of the people I see in the innovation space are not business or finance oriented. They simply ask themselves, "Do I understand the problem, and can I find a technical solution?" The people who are doing SWOT analysis are the ones who are trying to run a full-fledged business.

But running a SWOT analysis (Strengths, Weaknesses, Opportunities, Threats) on an issue before you go down the rabbit hole trying to invent something or tweak something to solve a problem, to help you decide on a go/no-go situation, will save you thousands of hours, not to mention the costs of creating bids that are impossible to win.

There are all kinds of diverse ways to do a SWOT analysis. In this instance, you're doing it with a focus on the technology and the specific projects for which you're considering bidding. You're focusing on the appetite for technology versus how far advanced it is compared to competing solutions. Then you're looking at how readily available the funding is versus the cost-effectiveness of the solution compared to other solutions. That assessment will drive how much effort you put into a bid process.

Answer the following questions and consider how your chosen technology solution and funding route stack up against your competition:

- Is your chosen TECHNOLOGY something the government is eager to push through?
- How far ADVANCED, or behind, the competing technologies is your development?

- Is FUNDING readily available for the necessary development?
- How COST-EFFECTIVE is your solution compared to others?

Complete an Innovation TAFE Analysis as shown in Figure 17 for your business, and one for each of your main competitors/alternative technologies, before embarking on a major project.

TAFE INNOVATION ANALYSIS

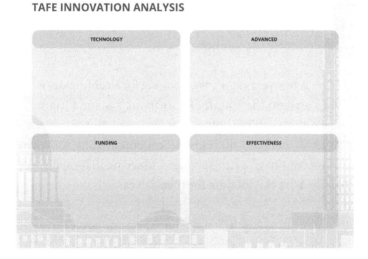

TECHNOLOGY

ADVANCED

FUNDING

EFFECTIVENESS

Figure 17: TAFE Innovation Analysis.

Let's say, for instance, you're building a prototype, and you plan to take the solution through testing to production. If the solution is something the government wants and is pushing for, you will be working with the government procurement specialist and technical specialists throughout the process. They will be talking to you about follow-on funding and eventual procurement because they need the solution.

If the government isn't so keen to walk the solution through the development process, you will need to have done your technical analysis and identified a funding route in your **Federal Business Game Plan**. You may still be able to identify opportunities to get funding, or the lack of a clear route could be a problem.

As another example, let's say you built an initial prototype and the government gave you the initial data package. You know a material you use to create the solution is relatively rare, or that there are only one or two suppliers. That's a potential issue because if you can't secure the material, you can't complete the solution.

A few years ago, I was looking for a cabling device to extend the length of a weapons system. Originally, the solution required both a fiber optic and copper cable, but there was a copper shortage. So, an opportunity was there for someone to go to the supplier and secure that supply, and thereby wire the solution for themselves.

If you're thinking like a businessperson, you know you need to secure the supply, possibly by getting an exclusive deal with one of those suppliers. You've moved something from the threats column to become one of your strengths, a unique characteristic you can offer. As a bonus, you've also potentially added an item to your competitors' weaknesses column.

Look for aspects of your solution that, as you build it for the government to go back and test, could become baked into the requirements—especially if you can find something that impacts function. Your strengths could be that you already have experience in building your solution, or you have a production line set up because you already produced three prototypes.

Look at your past experience and ask how you apply that to the current problem/solution.

- How does that put you ahead of your competition?
- How does it put you behind?
- How can you close the gaps or switch the focus of the procurement onto your strengths and away from your weaknesses?

You will, of course, have many other decision-making tools at your disposal. You should not consider the TAFE analysis a one-and-done process.

POWER PLAY: *Keep the grid in front of you and check regularly that the things you have counted as strengths and opportunities are still valid. Work on reducing items in the weaknesses and threats columns. This way, you will always have a simple compass guiding you toward working on a technology that the government wants and can pay for.*

But how do you go about creating the solution? What if all you have is an idea?

INNOVATION DEVELOPMENT CYCLE

Fortunately, you don't have to waste a lot of time to invent a product or solution. We already have a well-established innovation development cycle that pretty much all technology goes through in one way or another.

- First, you get someone to propose a theoretical solution.
- Then you get someone to build it and make it functional.
- Then it goes through several rounds of testing.
- Only when it is near completion do we think about packaging and delivery.

There are several different Innovation Development Cycle structures, but NASA refers to Technology Readiness Levels. Let's take a closer look at those now before we look at funding R&D.

 TECHNOLOGY READINESS LEVELS

If you're working in the innovation space, the chances are you're already familiar with NASA's Technology Readiness Levels (TRLs).[113] But for anyone new to the game or looking to break in, let's just remind ourselves of what those levels are and what they represent:

- **TRL 1—Applied Research:** Theoretical research is evaluated and approaches for applied research formulated. This is the level of looking for possible use cases for emerging knowledge. It might include grants for publishing scientific papers, literature reviews, or "think tanks."
- **TRL 2—Early Invention:** Early invention might include design diagrams, technical requirements, and potential

---

113 NASA, 2017.

materials to test. We're not actually building anything here, just formulating an idea of how the solution might look and work, and the constraints within which it would have to work. Supporting evidence may come from similar inventions, or theoretical analysis of the prospective design.

- **TRL 3—Proof of Concept**: Proof of concept might come from laboratory studies and experiments testing individual parts or components of the design and modelling the results of the design using simulation software. Individual components may be tested in extreme laboratory conditions to establish critical parameters.

- **TRL 4—Pre-Prototype**: The first working iteration of a prototype may be a cobbled-together breadboard in a lab consisting of ad hoc equipment. It may bear no resemblance to the practical design, as it is merely the first working example of the solution. It needs to be supported by observations about how the working solution differs from the theoretical one, and it needs to be replicable.

- **TRL 5—Simulation Prototype**: Once the parts are tested and assembled, they need to fit into the practical design for use in the real world. But first they will undergo various simulations. This is the refinement stage. Components will be honed to meet requirements, perform optimally, and fit the design. The overall design may be tweaked to solve issues that diverge from the goal. All this needs to be carefully documented, and remaining issues addressed.

- **TRL 6—Working Prototype**: The working prototype is a fully functional, high-fidelity design. To pass TRL 6, technology needs to be tested and proven to work in a relevant environment. This might be a high-fidelity laboratory simulation (where real-world testing is not possible, such as for aerospace) or a simulated operational environment, such as army exercises. Observations need to be made to show how the prototype performed in the relevant environment, what issues remain, and any new challenges that surfaced.

- **TRL 7—Operational Prototype**: This is the first test of a solution in its intended environment. The prototype will be as close as possible to the final solution design and it will be tested in real world circumstances. Everything still needs to be logged, with issues identified and ideally solved. If issues remain, a solid plan needs to be in place to resolve them before moving on to the next stage.
- **TRL 8—Production Prototypes**: With the design tested and proven in its final form and in operational condition, the final test is production in quantity or installation. Final tests may include inducing extreme conditions, evaluating adoption and training needs, and gathering feedback from users for use with future iterations.
- **TRL 9—Mission Readiness**: The solution is ready to go. Buyers may need to perform in-situ testing under mission conditions.

Sometimes, it helps to think less in terms of TRLs and more in terms of simpler stages of development, which have some overlap.

- **Basic technology** research will cover TRLs 1 and 2.
- **Feasibility** research might cover levels 2 through 4.
- **Technology development** covers levels 3 through 5.
- **Technology demonstration** covers levels 5 and 6.
- **Systems development** covers levels 6 through 8.
- **Systems launch, test, and operations** covers levels 8 and 9.

Figure 18, adapted from a thermometer image created by NASA, might make it easier to see the overlap, and how you might follow a funding route from basic technology research through technology development to systems development without skipping any levels.

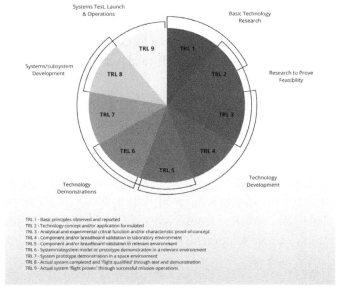

Figure 18: Technology Readiness Levels and development stages.

Sometimes several entities will be involved in the process. The initial research may come from academia. The initial proof of concept and design work may be done in a lab, with prototyping done by one company, testing and development by another, and licensing the technology by a production company. Some of these companies might be just one or two people, while others might be larger enterprises. In other cases, you might have a business set up to take a single idea from concept to maturation.

It's worth bearing in mind that the costs involved to move through the lower TRLs are lower, and the testing requirements to move up through the levels become more stringent and cost-prohibitive the higher up the ladder you go. So early-stage research and development may be an easier entry route for smaller businesses. You will need to weigh the potential return on investment against the higher barriers to entry at the higher levels and consider licensing or selling intellectual property rights to a larger company to take a product through the later levels to maturation.

 MAP YOUR TECHNOLOGY TEAM SPORT TO TRLS

Look at the **Development Stage** of your **Technology Team Sport** on your **Federal Business Game Plan**. Identify the TRLs you will be working at on your **TRL Relay Map**. Do you have an existing solution already at TRL 8 or 9? Do you plan to take solutions from levels 3-6, for example, or are you taking a single solution all the way from TLR 1 to TRL 9?

 TESTING REQUIREMENTS

Testing is important because it's a gateway for validation to moving on to the next technology readiness level. I have seen some companies who will say they have done testing, and thus are ready to talk to a procurement officer. When you peel back the onion, you realize they have only done breadboard testing in a lab. That's not the gateway to procurement. It has nothing to do with you making a prototype, nothing to do with hardening a solution, or environmental testing, or any of the other critical things you would do at various stages of technology maturation.

You can't go to technology readiness levels five, six, or seven without first doing the testing required at the earlier stages. There's no point in approaching the procurement community looking for a procurement to supply an entire army until you've successfully completed field trials and done all the testing required. You need to understand which activities need to be completed in each stage. Often, a procurement officer will talk to an innovator with a solution in early-stage development and tell them to come back when the final solution has passed testing.

When that happens, the government usually means they want to buy in significant quantities to meet a capability gap for a specific group of end users, but they need a solution that is ready to go in large quantities now. That might mean you need to do **field testing** prior to them procuring quantities to supply an entire agency or brigade.

If they had no interest in the solution, they would tell you as much. If they tell you it's not in the budget, that means they may like the idea, but either your solution is peripheral at best, or the technology is too expensive at this time.

I worked with a lot of older scientists and innovators in a military setting who struggled to understand why they were not getting funding. Often, it was because they had funding that required them to deliver a prototype. A lot of them didn't understand the various levels of prototypes. So, they would get to the pre-prototype stage and think they had delivered to requirements. They may have been required to deliver a simulation prototype or a working prototype. They hadn't done anywhere near the level of testing and development required to progress. They would claim that they had completed testing similar to that conducted at TRL 4 and maybe 5, which is breadboard testing, BUT they were approaching a procurement customer such as a Program Manager (PM) or Program Executive Office (PEO) who was in charge of fielding to an entire army. They hadn't gone through operational testing in an actual environment, which is typically done at TRL 7.

In the Introduction, I talked about getting the SWIPES system through military testing. As the Army RD&A Manual explains, that means three rounds of testing that are "tougher and more demanding than anything the soldier will encounter on the battlefield."[114] The first round is designed to ensure the equipment is useable and safe, and that it is complete and fully functionable. The second round follows a specific test plan designed to test equipment to its limits, and the third round evaluates the data supplied in the first two. That means every piece of equipment needs to be developed to exceed the stated requirements. You really need to bake over-delivery and the "wow" factor into your development process because once the military get their hands on it for testing, they are going to do everything they can to try and break it before they buy it.

So, what do you do? You align your funding to your level or development.

Now that we know what we mean when we're talking about specific TRLs, let's look at what that means in terms of funding from innovators within the Federal Procurement Arena.

---

114 Army Materiel Command, 1983.

INNOVATION FUNDING ALIGNMENT

If a government agency tells you they like your solution and to come back after testing, they're NOT fobbing you off; they're telling you to do the testing. If you read between the lines, they may be telling you subtly that they have the funding to buy the finished product, but not to fund its development. That does not mean, however, that the entire government does not have the right type of funding for it. You just need to speak to the right people.

It pays to look at the agencies with research dollars in your area of interest as early as possible. Often only recipients of Phase 1 grants in a specific program are eligible to apply for Phase 2 grants, as with the Office of Energy Efficiency and Renewable Energy's Small Business Innovation Research (SBIR) and Small Business Technology Transfer (STTR) grants.[115]

From levels 1 through 4 or 5, you need to speak to people in the science, technology, and engineering community. Look for SBIR Phase 1 grants. Once you get to levels 5 or 6 and up, you'll need to speak to the RD&E community and look for Phase 2 grants.

When you get to levels 8 or 9, it's time to start talking to the procurement and acquisitions people because the acquisition procurement community isn't going to award a major contract to something that's still at TRL 5 or 6. They have no clue if it will work in the operational environment. They

---

115 Office of Energy Efficiency and Renewable Energy, 2020.

don't have dollars earmarked for R&D or testing; they have procurement dollars.

Figure 19 shows how various types of RD&E funding align with the technology readiness levels.

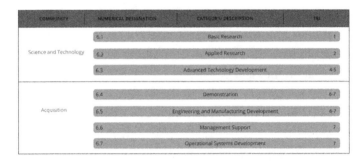

Figure 19: Funding and Technology Readiness Level Alignment.[116]

Different government organizations or programs are often funded with specific types of funding, which often align with certain activities. You can't use procurement dollars for TRL 5 level activity. By the time you get to procurement, the dollars are not used for development; they just procure an item. Figure 20 shows how various past and present funding programs have aligned with Technology Readiness Levels.

---

116 Espy, 2006.

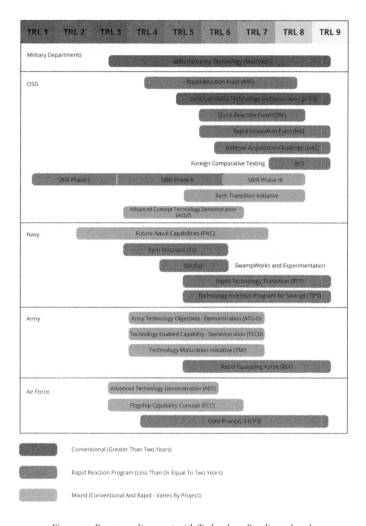

| TRL 1 | TRL 2 | TRL 3 | TRL 4 | TRL 5 | TRL 6 | TRL 7 | TRL 8 | TRL 9 |

Military Departments
Manufacturing Technology (ManTech)

OSD
Rapid Reaction Fund (RAF)
Joint Capability Technology Demonstration (JCTD)
Quick Reaction Fund (QRF)
Rapid Innovation Fund (RIF)
Defense Acquisition Challenge (DAC)
Foreign Comparative Testing   FCT
SBIR Phase I   SBIR Phase II   SBIR Phase III
Tech Transition Initiative
Advanced Concept Technology Demonstration (ACDT)

Navy
Future Naval Capabilities (FNC)
Tech Solutions (TS)
SW/Exp   SwampWorks and Experimentation
Rapid Technology Transition (RTT)
Technology Insertion Program for Savings (TIPS)

Army
Army Technology Objectives - Demonstration (ATO-D)
Technology Enabled Capability - Demonstration (TECD)
Technology Maturation Initiative (TMI)
Rapid Equipping Force (REF)

Air Force
Advanced Technology Demonstration (ADT)
Flagship Capability Concept (FCC)
Core Process 3 (CP3)

Conventional (Greater Than Two Years)

Rapid Reaction Program (Less Than Or Equal To Two Years)

Mixed (Conventional And Rapid - Varies By Project)

Figure 20: Program alignment with Technology Readiness Levels.

Figure 21 gives budgetary amounts requested by the department in the fiscal years 2018-2020 presidential budget assigned to R&D.[117] The DoD receives quite of bit of Research Development Testing and Evaluation (RDT&E) funding because they have to set a lot of "applied" solutions in the operational environment.

Table 1. Federal Research and Development Funding by Agency, FY2018-FY2020
(budget authority, dollar amounts in millions)

Department/Agency	FY2018 Actual	FY2019 Enacted	FY2020 Request	Change, FY2018-FY2020 Dollar	Change, FY2018-FY2020 Percent, Total	Change, FY2019-FY2020 Dollar	Change, FY2019-FY2020 Percent, Total
Department of Defense	$52,386	$55,832	$59,463	$7,077	13.5%	$3,631	6.5%
Dept. of Health and Human Services	36,942	38,647	33,693	-3,249	-8.8%	-4,954	-12.8%
Department of Energy	17,482	17,793	14,718	-2,764	-15.8%	-3,075	-17.3%
NASA	11,755	n/a	11,280	-475	-4.0%	n/a	n/a
National Science Foundation	6,327	n/a	5,760	-567	-9.0%	n/a	n/a
Department of Agriculture	2,618	n/a	2,464	-154	-5.9%	n/a	n/a
Department of Commerce	2,029	n/a	1,694	-335	-16.5%	n/a	n/a
Department of Veterans Affairs	1,286	1,342	1,325	39	3.0%	17	-1.3%
Department of Transportation	1,043	n/a	1,076	33	3.2%	n/a	n/a
Department of the Interior	885	n/a	753	-132	-14.9%	n/a	n/a
Department of Homeland Security	725	n/a	507	-218	-30.1%	n/a	n/a
Environmental Protection Agency	492	n/a	285	-207	-42.1%	n/a	n/a
Smithsonian Institution	357	n/a	315	-42	-11.8%	n/a	n/a
Department of Education	257	258	224	-33	-12.8%	34	-13.2%
Other	1,181	n/a	540	-641	-54.3%	n/a	n/a
Total	**135,765**	**n/a**	**134,097**	**-1,668**	**-1.2%**	**n/a**	**n/a**

Source: CRS analysis of data from EOP, OMB, *Analytical Perspectives, Budget of the United States Government, Fiscal*

Figure 21: Departmental R&D Budgetary Requests in Presidential Budgets 2018-2020.

---

117 Congressional Research Service, 2020.

You will want to learn to read budget sheets. If a government client has NO money, the prospects of getting a contract are more challenging. You can have GREAT meetings and spin your wheels working with a customer who may or may not realize they have no money.

Figure 22 shows a budget sheet with no money planned for 2020, while Figure 23 has a budget through to 2025.[118] Figure 24 shows an Army Program with RDT&E planned, and Figure 25 one with no budget.[119]

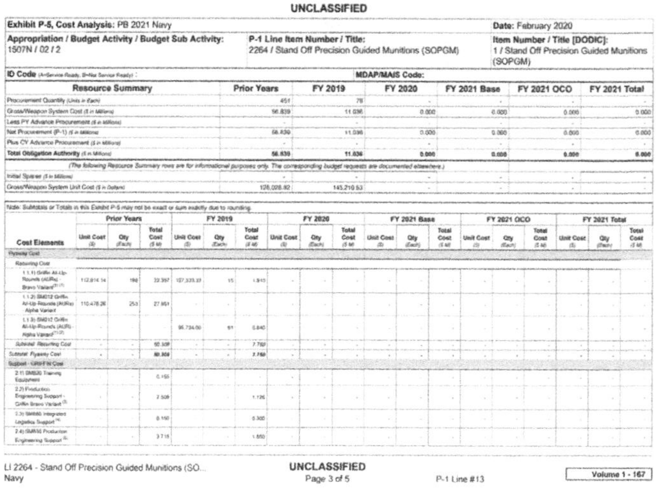

Figure 22: This program has NO money planned for 2020.

118 U.S. Department of the Navy, 2020.
119 U.S. Department of the Army, 2018.

Exhibit P-40, Budget Line Item Justification: PB 2021 Navy											Date: February 2020	
Appropriation / Budget Activity / Budget Sub Activity: 1507N: Weapons Procurement, Navy / BA 02: Other Missiles / BSA 2: Tactical Missiles					**P-1 Line Item Number / Title:** 2280 / Aerial Targets							
ID Code (In-Service Ready, B-Not Service Ready): B				Program Elements for Code B Items: N/A				Other Related Program Elements: N/A				
Line Item MDAP/MAIS Code: N/A												

Resource Summary	Prior Years	FY 2019	FY 2020	FY 2021 Base	FY 2021 OCO	FY 2021 Total	FY 2022	FY 2023	FY 2024	FY 2025	To Complete	Total
Procurement Quantity (Units in Each)												
Gross/Weapon System Cost ($ in Millions)	3,927.996	133.937	150.561	174.336	0.000	174.336	170.948	177.239	178.608	180.466	Continuing	Continuing
Less PY Advance Procurement ($ in Millions)	-	-	-	-	-	-	-	-	-	-	-	-
Net Procurement (P-1) ($ in Millions)	3,927.996	133.937	150.561	174.336	0.000	174.336	170.948	177.239	178.608	180.466	Continuing	Continuing
Plus CY Advance Procurement ($ in Millions)	-	-	-	-	-	-	-	-	-	-	-	-
Total Obligation Authority ($ in Millions)	3,927.996	133.937	150.561	174.336	0.000	174.336	170.948	177.239	178.608	180.466	Continuing	Continuing
(The following Resource Summary rows are for informational purposes only. The corresponding budget requests are documented elsewhere.)												
Initial Spares ($ in Millions)	-	1.551	2.516	2.407	-	2.407	2.175	2.653	4.137	4.220	Continuing	Continuing
Flyaway Unit Cost ($ in Thousands)	-	-	-	-	-	-	-	-	-	-	-	-
Gross/Weapon System Unit Cost ($ in Thousands)	-	-	-	-	-	-	-	-	-	-	-	-

Description:

The Aerial Targets program provides threat representative aerial targets for test and evaluation (T&E) and fleet training events. Assets procured under this line item are used to simulate and replicate currently fielded subsonic and supersonic Anti-Ship Cruise Missile (ASCM) threats. The threat representative targets are used to test and evaluate Navy ship self-defense systems currently in development, and are required for the successful completion of independent operational test and evaluation prior to fielding the systems to the fleet. Some variants are also used as fleet training assets to support fleet readiness. All assets procured by the Aerial Targets program are critical elements in improving the warfighters ability to counter threats and improve threat readiness capability. This program is composed of four primary components: (1) Subsonic Aerial targets, (2) Supersonic Targets, (3) Full Scale Aerial Target (FSAT), and (4) Auxiliary/Augmenting Systems.

(1) Subsonic Aerial Targets

The subsonic aerial targets portfolio is composed of production and sustainment programs that consist of the BQM-177A, BQM-34, BQM-74E and other various aerial target programs. The BQM-177A SSAT provides dynamic, high subsonic, sea-skimming, Anti -Ship Cruise Missile threat emulation for fleet training and for the testing of USN ship self-defensive weapon systems and other surface-to-air systems. The BQM-177A is the replacement subsonic target for the BQM-74, which is scheduled for sundown in FY 2021. Funding is used for the procurement of the BQM-177A and to procure associated hardware and mission kits, avionics upgrade kits, modifications, Engineering Change Proposals (ECPs) and software upgrades as required. The BQM-34 is a jet powered, high subsonic speed aerial target that provides a multitude of payloads for threat emulation. Funding efforts for the BQM-34 are for modifications to allow for continued utilization of current inventories as required to mitigate critical subsonic inventory shortfalls of the BQM-74 and to support Fleet Live-Fire training until the BQM-177A is fully fielded. These SSAT assets are recoverable and reused dependant on the objectives of each event. Funding may also be used to procure other subsonic targets in support of unique and emerging threat simulations.

(2) Supersonic Targets

The Supersonic targets program consists of the GQM-163A Supersonic Sea Skimming Target (SSST). The SSST is a non-recoverable target capable of speeds in excess of Mach 2.5 and cruise altitudes from 15 to 66ft. Additionally, SSST has successfully demonstrated a high dive threat profile capability. SSST replicates a family of supersonic sea-skimming targets and Anti-Ship Cruise Missile (ASCM) threats to meet critical T&E requirements of USN ship self-defense systems along with providing fleet training Live Fire with a Purpose (LFWAP) events. Funding is also used for Engineering Change Proposals, production modifications and software upgrades to help the supersonic Targets keep pace with emerging threats.

(3) Full Scale Aerial Target (FSAT)

LI 2280 - Aerial Targets
Navy

UNCLASSIFIED
Page 1 of 26
P-1 Line #14

Volume 1 - 171

Figure 23: This program has funding planned until 2025.

Exhibit R-2, RDT&E Budget Item Justification: PB 2019 Army											Date: February 2018	
Appropriation/Budget Activity 2040: Research, Development, Test & Evaluation, Army / BA 5: System Development & Demonstration (SDD)					**R-1 Program Element (Number/Name)** PE 0604807A / Medical Materiel/Medical Biological Defense Equipment - Eng Dev								

COST ($ in Millions)	Prior Years	FY 2017	FY 2018	FY 2019 Base	FY 2019 OCO	FY 2019 Total	FY 2020	FY 2021	FY 2022	FY 2023	Cost To Complete	Total Cost
Total Program Element	-	36.237	39.238	44.542	-	44.542	48.665	50.022	49.735	57.298	0.000	325.737
812: Mil HIV Vac&Drug Dev	-	0.876	1.183	1.179	-	1.179	1.201	1.230	1.067	6.060	0.000	12.805
832: Field Medical Systems Engineering Development	-	19.733	24.812	28.852	-	28.852	31.484	32.382	31.788	34.048	0.000	203.099
849: Infec Dis Drug/Vacc Ed	-	15.520	13.243	14.511	-	14.511	15.980	16.410	16.880	17.181	0.000	109.725
VS8: MEDEVAC Mission Equipment Package (MEP) - End Dev	-	0.108	0.000	0.000	-	0.000	0.000	0.000	0.000	0.000	0.000	0.108

A. Mission Description and Budget Item Justification

This Program Element (PE) funds advanced development of medical materiel within the System Demonstration and Low Rate Initial Production portions of the acquisition life cycle using 6.5 (System Development and Demonstration) funding. It supports products successfully developed in the Systems Integration portion of the Systems Development and Demonstration phases through completion of the Milestone C Decision Review. Commercially-off-the-shelf (COTS) medical products are also tested and evaluated for military use, when available. This PE primarily includes pivotal (conclusive) human clinical trials necessary for licensure by the Food and Drug Administration (FDA).

Projects in this PE include the following:

Project 812 funds military relevant human immunodeficiency virus (HIV) medical countermeasures. These funds provide for engineering and manufacturing development of candidate vaccines and drugs for pivotal large-scale field testing. Development focused on military unique needs effecting manning, mobilization, and deployment. Products from this project will normally transition to Department of Defense (DoD) Health Programs or Other Procurement, Army (OPA) Funds.

Project 832 funds the engineering and manufacturing development of medical products for enhanced combat casualty care and follow-on care, including rehabilitation. Mature COTS medical products are also evaluated for military use. Consideration will also be given to reduce the medical sustainment footprint through smaller weight and cube volume, or equipment independence from supporting materiel. Products from this project will normally transition to OPA Funds.

Project 849 funds development of candidate medical countermeasures for military relevant infectious diseases. These products fall in four major areas: vaccines, drugs, diagnostic kits/devices, and insect control measures to limit exposure and disease transmission. FDA approval is a mandatory obligation for all military products placed into the hands of medical providers or service members for human use. Products from this project will normally transition to DoD Health Programs or OPA funds.

Figure 24: Army Program with RDT&E planned.

246 · FEDERAL CONTRACTING PLAYBOOK

| Exhibit R-2A, RDT&E Project Justification: PB 2019 Army | | | | | | | | | | | Date: February 2018 | |

| Appropriation/Budget Activity 2040 / 5 | | | | R-1 Program Element (Number/Name) PE 0604805A / Command, Control, Communications Systems - Eng Dev | | | Project (Number/Name) 593 / Joint Battle Command - Platform (JBC-P) | | | | | | |

COST ($ in Millions)	Prior Years	FY 2017	FY 2018	FY 2019 Base	FY 2019 OCO	FY 2019 Total	FY 2020	FY 2021	FY 2022	FY 2023	Cost To Complete	Total Cost
593: Joint Battle Command - Platform (JBC-P)	-	4.166	9.910	15.970	-	15.970	12.595	0.431	14.221	23.631	0.000	80.924
Quantity of RDT&E Articles	-	-	-	-	-	-	-	-	-	-	-	-

A. Mission Description and Budget Item Justification

The Joint Battle Command - Platform (JBC-P) program is the cornerstone of Joint Forces Command and Control (C2) Situational Awareness (SA) and communications. JBC-P includes a network which enables the movement of data and provides secure Blue Force Tracking (BFT) capability in Platforms and Command Posts, providing soldiers and commanders a map-based Common Operating Picture of the battlefield, as a result, reducing fratricide.

PdM JBC-P, under PM Mission Command (MC), is collaborating with the Communications-Electronics Research, Development and Engineering Center's (CERDEC) Space and Terrestrial Communications Directorate (S&TCD) on evolving BFT network. Systems engineering studies/planning activities are underway to develop the evolution path of the BFT network. In addition, there are two RDT&E contractual efforts underway for FY 2018 and FY 2019 that will aid in assessing the feasibility of reusing existing BFT-2 transceivers (hardware) and replacing it with advanced, government owned hardware/software. The goal is to have a BFT-3, full and open solicitation to industry, ready for FY 2020.

To better understand how potential changes to the BFT network would affect overall operations, funding was increased in both FY17 and FY18 to assist PdM JBC-P to fully model the operational BFT network; S&TCD is working on developing a model of the current BFT-2 waveform to test in the BFT portion of their Network Test Lab. This Test Lab provides the Government the ability to test proposed fixes, conduct regression testing of future Software and Firmware releases, and replicate any problems the system may experience without impacting the operational network.

FORSCOM users have identified a need for an expeditionary JBC-P capability to better connect the Lower Tactical Internet (LTI) to the BFT network when dismounted. PdM JBC-P has partnered with CERDEC's Command, Power and Integration Directorate to developed capability.

B. Accomplishments/Planned Programs ($ in Millions)

	FY 2017	FY 2018	FY 2019 Base	FY 2019 OCO	FY 2019 Total
Title: Software Development	0.355	0.200	-	-	-

Description: Develop capabilities, product applications, platform interoperability, and system services across the JBC-P family of systems, to include the development of capabilities to meet Key Performance Parameters (KPPs), and other system attributes. Develop Multi-Level Security Domains for Network, Users, and Information.

FY 2018 Plans:

PE 0604805A: Command, Control, Communications Systems.
Army

Figure 25: Army Program with no RDT&E planned.

If you are working on a technology that aligns with DoD and looking for funding for the entire development process (TRL 2–TRL 9), then you'll need funding that aligns with all those activities. More precisely, you will need 6.2 thru 6.7 funding. Table 3 and Figure 26 show how definitions of R&D differ across government agencies, and specifically the DoD.[120]

---

120 Adapted from Moris, 2018.

Table 3: Definitions of R&D

	Government-Wide OMB Circular No. A-11 (1998)	Department of Defense DoD Financial Management Regulation (Volume 2B, Chapter 5)	
Conduct of R&D Basic Research	Systematic study directed toward greater knowledge or understanding of the fundamental aspects of phenomena and/or observable facts without specific applications toward processes or products in mind.		S&T Activities Basic Research (6.1)
Applied Research	Systematic study to gain knowledge or understanding necessary to determine how a recognized and specific need may be met.		Applied Research (6.2)
Development	Systematic application of knowledge toward the production of useful materials, devices, and systems or methods, including design, development, and improvement of prototypes and new processes to meet specific requirements.	Efforts that have moved into the development and integration of hardware for field experiments and tests.	Advanced Technology Development (6.3)
		Efforts necessary to evaluate integrated technologies in as realistic an operating environment as possible to assess the performance or cost reduction potential of advanced technology.	Demonstration and Validation (6.4)
		Projects in engineering and manufacturing development for Service use but which have not received approval for full rate production.	Engineering and Manufacturing Development (6.5)
		R&D efforts directed toward support of installation or operations required for general R&D use such as test ranges, military construction, maintenance support of laboratories, operations and maintenance of test aircraft and ships, and studies and analyses in support of R&D program.	RDT&E Management Support (6.6)
		Development projects in support of development acquisition programs or upgrades still in engineering and manufacturing development, but which have received Defense Acquisition Board (DAB) or other approval for production, or for which production funds have been included in the DoD budget submission for the budget or subsequent fiscal year.	Operational System Development (6.7)
		Efforts associated with engineering or support activities to determine the acceptability of a system, subsystem, or component.	Developmental Test and Evaluation
			Operational Test and Evaluation
R & D Equipment	Acquisition of major equipment for R&D. Includes expendable or movable equipment, office furniture and equipment. Routine purchases of ordinary office equipment or furniture and fixtures are normally excluded.	Major equipment dollars are mixed with the dollars for the "Conduct of R&D" and carried in the RDT&E accounts (i.e., 6.1 through 6.7) listed above.	
R & D Facilities	Includes acquisition, design, construction major repairs or alterations of all physical facilities for use in R&D activities. Includes land, buildings, and fixed capital equipment for government or private organizational use, regardless of ownership. Includes such fixed facilities as reactors, wind tunnels, and particle reactors. Excludes movable R&D equipment.	In FY 1998, close to 90% of the $67 million requested by DOD for R&D Facilities was carried separately in Military Construction accounts. The rest were included in the costs of major development programs and are mixed with the dollars for the "Conduct of R&D" carried in the RDT&E accounts (i.e., 6.1 through 6.7) listed above.	

Funding	6.1	6.2	6.3		6.4	6.5	6.7	
Funding	Research, Development, test and Evolution						Procurement	O&M
TRL	TRL 1-3	TRL 4	TRL 5		TRL 6	TRL 7	TRL 8	TRL 9
ACQ Milestone/ Phase	Pre-Concept	Mtrl. Solution Analysis	Technology Development		Engineering & Manufacturing Development		Production & Deployment	Sustainment & Maintenance
MRL	1 2 3 Feasibility Concepts	MRL 4 Lab Environment	MRL 5 Prototypes Components	MRL 6 Prototype System	MRL 7 Systems in Production Environment	MRL 8 Pilot Line - Low Rate Production	MRL 9 Begin Full Rate Production	MRL 10 Lean Production Practices

 Defense Acquisition Milestones

Figure 26: Funding Alignment of R&D definitions.[121]

FUNDING VERTICAL ALIGNMENT

The other thing to bear in mind in this funding mapping process is that the funding must be available for the right *kind* of technology development as well as for the appropriate technology readiness level. So, for example, if you're trying to develop a better radar system, you can't use biochemical research dollars to fund that; you would need naval or aviation funding. Similarly, you can't use aviation funding to fund medical research.

As well as looking at your technology readiness level and the agency that has funding, you need to consider the problems they are trying to solve and the issues for which those dollars are earmarked.

Another thing to consider when you're planning your route to market funding is that budgets are calculated and announced multiple years in advance. You can't expect to apply for

---

121 Atchison, 2013.

funding today and receive it tomorrow. As with procurement, grant applications are a slow process. In terms of not getting stuck creating an obsolete product, possibly the biggest thing you can do is use the Broad Area Agency announcements to inform your development efforts and ensure what you're trying to create actually answers a specified need.

YOUR GOLDILOCKS INNOVATION AREA

If your target agency has an identified requirement for your technology solution, but not the funding to take your early-stage prototype through testing, you may have to find alternative sources of funding before you can approach the procurement office.

If your target agency has an identified need and the funding to take a solution through testing to procurement, but your technology isn't a good fit, you need to pivot your technology to meet the agency's needs.

If the funding to take your technology through testing to maturity is in place, but your target agency has no identified need for it, you need to find the agencies or commercial customers who do have that need.

Your **Goldilocks Innovation Area,** as shown in Figure 27, is the intersection of your target agencies' REQUIREMENTS with innovation FUNDING sources that play into your TECHNOLOGY vertical.

YOUR GOLDILOCKS INNOVATION AREA

Your Goldilocks Innovation Area is the intersection of your target agencies' REQUIREMENTS and the innovation FUNDING sources that play into your TECHNOLOGY vertical.

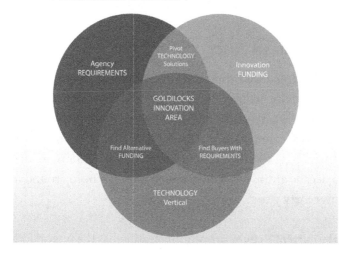

Figure 27: Goldilocks Innovation Area.

 POWER PLAY: *Dig deep into the USASpending.gov and beta.sam.gov site data and make sure you understand the budgets of your target agencies and how they break down programmatically. Investigate funding sources and consider pivoting your technology or finding alternative funding sources for development funding gaps. Keep digging until you find your Innovation Goldilocks Area, and focus your efforts on that.*

WIDER INNOVATION CYCLES

There's always the possibility that the political landscape could shift, priorities could change, and funding could be cut at short notice. So, it pays to be aware of certain cycles and how they might affect your innovation efforts.

 CYCLES IN POLICY

At the time of writing, the government is placing a lot of emphasis on artificial intelligence. Machine learning, robotics process automation, blockchain, and those sorts of things are also technical solutions, but they're not so innovative anymore. They have been in the marketplace for more than a decade already. Robotics automation has been around for over forty years.

The current Republican administration has the typical ideal of cutting back the government. They are trying to reduce the size of the federal workforce by automating processes that have previously been handled by humans, with the hope of reducing the overall size of the government.

I would argue that historically, these types of automation technologies result not in needing less people, but in a shift in the nature of the work. There's always a tendency to think that by automating a process you can reduce the workforce and have just one person maintaining everything.

That's not how it usually goes. If you have more technology and equipment, then you need more technicians to maintain that, and more programmers and developers to keep pace with changes in the code, secure it against hackers, etc. Then you need analysts to interpret the results, and specialists to make decisions based on those insights, or at least to handle oversight. Of course, you also need to train all these people, so you need educators and technical writers to compile support materials, and so on.

Another major trend in procurement is currently to push for the use of Commercial, Off-the-Shelf (COTS) solutions over custom ones. There's a move toward buying commercial products. But there are pockets of the government pushing the bounds of innovation, where COTS solutions simply aren't available or suitable, such as in enhanced radar detection, intelligence defense, and in bioengineering, etc.

What we're seeing right now is a dichotomous split between buying COTS solutions wherever possible, and the introduction of those small innovation teams designed to shorten the development process when COTS solutions aren't available. It's all about speeding things up and shortening the gap between identifying a need and filling it, about reducing waste through wait time.

We also have a swing toward category management and awarding contracts to large primary contractors, or to conglomerates or groups of smaller businesses. The idea is to have a single vendor who delivers products according to that category.

The Obama administration did the opposite because the old boys' network had remained unchallenged for years. There was a preponderance of large incumbents constantly wiring contracts for themselves and making it impossible for new vendors to break in.

The rules and policies were adapted to make it easier for newer and smaller businesses to win contracts because small business and innovation are the lifeblood of the economy. Set-asides for small businesses, women-owned businesses, and disadvantaged businesses were put in place, and the requirements to get more bids were all aimed at opening the marketplace to new competitors. The emphasis on past performance was relaxed to reduce the advantage of existing incumbents and make new businesses eligible to compete.

But these things are circular, and whenever we have a change in government, priorities change, and policies with them. Currently the pendulum is swinging back toward the old boys' network and assigning huge contracts to a small group of people who have been in the space for a long time.

Even so, the emphasis on innovation and reducing the procurement cycle remains a priority, which is good news for innovators in general.

Those are the major cycles at play in the **Federal Procurement Arena** now, but there are also other cycles you need to consider.

💡 CYCLES IN INVENTION

One thing I have learned is that it's always difficult to predict the trends of the future. We were fighting an asymmetrical war, armed with far more advanced technology than our enemy. But our enemy was using non-standard tactics such as jungle warfare, and weaponry and bombs we hadn't seen since World War II, such as improvised explosive devices (IEDs).

 Some of the most effective solutions we came up with were also revivals of older solutions, such as dogs and dog handlers. Although there were some highly innovative solutions, a lot of them were low-tech. We had to retrain and retool production lines or reverse engineer the solutions that had been mothballed for decades to counter those devices and tactics. An excellent example would be interrogation lathes, which were basically long knives used to slice into the ground and probe for IEDs. They were an iteration of the soldier's bayonet, which used to be tied to the end of a rifle for close-quarters combat.

>  **POWER PLAY:** *Never overlook the simple, low-tech solution. When you're looking for a solution, always ask if similar problems have cropped up before, and how they were resolved.*

CYCLES IN INDUSTRY

Finally, although policies and developments are cyclical, you also need to be aware of the cyclical nature of industries, and disruptive technologies. Every industry was at one time a disruptive new idea. Even farming, thousands of years ago, was a novel idea to hunter-gatherers. Industries go through stages of innovation, early adoption, and wide acceptance, then through to maturity and eventual decline. That decline might be slow and drawn out, or it might be swift and sudden in response to a new disruptive technology making it obsolete.

Think about the horse and cart, with everyone trying to invent a better harness. Just a few short years after the invention of the automobile, the entire industry had become a niche, the province of artisans. All the innovators were busy trying to build a better engine, a better chassis, etc. How do you ensure you don't get left behind?

Well, there is no guarantee against it. You can never know what's around the corner. But you can stay up to date with your industry. You can read science journals for a glimpse of what's coming, and you can be aware of your own industry's maturation level.

Table 4 shows a rough and ready guide to identifying where your industry is in the maturation cycle.

Table 4: Industry Maturation Cycle

When you tell someone what you do, what's the most common response?	
Response	Industry Maturation Level
What's that?	Emerging
Really? Tell me more.	Early Adoption
Oh, I have a friend who does that.	Wide Acceptance
Oh.	Maturation
Really? Aren't you worried about [new option]?	Decline
I didn't think people did that anymore.	Obsolescence

There will always be areas that need innovation. What made a place like JIEDDO work was that people were able to submit ideas and solutions from all walks of life (so long as they were US citizens). It created an environment that included diversity of thought by engaging with universities, labs, operators, scientists, former and current military, young and old together under one roof. Diversity of thought was baked into the culture by bringing everyone together from different disciplines. With respect to the REF, soldiers from all ranks and walks were able to submit problems, no matter how small to us. We were able to reach out to almost everyone across the US to consider solutions.

My former director at REF is part of a growing movement to take "think tanks" into universities and academic institutions, and to expose the younger generation to big problems they would never be exposed to. Much in the way the government reached out to Bell Labs in the twentieth century and the multidisciplinary innovation teams of this century, there's a trend toward pulling in the best and brightest from wherever they are. That means going to them and gathering ideas and input from people who would never normally be a part of the process.

Young people who haven't yet chosen a discipline, and who are not married to a certain theory or way of working, often come up with some of the best innovative ideas. They often find it easier to think in terms of possibilities rather than obstacles. Youth outreach programs are one way the government is trying to reverse the current commercial technology brain drain that has been luring the best innovators away from public service with huge salaries after the collapse of the financial industry. The government is also pairing them with organizations staffed with people and problems who have experience, operational wisdom, and technical know-how. In many ways, they are recreating that same diversity of thought we had at JIEDDO, in some areas of the REF, and even within the work at Bell Labs.

POWER PLAY: *Track the government-sponsored "think tanks" at universities near you and find out what problems they are being asked to consider. These are the problems you need to focus on if you want to stay focused on serving the government in the future.*

Congratulations, you have now done all the background work. You have your **Team Roster** and teaming plans in place, you have your **Business Strength Training System** up and running, and you have identified your **Goldilocks Innovation Area**. You have identified potential buyers and sources of development funding, and you're working in a viable technology vertical in an emerging **Open Playing Field**. In other words, you're all set to make your **Federal Procurement Arena** debut.

In Part Three, "**Go!**", we're going to learn the last two skills for winning, **Playing to Win** and **Delivering Value**, and then enter the final two **Zones of Innovation Excellence**: The Pitching Zone and The Performance Zone. We'll put together your **Pitch Perfection Program**, your **Proposal Set Pieces**, and your **Program Management Practice** as we walk through the process of preparing a proposal and delivering your first government contract.

Are you excited? I am. Let's go!

PART THREE:

GO!

Make sure you're Playing to Win and Delivering Value before entering The Pitching Zone and The Performance Zone.

11

PLAYING TO WIN

Everything we have covered so far has been designed to help you find your place and fit in the **Federal Procurement Arena**. But knowing your place and fitting in won't help you win grants and contracts; for that, you need to stand out—in the right way.

In **Playing to Win**, I'm going to show you HOW to seal the deal.

Here you'll focus on distinguishing yourself from the pack and avoiding the trap of complacency. You'll start to develop your **Proposal Set Pieces**: the words, phrases, and themes you will use throughout your business capture activities to cement your unique value proposition in the buyer's mind. Then you're going to use those "Win Themes" in your everyday correspondence and conversations with your buyers, until they're so natural that when buyers see them in your proposal, they feel authentic.

You're also going to do everything you can to embed your win themes into the language of the Request for Proposal so that your bid stands out from the competition and seems like the natural choice.

Of course, that's a tall order, and you must remember all of your competition is trying to "wire" the proposal in their favor. It is, after all, a competition.

First, let's talk about finding your value.

FIND YOUR VALUE

I have seen people offer a product that did not deliver value beyond the existing solution. If it doesn't offer a significant saving, it won't be effective.

For example, inside aircraft hangars are standard-sized pallets for transporting goods. These pallets have been in use for decades. I came across a company lobbying to replace these pallets with their own.

The problem was that their pallets would not significantly reduce costs, improve performance, or introduce any other benefits. They weren't lighter, stronger, or more durable to any significant extent. Thus, there was no incentive for anyone to want to change from an existing product with a long service history that people were trained on how to use, maintain, etc.

Worse, since the pallets were a different size, it would have meant disposing of a lot of existing stock, retooling equipment and machinery, and retraining personnel unnecessarily.

There simply was no value proposition.

When you're preparing and pricing your pitches, you must bring something of value to the table. The more friction would be involved in switching from an existing solution to the proposed one, the bigger the payoff needs to be.

You need a system that challenges your exuberance and assumptions. You need to address the issues of inertia and guarantee your proposed solution is a step forward and not sideways.

Let's take a look at a single product idea that has evolved over the years, to give you an idea of what product advancement might look like.

Road Studs—the little markers used to light the road at night—are a great example of innovations on a basic idea that have introduced safety improvements or other benefits to encourage governments around the world to upgrade road markings.

- **Cats' Eyes**—These were developed in the UK in 1934 and so-named because they were inspired by the reflection of the inventor's headlights in the eyes of a stray cat on a dark road at night. They used reflective strips, were raised on the road, and were prone to damage tires or become loose and fly off, damaging passing vehicles.

- **Botts' Dots**—An early American adaptation of cats' eyes—while stuck on the road, these were lower profile and less likely to cause damage. However, they were simply silver reflective metal disks.
- **Colored Road Studs**—The introduction of different colored road studs to delineate junctions, land divisions, and verges made navigating at night easier.
- **Depressible Road Studs**—The introduction of depressible studs made them less likely to cause damage or to be damaged and introduced a self-cleaning mechanism that prolonged their use.
- **Solar-Powered LED Road Studs**—More recently, solar-powered LED studs have increased road safety.
- **Smart Studs**—The introduction of smart studs, controllable at junctions to illuminate active lanes, has reduced the incidence of collisions at major junctions. They can even be used to warn when cars are too close in transit, reducing tailgating and collisions.

These are all tangible benefits that equate to lives saved and thus warrant the investment required to upgrade infrastructure.

 TECHNOLOGY PRVOGRESS LADDER

Draw up a similar progress ladder for your technology, then answer the following questions:
- What are the outstanding issues?
- How does your solution solve the problem better than other solutions?
- Will your solution save time, money, or energy?
- Will it reduce errors? How?

The answers to these questions will tell you what value you bring to the table. Now consider:

- How easily can the transition from the existing solution to yours be made?
- What issues of retooling, retraining, or disposing of the old technology must be considered?
- How can you turn these to your advantage to incentivize the switch?

Once you know your value proposition, you're going to start laying the groundwork with your buyers so that the language you use in your proposals matches the language you use from the outset.

 ## WATCH YOUR LANGUAGE

The language you use in your pitches and presentations should not be something you think about at the end of the cycle when you're putting those things together. You do not start practicing your passes when you turn up for the game; you drill them beforehand until it's muscle memory.

Table 5 gives a short Federal Procurement Arena vocabulary lesson.

Table 5: Federal Procurement Vocabulary

Don't say	Say instead
Sales	Business capture
Buyers	Procurement personnel
Buy	Obtain/acquire
Sell	Offer/provide
Sales activities	Business capture pursuits
Sales strategy	Win strategy/business capture strategy
Buzz words/taglines/slogans	Win themes

You must have a sound business capture strategy, or win strategy, just like sports competitions. Win strategies help you run a business capture pursuit in a way that helps you stand out. Win themes describe your value proposition consistently for Inside Track runners.

Your win strategy should include a succinct set of statements that can be reviewed regularly and adjusted as necessary. After defining your win strategy, you will put together an action plan with clear priorities, deadlines, and targets assigned to each task. This plan should then be entered into your **Business Strength Training Center** and disseminated to all personnel who interact with government personnel.

In team sports like soccer and football, teams have set pieces, which are plays practiced over and over in response to situations that come up regularly within a game. Then, when those situations come up, the team knows what to do instinctively, and works together with little instruction or communication. Set pieces statistically increase the chances of winning in many sports.

To help you define your win themes, let's run through a few set pieces.

PROPOSAL SET PIECES

You have three types of set pieces in terms of winning strategies: Unique Strengths, Supporting Strengths, and Reversible Negatives. Use a Unique Strengths template as shown in Figure 28 to complete this exercise.

PITCH PERFECTION PROGRAM
Unique Strengths

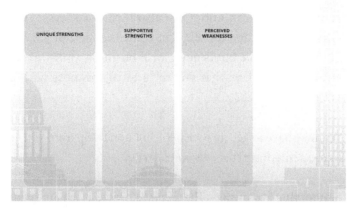

Figure 28: Unique Strengths.

Unique Strengths—Your first set piece is to find your unique strengths, and to phrase them in a way that communicates your value in a way government personnel will both remember and associate with you. Unique strengths only count if they are totally unique to you—either in the world or in your competitive arena—AND they are valued or sought after by the client in the context of the solution.

To find your unique strengths, go back to your **Innovation TAFE analysis** and **Find Your Value** in this chapter, and list all your strengths. Then list the strengths of all your known competitors.

Cross out any on your list that appear on your competitors' lists as well, even if you think you are better at that than they are.

If you're left with nothing, look for a combination of strengths that only you have. If, for example, you had listed "local business" and "national presence" as strengths, and your competitors 1 and 2 are also local businesses, but don't have a national presence, while competitor 3 has a national presence but is not a local business, your unique strength would be that you're "a local business with a national presence."

You may have to get creative here, but don't stop until you've found something that sets you apart.

Supporting Strengths—The second set piece is to name your supporting strengths and use them to balance out as many of your competitor's unique strengths as possible. These are the items you crossed out on your strengths list because your competitors have them, too.

Even if everyone in the field can do these things, you must talk about them to make it clear you have the capability. You don't want to inadvertently create a perceived gap. For example, if your customer cares about small business and likes lots of personal contact, you could say, "We are a small business that considers each customer vital."

Perceived Negatives—Your third set piece is to acknowledge existing real or perceived negatives and use them as opportunities for turnarounds or comebacks. These would be the strengths on your competitors lists that you can't add to your list. To balance these out, try to pair them with one of your strengths. So, for example, if you are a local company going up against national ones, you might say, "Unlike bigger companies, we focus on local issues, and know them intimately because they affect us, too."

Perceived negatives also include past failures, such as your company not delivering on a project or getting a poor past performance reference. You can make your blunders work for you when you represent them as a valuable lesson learned.

Ghosting—A fourth set piece you might employ with caution is a technique called ghosting. Ghosting is when you point out to the customer your competitors' unique disadvantages indirectly and subtly. You don't name your competitor but point out a problem they have.

For example, if your competitor is about to be sold, you might say, "We are not going to be divested in a year, causing turmoil and employee turnover." You can then talk about your stability, customer focus and proof of delivering similar programs as well.

If you choose to use ghosting, be aware that negatives you're trying to flag up in your competitor's case can be erroneously assigned to you in the customer's mind if you're not careful.

POWER PLAY: *Write your set pieces using your audience's language from the notes you collected in your Business Strength Training Center.*

So now you have some **Proposal Set Pieces**, you will want to disseminate them as approved language in your **Business**

Strength Training System to ensure all staff use the same language in all communications with government personnel. You might want to start a file or folder called "approved language" and include in it your set pieces and win themes with examples of when they might be used.

CREATE WIN THEMES

You will use **Win Themes** in your communications with key players and carry them through to your proposals. These are phrases, mantras, and punchlines that support your **Federal Business Game Plan**. **Win Themes** convince your customers, help them remember your proposal over those of others, and even lend them the language to justify to others why they want to award this proposal to you.

The secret of developing a powerful **Win Strategy** is counterintuitive: start with **Win Themes**. Win Strategies will fall out of the action items that your Win Themes will drive. Why is that?

Just like you would with any good strategy, you start with the end in mind. In this case, that's persuading your customer to select you. You start by looking at the customer's concerns and priorities and working out what it will take to get them to choose you over your competition.

At this point, you might want to go back to your strengths list and **Innovation TAFE Analysis** and consider the list from the buyer's perspective. Which are the most important?

Which are vital, and which are nice to have? Structure your language to lead with the most important things to the buyer first, even if they're not your biggest strengths.

Your **Win Themes** are the main tool of customer persuasion, but how do you put them together?

There are three mandatory elements in a Win Theme: feature, benefit, and proof.

Most people are not certain what a great Win Theme should look like. Hence most proposals read like technical papers. This is the case because the Win Theme can be many different things, including the following:

Slogans—A recurring thought, a slogan, a tagline or a punchline—for example, a way to identify your team with attributes that your customer wants.

Let's say your buyer is looking for better security. A Win Theme might be *Serving [Area] Vigilantly since [Year.]*

If they've had a budget cut, you might talk about *"Cutting costs, not corners: $xxx saved last year alone."*

Use the template as shown in Figure 29 to complete this exercise.

SLOGANS

A recurring thought, slogan, tag line, or punchline — for example, a way to identify your team with attributes your customer wants.

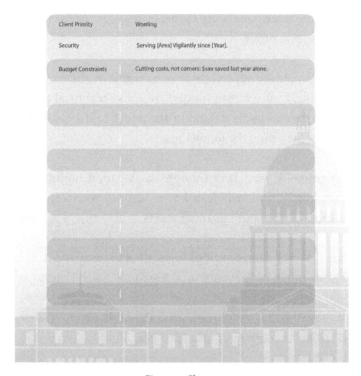

Client Priority	Wording
Security	Serving [Area] Vigilantly since [Year].
Budget Constraints	Cutting costs, not corners: $xxx saved last year alone.

Figure 29: Slogans

Benefit Statements—These are often the bullet points in sales literature, and they will make up a large part of your business capture literature, too. Benefit statements package a feature of the proposed solution, service, or product, with the stated benefit and an element of supporting proof:

For example, if you say: "Our proprietary technical solution enables us to meet the reporting schedule using only six analysts instead of eight, cutting the total project cost by 25 percent," your *proprietary technical solution* is the feature. The stated benefit is *cutting the total project cost by 25 percent*. The supporting proof is the explanation that this will be achieved by needing fewer staff, in this case, *using only six analysts instead of eight*.

Use the template as shown in Figure 30 to complete this exercise.

BENEFIT STATEMENTS

These are often the bullet points in sales literature, and they will make up a large part of your business capture literature too. Benefit statements package a feature of the proposed solution, service, or product, with the stated benefit and an element of supporting proof.

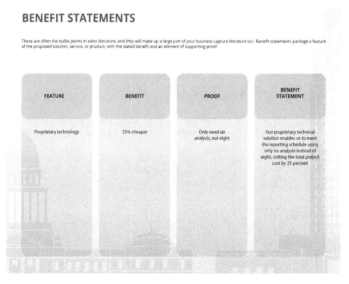

FEATURE	BENEFIT	PROOF	BENEFIT STATEMENT
Proprietary technology	25% cheaper	Only need six analysts, not eight	Our proprietary technical solution enables us to meet the reporting schedule using only six analysts instead of eight, cutting the total project cost by 25 percent

Figure 30: Benefit Statements.

Value-Added Propositions—A value-added proposition is an unasked-for extra. It's your promise to over-deliver. This needs to be something that isn't in the government's specs or request, but that you will deliver naturally.

Ideally, these need to speak to one of the three major points of the **Project Management Quality Triangle**, which states that the quality of any project is constrained by the intersection of time, money, and scope of the project.

For example:
- "We will cover the costs of transition to our service" speaks to the cost center of a project.
- "We can deliver in three months instead of four" speaks to deadlines or time.
- "Our product is future-proofed with open-ended connectivity" speaks to scope.

Use the template as shown in Figure 31 to complete this exercise.

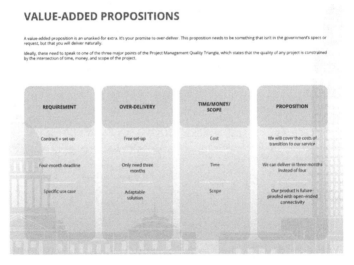

VALUE-ADDED PROPOSITIONS

A value-added proposition is an unasked-for extra. It's your promise to over-deliver. This proposition needs to be something that isn't in the government's specs or request, but that you will deliver naturally.

Ideally, these need to speak to one of the three major points of the Project Management Quality Triangle, which states that the quality of any project is constrained by the intersection of time, money, and scope of the project.

REQUIREMENT	OVER-DELIVERY	TIME/MONEY/ SCOPE	PROPOSITION
Contract + set-up	Free set-up	Cost	We will cover the costs of transition to our service
Four-month deadline	Only need three months	Time	We can deliver in three months instead of four
Specific use case	Adaptable solution	Scope	Our product is future-proofed with open-ended connectivity

Figure 31: Value-Added Propositions.

Discriminators—Discriminators or differentiators frame your strengths in relation to your competition. These could include references to awards you have won, patents you hold, or other achievements that set you apart. But even if you do not have those credentials, your Unique Value Proposition should be framed this way.

Example:
- Only we can bring the XYZ technology to this project.
- Unlike the competition, we have extensive experience in ABC.
- The only company you can trust to...

Use the template as shown in Figure 32 to complete this exercise.

WIN THEMES

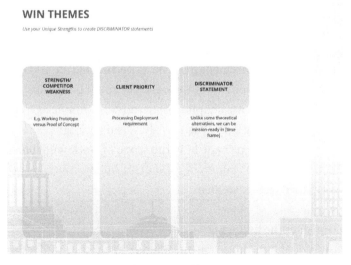

Figure 32: Win Themes.

> 🏆 **POWER PLAY**: *Develop your win themes using your buyer's language. Echo their complaints back to them in your solution, and they will instinctively "get it."*

Create your Win Theme approved language and disseminate it through your **Business Strength Training System.**

Then, start using that language in your communications, both spoken and written, with government personnel. If you think it sounds odd or forced, practice saying it out loud until it feels natural.

GET ON THEIR TEAM

If you haven't already, make sure you're offering procurement personnel in your target agencies helpful advice, and playing on their Procurement Relay Team.

Look at the requirement from the government side and consider the numerous ways the contract could be set up. The whole time you are shaping your solution, you need to be acting as an MVP or Trusted Advisor to your buyers. That way, you can help shape how the scope of work will appear in a perspective statement, statement of objectives, or performance work statement.

Consider the following:
- Would it be more beneficial to keep the scope under one procurement versus splitting it up across multiple procurements (and potentially different contractors)?

- Would a defined scope of work be beneficial? If so, you might suggest it be issued under a fixed price contract with a specific budget.
- Would it benefit the project (and you) to have more wiggle room to execute? Suggest a cost-plus or a performance-based vehicle.
- Would it benefit you if you had solid performance metrics you could apply?
- Could the work be phased into a series of purchase orders under the $250,000 threshold where all the work must go to a small business?
- Could the work be contracted as a single contract with options versus a series of successive contracts?
- If you have **POWER UP**s available to you because you are a small business or a small disadvantaged business, it is a no-brainer to argue for a set-aside; there just has to be another viable small business competitor in accordance with the rule of two, and the procurement automatically has to become a small business procurement.
- If you are someone for whom the field or customer is new, you might want more time, a draft RFP, and a longer proposal process to have the time to react and develop a better offer.
- Should certain incumbent documentation be released to other contractors (including you) to make it fairer and easier for small innovators to bid?

You might not be able to influence the wording of the evaluation criteria, but you can suggest increasing the relative importance of those criteria where you would score highly, or decreasing the importance where you would not fare well.

> 🏆 **SUPER POWER PLAY:** *Argue for Organizational Conflict of Interests (OCI) considerations to be taken into account if you know your competitors have been working on too many contracts with this customer, or if you feel the agency might have exposed information that would provide them with an unfair advantage and compromise procurement integrity.*

Orals are when you present your proposal in an oral form, with a PowerPoint presentation instead of or in addition to a written proposal. Orals can be challenging and take a tremendous amount of preparation and practice, as well as staff readily available to put together and deliver the presentation. Those good at orals could beat those who are not.

Do you have a model ready for what you are selling that could absolutely blow away the competition through an amazing demo? If so, push for an oral presentation/demonstration.

As well as arguing for the procurement vehicle that best suits your solution and business type, you want to influence the performance requirements of the contract in several areas.

TALK PERFORMANCE FACTORS

Consider how you would deliver the contract, and how your competitors might perform. Again, you want to emphasize your strengths and downplay your weaknesses.

Here are some things to consider:

- **Past performance, key personnel, and resume requirements.** As a small innovator, you may not have a past performance record. You want to emphasize your qualifications and credentials.
- **Requirement Specifics.** If you have specific qualifications or facilities, it makes sense to emphasize those as essential requirements. At the same time, you might want to downplay those you do not have as non-essential.

You need to look at every area of performance and define the minimum requirements that would enable you to complete this project with a high degree of quality.

 ## TALK LEGAL AND INSURANCE REQUIREMENTS

You might not think building legal and insurance requirements into the RFP would be beneficial. But like every other aspect of the contract, it could be set up to favor or disadvantage you. Consider the following:

- Do you have an invention or technology where you might have to relinquish your intellectual property rights to the government? Or will you have the government license it from you? How would it impact you and the competition?
- Are you willing to accept a bid bond requirement?

Remember this: your competitors will all be trying to shape the solution and requirements in their favor. If you're not playing the game, you may get shut out by someone who is.

Remember how we talked about Boeing when we first investigated the size of the **Federal Procurement Arena**? Well, those **Major League players** are also arguing their case, and lobbying the government on all sides to ensure they get their piece of the pie.

According to *The Washington Post*, "Boeing was among the top companies spending money last year [2018] trying to influence U.S. government decision-making. The Chicago-based aerospace giant spent $15.1 million lobbying the federal government, employing about 100 lobbyists on its behalf."[122] Boeing, they say, through its Political Action Committee, donated $2.4 million to political candidates in 2017 and 2018.

In defense of their practices, Boeing released a statement saying, "As the nation's largest exporter and a leading producer of both commercial and defense aerospace products, there are a number of significant policy issues at the federal, state and local levels with the potential to impact our business, our diverse workforce, and our supply chain. Our team is focused on telling Boeing's story and supporting policies that advance the aviation industry and U.S. manufacturing in the communities where we live and work."

This is what you are up against.

The biggest and most established companies in the country are "telling their stories" and "supporting policies" that advance

---

122 O'Connell and Lamothe, 2019.

their own goals. If you want to play to win, you need to tell stories and support policies that advance your goals.

Also, the government is always trying to level the playing field. This raises two points:

- If it isn't specifically prohibited, and doesn't expose anyone to accusations of impropriety, you can consider it.
- You need to stay abreast of changing rules and regulations because something that could be considered okay today could be prohibited tomorrow.

The reason the government does not want the procurement process to appear biased is that they would risk protests if it did. Often, an incumbent will raise a protest just to extend a contract that has been awarded away from them for the year it takes to investigate the protest.

For a procurement professional, there is nothing worse than a protest that triggers a General Administration Office (GAO) audit, draws attention from Capitol Hill with requirements to appear in front of Congress, and brings negative press.

You must take this into consideration when working with federal employees: be strategic, be smart, and think for the government. You have a much better chance to create a clever solution by thinking through all objections first, rather than being caught off guard.

So, go out and tell your stories. Use your **Win Themes** throughout your communication to emphasize your strengths and downplay your weaknesses, all while working on moving weaknesses and threats into the strengths and opportunities columns of your **Innovation TAFE Analysis**.

Become a trusted MVP to your potential buyers and help them shape their requirements into ones you can fulfill better than your competition. As you do that, you will grow ever closer to entering **The Pitching Zone**. But before you do, you have one last skill to learn: **Delivering Value**.

12

DELIVERING VALUE

In **Playing to Win,** you identified your Unique Value Proposition, and developed your **Win Themes**. In **Delivering Value**, we're going to look at how you measure performance, and bake delivering that value into your **Federal Business Game Plan.**

I have seen far too many innovators pitch products and solutions with no consideration for the value proposition. If you hope to win contracts, you absolutely must ensure your proposal has real value.

How are you going to deliver value? By having a **Win Strategy** guided by your **Win Themes** and embodied in your **Proposal Set Pieces**, which were driven by your customers' language and identified needs.

DEVELOP YOUR WIN STRATEGY

It can take companies days of brainstorming to develop **Win Strategies**, yet after all the effort the emerging strategies often are still weak. You can turn all of this around by training your team to use the right process for **Win Strategy** development.

CHOOSE YOUR PROJECT BUSINESS CAPTURE TEAM

Assign a project leader and ensure you have at least one team member from each of your **Relay Teams** (Business Capture, Innovation, Operations) assigned to the project. You will probably also need a **Champion** to be the face of your business in negotiations, as well as a bid writer and legal and financial professionals. However you structure your team, make it clear who is responsible for what, and who has the final say in decision-making.

HOLD A BRAINSTORMING SESSION

Start the first team meeting with a presentation on the opportunity background. Run through roles and responsibilities and introduce team members who are not already familiar with each other.

Don't try to do too much in one sitting. Use a series of short sessions to maximize productivity from the attendees. Break for homework assignments for a couple of days after the initial introductory session. Use video conferencing rather than the telephone for remote members.

REFINE YOUR WIN THEMES

The Win Themes you developed in **Playing to Win** were broad. Each project team needs to develop **Win Themes** specific to their **Win Strategy** for that project. That said, your existing **Win Themes** should provide a healthy "shopping basket" for project teams to start from.

Develop at least one **Win Theme** for each of your unique skills, one for your supporting strengths, and one for your reversible negatives as they apply to this project. If necessary, update any preexisting **Win Themes** to reflect changes.

 ### CREATE YOUR WIN STRATEGY

Use your **Win Themes** to create an **Action Items List** that ensures you will deliver what you promise. If your Win Theme is "We can hit the ground running," make sure you know how many personnel the project requires, and set deadlines in place for recruitment, background checking, etc., to ensure you will be able to do what you promised.

Similarly, let's say your **Win Theme** is "We will have XYZ technology to Technology Readiness Level 5 by [deadline]." Create a list of things that need to happen before then for that to happen. Work backward from the last thing that must happen for you to meet your goal, and step backward from that one action at a time until you reach where you are now.

Then assign time frames to each step and assign the action steps to personnel as shown in Figure 33.

WIN STRATEGY
Walkback

For each Win Theme, walk backwards through what must happen for that to happen until you reach where you are now. Then create deadlines and assign your action steps to individuals or departments.

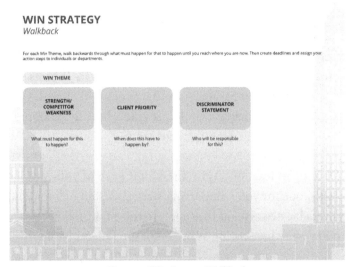

Figure 33: Win Strategy Walkback.

When you have done this for each **Win Theme**, combine your action steps chronologically to complete your Win Strategy as shown in Figure 34.

WIN STRATEGY
Chronology

When you have completed your walkback for each Win Theme, combine your action steps chronologically to complete your Win Strategy.

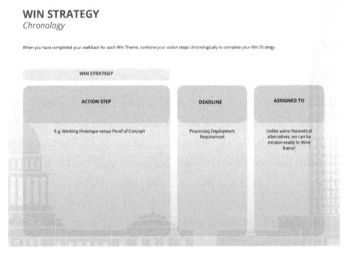

Figure 34: Win Strategy Chronology.

SHARE YOUR WIN STRATEGY

Once you have your **Win Strategy**, teach people what the **Win Themes** are and how you're going to go about delivering them. Disseminate your **Win Strategy** through your **Business Strength Training Center**. Make sure everyone who plays a part in the Win Strategy is familiar with it and their role in it.

Once you've invested time and energy in devising the language to highlight your **Win Themes** and **Proposal Set Pieces**, use them at every opportunity.

With your **Win Strategy** in place, you're almost ready to enter **The Pitching Zone**.

Almost.

There's just one last thing we need to talk about—and that's pricing.

 PRICE TO WIN

Before we talk about pricing, understand there's no way I can teach you everything you need to know about pricing your pitch in a single volume, let alone a chapter in this book.

Pricing is a complex issue, and you are going to need to hire a costing specialist unless you have one on staff full-time. You can't just think of a number and place your bets.

But the Federal Acquisitions Regulations (FAR) lays out certain requirements for showing your costing. As with everything else in the proposal, you must be compliant before you can be considered. With that in mind, I'm going to run you through some basics that will give you a basic grounding, to ensure you don't shoot yourself in the foot and make your proposal invalid.

 **PRICING 101**

As with everything, there are some basic initial questions you can answer to weed out a lot of unsuitable opportunities early on, before you invest too much time and energy considering them.

- Check the dollar value of an RFP. You can't win by bidding over budget; you will only exclude yourself from consideration. So, can you deliver under budget, and still make a profit? If not, don't waste your time and resources bidding.
- If there is an existing contract, find out who has it and what the overall amount for that contract was. Can you beat or match that? If not, unless your target agency has an increased budget and increased requirements that can justify the increased costs, you won't be able to win business there.
- Look at the evaluation basis. Was it "lowest price technically acceptable" or "best value?" That will tell you whether cost is the overriding factor, or whether you can win by adding value.

QUICK COSTING ESTIMATES

Before you get too far into the business capture process, you should have a clear idea of the buyer's requirements. Work through those requirements and calculate the costs of meeting them.

Calculate:

- Direct Materials costs
- Direct Labor costs
- Payroll Overhead (as a percentage applied to direct labor)
- Other Direct Costs
- Total Cost before General and Administrative (G&A) expense
- G&A Expense (as a percentage applied to total cost)
- Total Cost
- Profit (as a percentage of total cost)
- Proposed Price

POWER PLAY: *Don't be tempted to inflate costs and downplay profit. FAR 15.404 says that the government's objective is "to ensure that the final agreed-to price is fair and reasonable."*[123] *Further, paragraph (a)(2) states that (2) "Price analysis shall be used when certified cost or pricing data are not required." Paragraph (b)(1) defines price analysis as:*

  - *1. Price analysis is the process of examining and evaluating a proposed price without evaluating its separate cost elements and proposed profit. Unless*

---

123 FAR 15.404

an exception from the requirement to obtain certified cost or pricing data applies under 15.403-1(b)(1) or (b)(2), at a minimum, the contracting officer shall obtain appropriate data, without certification, on the prices at which the same or similar items have previously been sold and determine if the data is adequate for evaluating the reasonableness of the price.

Diving a little deeper down the rabbit hole, we learn at 15.403-1(b)(1) and (b)(2):

- *(b) Exceptions to certified cost or pricing data requirements. The contracting officer shall not require certified cost or pricing data to support any action (contracts, subcontracts, or modifications) (but may require data other than certified cost or pricing data as defined in FAR 2.101 to support a determination of a fair and reasonable price or cost realism)*
- *((1) When the contracting officer determines that prices agreed upon are based on adequate price competition (see standards in paragraph (c)(1) of this subsection);*
- *((2) When the contracting officer determines that prices agreed upon are based on prices set by law or regulation (see standards in paragraph (c)(2) of this subsection);*

And at paragraph (c)(1) and (2), we find:

- *(c) Standards for exceptions from certified cost or pricing data requirements -*
- *((1) Adequate price competition.*

- ((i) A price is based on adequate price competition when -
- ((A) Two or more responsible offerors, competing independently, submit priced offers that satisfy the Government's expressed requirement;
- ((B) Award will be made to the offeror whose proposal represents the best value (see 2.101) where price is a substantial factor in source selection; and
- ((C) There is no finding that the price of the otherwise successful offeror is unreasonable. Any finding that the price is unreasonable must be supported by a statement of the facts and approved at a level above the contracting officer.
- ((ii) For agencies other than DoD, NASA, and the Coast Guard, a price is also based on adequate price competition when-
- ((A) There was a reasonable expectation, based on market research or other assessment, that two or more responsible offerors, competing independently, would submit priced offers in response to the solicitation's expressed requirement, even though only one offer is received from a responsible offeror and if -
- ((1) Based on the offer received, the contracting officer can reasonably conclude that the offer was submitted with the expectation of competition, e.g., circumstances indicate that -
- ((2) The offeror believed that at least one other offeror was capable of submitting a meaningful offer; and
- ((ii) The offeror had no reason to believe that other potential offerors did not intend to submit an offer; and

- *((2) The determination that the proposed price is based on adequate price competition and is reasonable has been approved at a level above the contracting officer; or*
- *((B) Price analysis clearly demonstrates that the proposed price is reasonable in comparison with current or recent prices for the same or similar items, adjusted to reflect changes in market conditions, economic conditions, quantities, or terms and conditions under contracts that resulted from adequate price competition.*
- *((2) Prices set by law or regulation. Pronouncements in the form of periodic rulings, reviews, or similar actions of a governmental body, or embodied in the laws, are sufficient to set a price.*

All of which is a somewhat long-winded way of saying that so long as there are two or more contractors bidding for the contract, that the contract will go to the contractor whose bid offers best value, and that if there is no evidence to suggest it doesn't represent fair and reasonable value, you won't need to provide certified cost or pricing data, just reasonable pricing breakdowns. And unless you're digging on a DoD, NASA, or Coast Guard contract, the "rule of two" is fulfilled by the expectation of competition, even if the other possible contractor doesn't enter a bid.

So work your costs out realistically, and build in a "fair and reasonable" profit. And if you don't know what the government considers a fair and reasonable profit in your case, go back to USASpending.gov and beta.sam.gov and search previously awarded contracts, or consider the industry

average profit rates for similar work in your area of similar
complexity and risk.

This quick costing won't survive the bidding process. There will be items you've overlooked, underestimated, or overestimated. I'll say it again: you WILL need to hire a costing professional to help you with this part of your bid unless you have a specialist on staff already.

Pricing and costing alone could fill volumes, and we don't have space to dive deep into the variables in this book. In fact, Price to Win is just one pricing strategy. You might choose to Price to Deliver, or Price for Profit. If you price to win, you're basing your bid on the market; if you price to deliver, you're basing it on your costs plus a certain percentage. If you're pricing for profit, you're bidding based on what you guess the buyer is prepared to pay. In each scenario, your calculation will be different, and you will have constraints to consider, such as staying within competitive range determinations and Independent Government Cost Estimates (IGCE).

However, this quick costing exercise will flag up any major cost/budget mismatches that would make it impossible for you to win the business, and will save you spending hundreds or thousands of hours chasing a project you could never win or, worse, that would sink your business if you did.

So, now that you have learned all six **Skills for Winning**, it's time to enter **The Pitching Zone**, where we will create your **Pitch Perfection Program**.

13

THE PITCHING ZONE

Welcome to **The Pitching Zone**. In this chapter, we are talking about writing the perfect pitch proposal in response to a Request for Proposals (RFP). We're looking at the process from RFP to awarding of the contract. We're not really talking about smaller purchases that can be completed through a credit card purchase, or Other Transaction Authority. We're talking about bigger purchases and contracts.

Although the procurement cycle and business capture cycle are long in the **Federal Procurement Arena**, you may be surprised by just how short the proposal window is. You might feel like you have a lot of time to compile a proposal, but unless you are part of the shaping process and aware of the upcoming RFP before it happens, you really don't have much time to get a lot of things done.

A trend has developed in favor of shorter and more definite procurement cycles. The time between the RFP and the cutoff for submitting bids is getting ever shorter.

While there are some instances where you will still have for-ty-five days, thirty days is becoming more common. There are more RFPs coming out where you will have two weeks or even less to respond.

The best companies I have seen treat the RFP as the starting line, not the notice board. They are monitoring beta.sam.gov daily, waiting for the starting gun to fire on projects they know are about to come up. They're metaphorically in their race kit, in starting positions. They're not checking in once a week to see if there are any races being held, and having to go get their kit, get changed, go down to the track and warm up first. You can't win a marathon that way. Let alone a sprint!

So, let's make sure you know how this part of the process works, and what you need to do, and in what order, to make sure you're down there on the starting line with the pros when the firing gun sounds.

SHAPING THE RFP

Inexperienced or unsuccessful government contractors respond to RFPs; successful contractors help shape them. By being involved in the discovery process early on, and by achieving trusted advisor status, they wire the contracts for themselves, and seal the deal with the perfect proposal.

The good news is that you can wire the contracts to yourself, too.
1. Work toward becoming an MVP or trusted advisor. We've already talked about this.
2. Build or develop unique solutions that outperform the competition. In short, play to your strengths.

3. Make recommendations that solve the government's problem and meet its needs by filling a technical capability gap.

4. Show how the solution you come up with is in the best interests of the government.

Because you'll typically be introducing solutions they have never seen before, you may want to run it by them early. For example, what if your technology can get the job done with three people but they currently use ten? Questions you might need to ask include:

- Are they attached to the staffing levels?
- Are these people doing more work than the statement of work suggests?
- Do personnel report to different departments who like to have their own resources instead of sharing a person?
- How might this affect funding?

See if they approve your solution and tweak it with them if they do not. There may be times, however, when you do not want to expose your technology or innovative solution too soon. For example:

- If you are working in a highly competitive field of scientific advancement and on the verge of a breakthrough, you might not want to risk disclosing your solution before it's ready.
- If there are other contractors near the customer who could share information with team members and other partners.

In some pursuits, you should exercise caution and decide what you want to run by the customer, and which (if any) artifacts you want to leave with them.

Here's the important part: you have stretched your skills to provide the best solution and have shown the government customer why your proposed solution is the best for their problem. Now, you need to help the customer define the tasks and objectives that need to be accomplished to solve that problem—and what metrics apply—to make them fit your solution.

These are all questions you need to answer when you draw up your solution, so that you can help the contracting officer frame the requirement. And if you think that's in some way unethical, remember every other potential contractor will be doing the same. If you don't make your preferences known, the requirement will be shaped by your competition.

 THE PROPOSAL PROCESS

You should be in contact with the buyer for some time before the RFP comes out. However, if you're late to the game, or if you still have questions about the proposal when it is released, you will have a brief time during which you can ask questions. This is usually a seven-day period in which you can email your questions to the Source Selection Authority (SSA).

This is the only opportunity for communication you will have during the bid process unless there are open days during this period. So, if you have something you need to know, don't miss it, or you will be reliant on the RFP document alone for guidance. The Purchasing Officer or Source Selection Team will view all questions after the cut-off date and discuss them. They will answer them publicly, so everybody will be able to see their responses. You probably want to avoid asking questions here if the answer will give your competition a heads up on something they may not have considered.

Your job is to analyze the RFP document and to confirm you still want to bid on this opportunity. Compare the requirements to your preferred wording and see if it has been shaped to your strengths. This assessment will give you an idea of whether the buyer is leaning in your direction or toward your competitors.

If you still want to bid on the contract, you need to project-manage the process. You need to allow time to outline the proposal, schedule your writing, and then edit and format the document for delivery before the deadline.

Be very aware that the deadline is firm and will include both date and time. If you miss it, you will be disqualified. I have seen companies disqualified for non-compliance because they were not paying attention to both date and time deadlines and submitted their proposals an hour after the deadline.

On occasion a proposal might get extended, for exceptional circumstances, such as during a government shutdown. I have been part of RFPs where we had to extend the deadline because potential contractors were unable to obtain past performance input because the departments they were trying to contact were closed due to federal funding issues—although the smart ones used that time to complete other parts of the proposal. But even if you think an RFP may be extended, you cannot count on it until it happens. Reasons for extensions must be substantial, and extensions must be made across the board. The government cannot make exceptions for individual businesses in the interests of fairness. Poor organization will not cut it.

> **POWER PLAY**: *Build a buffer into your process for last-minute changes and delays. Never assume the cutoff time is midnight and any time on the closing date will do. The deadline might be the end of office hours, or at 12 noon. Make sure you know the exact time, and get your proposal in well before.*

It's important to remember, though, that your job is to win a contract, not just to complete the proposal by the deadline. With that in mind, you need to learn the proper process for developing winning documents.

 BATTING AVERAGES

While it's true you miss 100 percent of the shots you don't take, and you must be in the game to win, you only get so many swings at the ball. Even a small proposal is going to cost you thousands of dollars to put together properly. Bigger deals call for more complex proposals that might run into the tens of thousands to compile. If you disqualify yourself with rookie mistakes, or if you don't hit all the bases consistently, you're going to have a lousy batting average, and you can't sustain that for long.

If you try to skimp and save on a proposal instead of making every effort to impress to win, your win rate will suffer. Your content needs to be sharp. You need to make sure you don't fall into common traps such as skipping solution development or going with some boilerplate template from proposal to proposal.

Customers can see through that and get extremely annoyed, which results in losses. That's why I'm giving you worksheets and checklists, not templates. Every proposal is different, even to the same customer or the same service. Circumstances are always different, and these can lead to shifting customer priorities. You need to emphasize the current priorities and explain not just what you will do for the customer, but how you will do it. That means taking the time to think through the solution, and then describing step-by-step how you will implement it.

You need to realize your proposals are not technical papers—despite the dry technical requirements. They are sales documents. They need to be highly persuasive. Because of the government-wide allergy to sales, though, they must also be devoid of sales and marketing lingo.

Your proposal needs to be customer-focused, meaning it needs to talk about what the customer will receive and the results they will gain. It needs to echo your Win Themes; have crisp, clean graphics on every other page; and be professionally presented. Your writing must be grammatically correct, personal, and highly readable. Your proposal must affect your evaluators emotionally to sway them into trusting your abilities to do an excellent job if you get the award.

All that takes a lot of effort, skill, and time to get right. So, you can't write dozens of proposals and take a "throwing mud at the wall" approach, just hoping something will stick and land you a win. It's vital that you pick your battles well, and only bid on contracts you have a high chance of winning.

 YOUR CAPTURE PLAN

For every opportunity, you want to create a PowerPoint document in your **Business Strength Training System** entitled [Opportunity] Capture Plan.

In every business capture pursuit, it is vital that you document the valuable intelligence you collect, including both your conclusions and the raw data. As you collect information, document your conclusions immediately in the centerpiece of your capture efforts, the Capture Plan.

Your capture plan should include sections for:

- Summary
  - Client History
  - The Requirement introduction
  - Relationship with the client
  - Past/current performance
  - Recent interactions
- The Client
  - The Requirement in Detail
  - Hot Buttons/ Priorities
  - KPIs/Metrics
  - Procurement team
  - Decision-making process
  - Influencer map
- The Capture Team
  - Team roster roles and responsibilities
  - Meeting schedule
  - Action points
  - Project leader
  - Operations
  - Technical
  - Business Capture
  - Legal
  - Financial
  - Bid writing
- The Competition
  - Map of the Federal Procurement Arena
  - TAFE/SWOT Analysis per competitor
- Intelligence
  - Data collection
  - Data interpretation
- Strategy
  - TAFE Analysis
  - Unique Value Proposition
  - Win Themes
  - Win Strategy
- The Proposal
  - Outline
  - Rough draft
  - Technical draft
  - Operations draft
  - Sales draft
  - Legal draft
  - Financial draft
  - Final draft
  - Post award
  - Debrief
  - Contract
  - Implementation
  - Lessons learned

You may also want to use online team collaboration software such as Trello or Basecamp to organize group work on the Capture Plan.

The Capture Plan is your living, working document that describes the capture strategy and action items, but also provides a lot of detailed background information about the customer and the acquisition.

These documents become part of the proposal kick-off package to get the entire proposal team on the same page. It will help you make the decision to bid or not to bid.

TO BID OR NOT TO BID?

How do you decide which RFPs are worth your time and effort to bid on, if you can't just bid on everything that comes up that you might be able to?

First, look at the contract type and size, and consider your likely chances of a win.

If you're still trying to break into the space, and don't have past performance, you want to look for a multi-vendor Indefinite Delivery, Indefinite Quantity (IDIQ) program. A multi-vendor IDIQ means everybody who meets the minimum requirements will be added to the contract, allowing them to sell to the government. From the government's perspective, it's a license to shop around easily. From your point of view, it's a straightforward way to get into The Big Leagues and establish some past performance. All you have to do is not mess up.

Or look for small-dollar value contracts that may not be of high enough value to interest the bigger players in bidding. And when I say small-dollar value, I'm talking about less than $100 million. At that point, there's still plenty of scope for you to make money, but some of the bigger players have too much overhead in their rainbow teams to make it worth their while.

At the other end of the scale, high-value, single-vendor, fixed-price, fixed-term contracts are going to be tough to win as a small business or new vendor. Every major contractor that can meet the requirements is going to be going after that, and only one can win. Your likelihood of winning is low, and the expense incurred in generating a proposal will be high.

Those are obvious go/no-go scenarios.

Other obvious go bid determiners might be:
- You have been working with the Technical Point of Contact on the RFP shaping process.
- Like EFB in the Introduction, you have been working closely with a government representative.
- You are bringing an innovative solution to maturity that solves a pressing problem.
- You have no competition.

At the other extreme, no bid flags would be:
- The government has been working closely with the competition and show obvious signs of leaning toward their solution.
- You are selling an incomplete or poorly matched solution.
- There is so much competition and you could only compete on price.

Finally, consider the timeline. If an RFP has a two-week deadline, and you have no prior intelligence or involvement in the process, even if your solution appears at first glance to be a perfect match, chances are you won't have time to complete the proposal process to a sufficient standard to win. Additionally, chances are the RFP is a technical requirement and the decision is already made. At that point, your chances of swooping in and stealing the deal are slim at best.

So, once you've decided on a go situation, how do you increase your chances of winning?

 ## PITCHING PITFALLS

Writing government proposals can be rewarding but tough. When you venture into entering a proposal, you need training in writing persuasive proposals, professional help, or both. Fortunately, they are easily obtainable. You might find it useful to watch free instructional webinars on various aspects of proposal development online.

It is impossible to over-stress the importance of following the instructions in the RFP to the letter. First make a list of all the requirements, which as the criteria your proposal must meet to even be eligible for consideration. These are things you CANNOT afford to overlook, ignore, or get wrong. Always remember the Source Selection Authority must base its decisions on your proposal. They cannot overlook or ignore gaps in the requirements based on prior knowledge or informal conversation with you; what is on paper is the basis for consideration.

Pay attention to the details. And we're not talking only about the contents of the proposal here; your proposal's presentation is vital. I have seen proposals excluded from consideration because the formatting was wrong. If the RFP asks for proposals in a single font, double-spaced, and not to exceed twenty-four pages, and you submit a twenty-five-page document, single-spaced and with multiple fonts, it will be disqualified because you did not follow basic instructions.

While you may think that's unfair, or unreasonable, the government works with thousands of contractors, has myriad rules to follow, and bears a heavy burden to be fair and transparent. They need to know that when they award a contract, the appointee can follow basic instructions. Consider it part of the cost of entry and do exactly as it says.

Look at the sample formatting instructions below from a solicitation I worked on to get a feel for what your proposal may need to look like.[124]

L.8 GENERAL INSTRUCTIONS

The following instructions establish the acceptable minimum requirements for the format and content of your proposal. The Contracting Officer is the only individual authorized to legally commit the Government to the expenditure of public funds in connection with this requirement. By submitting a

---

124 Solicitation number 19-233-SOL-00098. Originally posted to FedBizOps, and now searchable on beta.sam.gov.

proposal in response to this solicitation, it is understood that your proposal shall become a part of the official contract file.

Your attention is directed to the requirements for the submission of technical proposals and business proposals contained in Sections L.9 and L.10 of the solicitation. Your proposal must be submitted in accordance with these instructions.

The proposal must be prepared in two parts: a "Technical Proposal" and a "Business Proposal." Each of these two parts shall be separate and complete so that the evaluation of one may be accomplished independently of the evaluation of the other. Offerors who fail to submit each of these two parts will be ineligible for award.

L.9 TECHNICAL PROPOSAL INSTRUCTIONS

Technical proposals shall be limited to 25 pages double-spaced, with 1-inch margins, and using not less than 12-point font on 8.5"x 11" paper. It is important to note that the text and font contained within charts or diagrams may be single spaced and no less than 9-point font. All other elements within technical proposals shall be double-spaced, with 1-inch margins and using no less than 12-point font. Offerors are encouraged to be succinct and economical in their Technical Proposal. Excessive volume and elaborate technical proposals are unnecessary. NOTE: The maximum page limit does not include the cover letter, executive summary, or table of contents.

It must address each Technical Evaluation Factor in sufficient detail to provide a clear and concise presentation that includes, but is not limited to, the requirements of the technical proposal instructions. The proposal shall contain a response to each of the factors and subfactors identified.

In terms of what the proposal needs to include, you really need to pay close attention to every item the government requests, down to every word. Much like answering those awful exam questions that would ask you to "compare and contrast" things, the terminology of an RFP is at once very precise and obfuscated. It's precise because certain words and phrases have extremely specific meanings for the procurement community, and obfuscated because the procurement community really isn't good at communicating what those meanings are to would-be suppliers. Sometimes it can feel like you're reading a foreign language.

For example, let's consider the following requirement:

"Offeror shall demonstrate the experience and ability to perform tasks required for Management Support (PWS 1.5.1.and subparagraphs)"

Before you can address this requirement, you need to unpack it and ensure you understand what it's asking for. Let's break down the difficult language below together.

Offeror shall demonstrate—Here, "demonstrate" is the key word. To demonstrate is to offer clear proof or evidence. You can't just say, "We can perform tasks required for Management Support (PWS 1.5.1. and subparagraphs)," and think you have covered this. You need to say, "Our ability to perform... is demonstrated by..." and then give concrete evidence. That evidence might be past performance, certification, or specifications that meet or exceed those required.

The experience and ability to perform tasks required—If the RFP asks for experience and ability, then you need to address those as two separate issues. You can't just say "we can do x"; you have to be able to say, "we have done x previously at y and z." And you can't just say "we have done this before"; you need to say, "we have performed at this level in the past at x and y, and we maintain our ability to perform by z."

Management Support (PWS 1.5.1. and subparagraphs)—If you are pointed to a section like this, you need to list out everything called for in that section and address them in order. Don't just address the top line of the item if it asks for subparagraphs; make sure you hit them all. In your draft, write them out with numbers, and map your evidence to them to make sure you don't risk being downgraded by not drawing the connecting lines for the procurement officer.

POWER PLAY: *When you are unpacking the RFP, pay attention to sections L and M. Those two sections lay out how the proposals will be evaluated and supply instructions for responding. Section J often has attachments. So, for example, requests for past performance may be included here. It's where you will find the list of documents you may need to collect and submit in support*

of your proposal. You'll also find design or project specif-
ics here. Those are the sections where I spend 90 percent
of my time when I'm writing RFPs or proposals.

Once you have a clear idea of what you need to include in your proposal, it's time to start thinking about how to deliver your pitch.

THE PITCHING PROCESS

Always remember, proposals are where you make your money. There's no point having a pretty office and expensive stationery if you can't write a sound proposal.

I have worked for a company that made that mistake. They went from having one or two small contracts to having multiple small ones and decided to roll them all into a bigger contract. At the time, the rules had changed to give preference to Native Americans, and the owner was a Pacific Islander. However, the owner was inexperienced and detached from the realities of the contract requirements. Instead, the owner focused too heavily on having the expensive office, creating an impression, attending events, and talking the company up.

But the proposals going in were not up to standard, and the government ended up breaking off parts of the contract and awarding them elsewhere. Because the owner refused to invest in professional proposal writing, and had existing staff writing them on top of their everyday work, the owner started losing work.

Major League players have entire departments or at least small teams dedicated to proposal writing. They have a codified system of proposal writing with blue, pink, red, green, gold, and white teams, each responsible for checking a proposal meets the RFP requirements to a specific set of criteria at various stages along the way. The blue team will review the outline, the pink team the rough draft, the red team the near-complete draft, the green team the pricing, the gold team the final draft, and then the white team will do a last proofread.

 A PITCHING PROCESS

If you're in **The Little Leagues** and writing one alone, or even in **The Big Leagues** as part of a small team, you are already an underdog. Don't make life harder for yourself by attempting to write the entire thing in one pass. Take a leaf out of **The Major League player's** playbook and break it down.

Here's a suggested approach:
1. Unpack the RFP—decode the language and write the request in plain English.
2. Make a **Master List of Requirements** you can use as your guide to check things off at each stage.
3. Start a spreadsheet with the requirements listed in Column A.
4. Title Column B "**Win Themes**" and then enter your win themes and phrases everywhere they fit in the requirements.
5. Title Column C "**Evidence**" and enter your supporting facts, figures, past performance, etc. where they fit.
6. In Column D, write rough sentences for each requirement.

7. Use proposal writing software to transfer your proposal **Win Themes** and **evidence** into a proposal document template in rough draft form. Your template should include from your **Capture Plan**:
   - Executive Summary
   - Key Personnel (short bios & resumes)
   - Past Performance (customer testimonials)
   - Statement of Work (as requested in the RFP)
   - Charts and Graphs (as requested in RFP or for ease of reading)
   - Quality Control Plan, Subcontracting Plan, or other required appendices
8. Have **technical** staff run through the proposal to check the language, facts, specifications, etc.
9. Have **operations** personnel run through the draft to ensure the business can meet the deliverables.
10. Get your **business capture experts** to run through it and ensure the customer pain points and buzzwords they use are incorporated into the language appropriately.
11. Get your **pricing** experts to run the numbers and make sure everything is priced properly.
12. Run the draft past a **legal** professional to ensure you're not creating obligations unintentionally or breaking any rules.
13. **Write** the proposal in polished form.
14. Get the **graphic designer** to create any graphics and do a first check on the formatting.
15. Smart businesses, especially those who are just starting out, hire a **professional proposal writer**, if not to write the entire proposal, then at least to **edit** and **format** it. RFPs are dense and complicated, and your proposal must hit every note. Get someone who "speaks the language" to tidy yours up at the very least.

16. **Review** the proposal against the **master checklist** one last time, ensuring nothing has been edited out that could disqualify it.

If you follow this plan, your proposal will at least meet the base requirements to be eligible for consideration. You will be ahead of the bulk of **Little League** proposals—and a fair few **Big League** ones—meaning you'll have a fair shot at winning if you've done your groundwork well.

Once you have completed your proposal and entered it, your job is done, for now. You can't ask the procurement personnel anything until after the award. All you can do is play the waiting game.

 THE WAITING GAME

You will have to wait until the date advertised to receive a decision, and you should not contact the procurement officer or any member of the committee until after the decision is made.

If you don't win, you can ask questions about how the decision was made during a debriefing period, which is usually three days after the decision is made public.

You also have the right to raise a protest if you feel the rules were not followed. You usually have only ten days to raise a protest, and the rules surrounding them vary from contract types and are strictly enforced. You can read more about how to protest a government contract at gao.gov/legal/bid-protests/faqs/.[125]

Fortunately, if you have followed the **Federal Business Game Plan** you set out, and followed the steps in this book, you won't have given anyone grounds for protest when you land your first (or next) contract.

Don't be too disheartened if you don't win your first proposal. Just make sure you learn everything you can from the experience and try again. Before long, you'll be entering the final Zone, **The Performance Zone.**

---

125 US Government Accountability Office, 2020.

14

THE PERFORMANCE ZONE

———

Congratulations! You landed your first government contract. Now what?

Well, you could consider yourself set for life, celebrate with a bottle of champagne, and then set about spending all that hard-earned cash on flash cars and fancy offices. I hope by now, however, you won't be too surprised to learn that's not what I'd advise.

Think of your first government contract as your tryout. You've been playing in **The Little Leagues**. Now, you've landed a spot in **The Big Leagues**, with a chance to try out for **The Major Leagues**. Do you think, if you rock up in your jeans and leather jacket like Maverick in *Top Gun*, and spend the afternoon sitting on the bleachers heckling the players, you're going to make the cut? No, of course not.

You need to show up looking the part, give it your best, and hope the coaches, managers, and talent scouts like what they see. Similarly, if you approach your first government contract with a take-the-money-and-run attitude, your first contract may well be your last. If, on the other hand, you show the procurement officer you are serious about over-delivering on the terms of the contract, and do everything in your power to make their life easier, you'll earn yourself some much-needed past performance feedback for when you make your next bid.

So, how do you ensure you're delivering everything you're required to deliver, and how do you monitor that?

 KPIS AND DELIVERABLES

As soon as you are awarded the contract, you need to go over it very carefully. Get a lawyer to look at it and compare it to your proposal. Make sure you are aware of any difference between them because if you don't address those now, the contract, not your proposal, will stand.

POWER PLAY: If you have issues, you need to raise them as early as possible. It may be possible to get the contract amended if it is in error, but if you don't do that early on, and issues arise later, you could find yourself without a leg to stand on.

Once you have satisfied yourself that you understand the contract, go through it again, pulling out everything you are required to deliver. Make a list, much as you did with the

RFP. These two lists should be almost identical. Pay attention to any differences, and double-check any wording that may be vague or confusing.

Now you know what's expected of you, measure that against your proposal and plans to implement it. Does anything need to change there? Can you still meet your aims and objectives and satisfy the contract?

Then assign a project manager who will be responsible for quality assurance, even if the contract doesn't call for one.

POWER PLAY: *Make sure your project manager is visible to the government buyer, checking in with them regularly, and sending in progress reports. The last thing you want is to get a request for a review; that's never a good sign.*

Assuming everything is good, it's a clever idea to draw up a set of reports that track the deliverables of the contract. If you have quotas to meet, or deadlines, design these into your reports. These will help you measure your performance.

 YOUR PROGRAM MANAGEMENT PRACTICE

First you learn the theory, then you put what you've learned to the test of real-life application. Then, you observe the results, evaluate, and modify your application for the next iteration of action.

You may have a natural tendency to shy away from delivering reports that are not specifically requested. You might think that, so long as you're not getting any complaints, all is well, and that raising your hand might attract unnecessary scrutiny.

I want you to approach this from another angle.

You may be interacting with the contracting officer on site every day or working remotely and rarely, if ever, have contact with the person evaluating your performance. Either way, their approval is vitally important. If they see you every day, you need them to see that you're working for them and getting results. If they never see you, you need to give them regular evidence of your progress.

There are several reasons you should stay in regular contact with the contracting officer or program manager and ask for feedback on your performance:

1. Your buyer might not be happy, but they might not be unhappy enough to deal with their complaints head on. They might just decide to put up with a subpar performance for the duration of the contract, put in negative past performance feedback, and assign the contract to someone else next time around. If you're not in regular contact, it's like playing a fast-paced game of basketball without a scorecard. If you're not getting that feedback, or measuring performance yourself, you might not even realize you're losing the game until it's over.

2. Your buyer might have an impression of you as underperforming when you're really on track. Sometimes

innovation can seem to be moving slowly or stuck, or conditions beyond your control can reflect on you and make it look like you're not delivering, when failed iterations may be part of the development process. What if the government personnel don't understand your solution, and are using it incorrectly? If you're not reporting regularly, the buyer might assume it's a delivery problem on your end and not a training issue on their end.

3. Even if you are underperforming, if you're putting in regular reports, you can frame that in your own terms and highlight any unforeseen issues that could be causing delays. Say you're supposed to be laying ten miles of fiber optic cabling a night, but the environmental parameters are not what the RFP specified, or conditions have changed. Even if you're stuck in a fixed-price, fixed-term contract and the government has no ability to amend it regardless of vendor experience, keeping the buyer abreast of the issues and how you are working to fix them will help.

4. If your program manager is meeting with the buyer monthly and providing weekly reports, they will develop a relationship where they will be able to find out where the customer is happy and unhappy. Building that relationship will give you the opportunity to gather intelligence that informs your future strategy.

The government is moving increasingly toward performance-based evaluation. If the contract doesn't have a performance-based evaluation structure, you might want to create your own because that reduces the subjective element of review.

Reporting gives you a track record to go back to when it comes time to appraise the contract. A buyer relying on memory to supply past-performance feedback may be vague or may only remember that one time when things went wrong. A buyer with a bunch of weekly, monthly, quarterly, and annual reports to refer to and an end-of-job report highlighting everything you did right and mitigating anything that went wrong is more likely to give you a glowing reference.

Don't settle for just monitoring performance, and doing just enough to get by, though. You need to take the initiative in ensuring you over-deliver on the contract, to ensure you get the positive past-performance feedback you need for future contracts.

Even if the government agency you're working with hasn't supplied forms for reporting and feedback, make sure you're recording your daily, weekly, and monthly performance against your deliverables. Make sure everyone working on your contract fills in reports in a timely manner as work is completed.

Don't allow form-filling to become a perceived waste of time or effort. Make sure everyone on the contract understands the importance of their work to the deliverables, and the importance of those deliverables to the continued existence of the business.

One of the best ways to keep reporting accurate and effective is to only measure the essentials, and to do it at frequent, regular intervals. Bonus points if you can find a way to turn this into a game for your personnel.

IMPROVING PERFORMANCE

Some government contracts are set up to incentivize and reward over-delivery. Others, while not having that baked in, may be open to renegotiation based on performance. Some of the best teams I have seen will be aware of the base threshold that the contract requires, and they will build in an over-performance buffer for their team. If the contract calls for the delivery of ten units per week, they will build in twelve. As well as over delivering on a regular basis, this builds in some leeway for downtime if setbacks and equipment failures occur.

 **INTERNATIONAL TELEPHONE & TELEGRAPH (ITT) CORPORATION**

One of the best companies and teams I ever had the pleasure of working with was called the International Telephone & Telegraph (ITT) Corporation (later Inc.). While some of my initial projects were worked with ITT, they eventually broke off their defense business line into a separate publicly traded company called Exelis in 2010.[126] Eventually Exelis was purchased by Harris Corporation for $4.75 billion in 2015.[127]

I began working with ITT in 2010 and had several projects that utilized its material solution. However, each project required unique integration work because of where the solution would be operated, the satellites it needed to talk to, and the platforms on which the solution needed to be integrated. Each project was separate and unique, AND

---

126 Ashworth, 2011.
127 Burke, 2015.

the team had no guarantee of a specific number of orders beforehand. Each effort required specialized military-level approvals and testing as it was employed in a different way with every requirement.

To compound this situation, many transitions were occurring in the background. The technology was originally developed by ITT Inc., which was then broken off. In the restructure the technology was placed under Exelis as a defense solution. Then Harris purchased the technology and the entire Exelis company. There was a LOT of confusion at the corporate level.

However, the director of business development, the program manager, and the technical team were simply outstanding. They were an extremely innovative, tight-knit crew. They understood the procurement space and really listened to my pain points. Together we developed solutions to address them.

They often leaned forward, purchasing some of the longest lead components far ahead of time so they had them on hand should I have a requirement. They took the time to understand their integration and production timelines so they could deliver on time. They were extremely responsive, often providing daily updates on the status of the solution—from development, to initial prototype testing, to integration testing, to deployment testing. They even had members of the same team available to ensure everything was working when the solution was deployed overseas.

Whenever there was a change or merger, they made sure they understood the legal "wickets" before I asked so they could provide quotes quickly. In my experience, even large companies often struggle with this, and typically take up to four weeks to provide a quote.

Because they did such excellent work and delivered such a high-quality product along with exceptional customer service for both myself (at the acquisition shop) in addition to the soldiers on the ground, we ended up providing some seed funding for iterations of that product in addition to other early-stage products to address other capability gaps. The solutions we created allowed soldiers to communicate efficiently and effectively, and ultimately saved lives.

This small team based in South Carolina really adopted and employed many of the concepts identified in this book and they continually received funding from us. Their operation stayed afloat even through all the turmoil and transition over a five-year period. Our work together, with a close-knit, five-man team, resulted in approximately $15 million to $18 million in revenue over that same period.

The other best way to improve performance is simply to ask the buyer what you can do to improve. Even if what they tell you is a stretch too far and you can't accommodate them, the fact that you're asking and looking forward will go in your favor. It speaks volumes, as a lot of contractors take the attitude that they have the contract and you must put up with the minimum delivery until it ends.

Good teams, on the other hand, having built up a track record of over-delivering, will go back to the buyer and use that to negotiate an extension or modification on the contract and increase the dollar value. This tactic is especially powerful if, in response to the stretch request for the customer, you can go back and say, "You asked us for this, but the contract doesn't really allow for us to do that. If we amend it this way, moving forward, it will allow us to…"

Now that you have past performance and a proven product, don't fall into the rut of thinking your current customer is your only customer. Ask yourself: who else within the government might have a use for your product? Which other departments do similar types of work? Who could use your product as it is, and who might use it with some modifications?

You're in **The Big Leagues** now. You made it to the Inside Track once. You can do it again. You might find it useful to work through the **Inside Track Framework** again now that you've "moved up" a level.

GO GET 'EM, TIGER!

Congratulations, you have reached the end of your **Federal Contracting Breakthrough** journey. You're now (hopefully) all set to serve the US government as an innovator and problem solver.

You're a multi-discipline zone warrior.

You've learned all about the **Government Procurement Arena**, identified your potential buyers, recruited your **Relay Teams** and partners. You are a relationship-building, intelligence-gathering, solution-stretching genius. You know how and where to go after the money, how to dot the i's and cross the t's to ensure your proposals pass muster every time, and how to dazzle 'em once you land the gig.

Now what?

If you're reading this book for intellectual purposes or as an academic exercise, you can safely put it down now and go on with your day. If this is your first read-through and you want to get something practical from the experience, though,

I would suggest you now go back to the starting blocks and work your way through the book again, doing the work in each chapter.

Using the tools and **Resources** in this book will help you move closer to winning your race and bringing YOUR vision of the world one step closer to reality.

After that, you can use it as a tactical playbook, a dip-in resource to remind you of the important principles and **POWER PLAYs** at each stage of the process.

Government contracting is not a static environment, though. Rules change; structures change. While the principles we have talked about in this book are timeless, the specifics may be subject to change.

Always double-check the accuracy of information before you act on it. As things change, I will endeavor to keep this book up to date.

As any coach does, I hope you utilize The Inside Track Framework because I want to see you on top of the podium with your Federal Procurement Arena gold medal. I hope to hear from you all about your successful government contracting endeavors. You can connect with me on LinkedIn at linkedin.com/in/janellebillingslea/.

In the meantime, good luck and God bless. Go get 'em!

RESOURCES

Find all the Inside Track Tools you need to complete your Federal Contracting Playbook

ONLINE RESOURCES

———

Below is a handy list of some of the online resources you will need:

- **General Services Administration** (GSA) website at www. gsa.gov for general help and advice for dealing with government agencies.

- **Dun and Bradstreet Request Service** at fedgov.dnb.com/ webform to request your free DUNS number.

- www.irs.gov/businesses for **Individual Tax Identification Number** (ITIN) or **Employer Identification Number** (IEN).

- **Small Business Administration** at www.sba.gov/ for business registrations.
  - www.sba.gov/size-standards/ Small Business Administration **Size Standards Tool** to determine Small Business Status standing.
  - www.sba.gov/federal-contracting/contracting-assistance-programs for current **Contracting Assistance Programs**.

- certify.sba.gov/am-i-eligible to find current and **check for eligibility for set-aside programs.**
  - SBA SubNet at eweb1.sba.gov/subnet/client/dsp_Landing. cfm for **subcontracting opportunities.**
  - Small Business Administration, "All **Small Mentor-Protégé program** at www.sba.gov/federal-contracting/contracting-assistance-programs/all-small-mentor-protege-program.

- NAICS Association **SBA Size Standards tool** at https://www.naics.com/sba-size-standards/.

- www.osha.gov/pls/imis/sicsearch.html for **Standard Identification (SIC) Codes** that apply to your business.

- support.outreachsystems.com/resources/tables/pscs for **Federal Supply Codes** and **Product Service Codes** that may apply to your business.

- www.sam.gov/SAM/ to register in **SAMS.**

- beta.sam.gov for **contracts and opportunities research.**

- USASpending.gov for **backdated awards information research.**

- **Office of Small Business** at www.osec.doc.gov/osdbu/.

- **Good Jobs First. "Subsidy Tracker"** at www.goodjobs-first.org/subsidy-tracker for researching historical government awards.

- **Grants.gov database** at www.grants.gov/web/grants/ search-grants.html to search the Catalog of Federal Domestic Assistance **(CFDA) for grants.**

- Breakdown of **Other Transaction Authority limits** by agency at aida.mitre.org/ota/.

- Defense Acquisition University's Contracting Cone aaf. dau.edu/aaf/contracting-cone/ visual representation of **Federal Procurement options.**

- www.ecfr.gov/cgi-bin/text-idx?tpl=/ecfrbrowse/ Title13/13cfr124_main_02.tpl Title 13 Part 124 of the **Code of Federal Regulations regarding small and disadvantaged businesses.**

- Clustermapping.us for creating **cluster maps.**

- Office of Science for map of **National Laboratories.** www.energy.gov/science/science-innovation/ office-science-national-laboratories.

- Office of the Under Secretary of Defense, Research and Engineering for map of **Defense Laboratories and Centers.** rt.cto. mil/rtl-labs/.

- **Bloomberg Government** research tool at BGov.com.

- **GovWin** from Deltek. Research tool at iq.govwin.com/neo/ home.

- **Department of Defense Subcontracting Directory** includes prime contractors with contract information and a **guide to marketing to DoD**. business.defense.gov/Acquisition/Subcontracting/Subcontracting-For-Small-Business/.

- **GSA schedule** at GSA E-Library. www.gsaelibrary.gsa.gov/ElibMain/ElibHome.

- Dynamics 365 **CRM Software** for Government Contractors from Information Strategies. www.infostrat.com/crm-for-govt-contractors.

- JAMIS **CRM Software**. jamis.com/products/jamis-prime-erp/customer-relationship/.

- Salesforce **CRM Software**. www.salesforce.com/solutions/industries/government/government-contractors/.

- Government Contractors **CRM Software**. https://www.governmentcontractors.co/crm-marketing-automation/.

LIST OF ABBREVIATIONS

AC	Alternating Current
AWS	Amazon Web Services
B2G	Business to Government
BAA	Broad Area Announcements
BGov	Bloomberg Government
CCTV	Closed-Circuit Television
CDDR	Combat Commander
CFDA	Catalog of Federal Domestic Assistance
CIA	Central Intelligence Agency
CMMI	Center for Medicare and Medicaid Innovation
CMR	Commercial Market Representatives
CO/KO	Contracting Officer
COCOM	Combatant Commanders
COTR	Contracting Officer's Technical Representative
COTS	Commercial, Off-the-shelf Solutions
CRM	Customer Relationship Management (software)
CS	Contracting Specialist
CSO	Commercial Solutions Opening
CUI	Controlled Unclassified Information
DARPA	Defense Advanced Research Projects Agency
DC	Direct Current
DCAA	Defense Contract Audit Agency

DoD	Department of Defense	IED	Improvised Explosive Device
DoE	Department of Energy	IG	Inspector General
DSVOSB	Service-Disabled Veteran-Owned Small Business	IP	Intellectual Property
		IRS	Inland Revenue Service
EDWOSB	Economically Disadvantaged Woman-Owned Small Business	ISO	International Organization for Standardization
EFB	Electric Fuel Battery	IT	Information Technology
EIN	Employer Identification Number	ITIL	Information Technology Infrastructure Library
EPLS	Excluded Parties List System		
		ITIN	Individual Tax Identification Number
EVM	Earned Value Management		
		ITT	International Telephone & Telegraph
FAR	Federal Acquisitions Regulations		
FOIA	Freedom of Information Act	JEDI	Joint Enterprise Defense Infrastructure
FPDS	Federal Procurement Data System	JIEDDO	Joint IED Defeat Organization
G&A	General and Administrative	JIDO	Joint Improvised-Threat Defeat Organization
GAO	Government Accountability Office		
		JV	Joint Venture
GSA	General Services Administration	KPI	Key Performance Indicator (used in the heading, not explained)
GTSI	Government Technology Services Inc.		
		MAC	Multi-Agency Contracting
IDIQ	Indefinite Delivery, Indefinite Quantity		
		MAC	Multi-Award contracts

MPT	Micro Purchase Threshold	PCO	Procuring Contract Officer
MVP	Most Valuable Player	PM	Program or Project Managers
NAICS	North American Industry Classification System	PMO	Program Management Office
NASA	National Aeronautics and Space Administration	PMP	Project Management Professionals
		POC	Point of Contact
NBA	National Basketball Association	POGP	Project on Government Oversight
NDA	Nondisclosure Agreement	POM	Program Objective Memorandum
NDU	National Defense University	POR	Program of Record
NIH	National Institutes for Health	PPE	Personal Protective Equipment
NRC	National Research Council	PRC	Procurement Center Representatives
NSF	National Science Foundation	PTAC	Procurement Technical Assistance Centers
OCI	Organizational Conflicts of Interest	PWS	Performance Work Statement
OCONUS	Operating Outside the US	RA	Research Announcement
OSBP	Office of Small Business Programs	R&D	Research and Development
OSD	Office of the Secretary of Defense	RD&E	Research, Development & Engineering
OSDBU	Office of Small & Disadvantaged Business Utilization	REF	Rapid Equipping Force
OTA	Other Transaction Authority	RFI	Requests for Information

RFP	Request for Proposal	SSP	Source Selection Plan
RTD&E	Research, Testing, Development & Engineering	SST	Source Selection Team
		STEM	Science, Technology, Engineering and Mathematics
SAM	Systems for Award Management		
		STTR	Small Business Technology Transfer
SAT	Simplified Acquisition Threshold		
		SWaP	Size, Weight and Power
SBA	Small Business Administration		
		SWIPES	Soldier-Worn Integrated Power Equipment System
SBIR	Small Business Innovation Research		
SETA	Systems Engineering and Technical Assistance	SWOT	Strengths, Weaknesses, Opportunities, Threats (analysis)
SME	Small to Medium Enterprises	TFCN	The Federal Contractor Network
SME	Subject Matter Expert	TPOC	Technical Points of Contact
SOW	Statement of Work		
SSA	Source Selection Authority	TRL	Technology Readiness Levels
SSAC	Source Selection Advisory Council	VOSB	Veteran-Owned Small Businesses
SSEB	Source Selection Evaluation Board	WAG	Widely Attended Gathering
SSEB	Source Selection Evaluation Board	WOSB	Women-Owned Small Businesses

INSIDE TRACK TOOL TEMPLATES

———

Use the Inside Track Tool Templates to create your Federal Contracting Playbook and supporting documents

 YOUR GOVERNMENT SERVICE OBJECTIVE

I want to ....

for ....

and get .... while doing it.

YOUR QUICK WIN GOAL

I can ....
....
....
....
.... to get a quick win goal.

YOUR TECHNOLOGY TEAM SPORT

My Technology Team Sport is bringing an

(Enabling/ Component/ Integrated)

Technology at the

(Early/ Late/ Mature)

Development stage to a

(Product/ Service/ IP/ Hybrid) market.

MY FEDERAL BUSINESS GAME PLAN

I am .... helping .... to .... in exchange for ....

My Quick Win Goal is ....

TECHNOLOGY POSITION	DEVELOPMENT STAGE	BUSINESS MODEL	PROCUREMENT LEAGUE	ALTERNATE FUNDING SOURCES	PLAYING FIELD	MARKET/ END USER
Enabling	In-House Ideation	Product	Little Leagues*	State & Local	Defense	Federal
Component	Early Development	Services	Big Leagues**	Private Sector	Intelligence	State & Local
Integrated	Late Development	Hybrid	Major Leagues***	Internal Financing	Health	B2B
	Mature	IP		External Investment	Other Federal	B2C
					Energy	
					Other****	

POWER-UPS	POWER-UPS	POWER-UPS	POWER-UPS
Get Found	Small Business	Scalable	Non-Profit

* Little Leagues: Credit Cards OTA / Small Business Set Aside/ Multivendor IDIQ
** Big Leagues: Verify interest, Need, Authority, Vehicle. Single-vendor contract over the simple procurement thresholds.
*** Major Leagues: frame vendor competition. Contract value over $10 million. Program of Record.
**** Other: Find an intractable problem with a partial solution, design a better solution, find the right buyer at the right agency, get your solution in front of them.

 ## BUYER ARENA CLUSTER MAP

 **TEAM ROSTER**

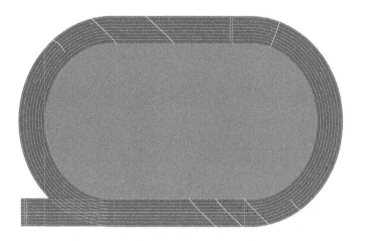

**BUSINESS STRENGTH TRAINING CENTER
QUESTIONING SETS**

Set 1: Greeting the contact • How have you been? • How is work treating you? • Has anything changed since we last spoke? • Is there anything I can help you with?	**Set 2: Digging for Dissatisfaction** • Are there any contracts due for renewal? • Who are the present incumbents? How is that working out? Would you do anything differently next time? • What's the present contracting vehicle? Is it an existing contract or does the government plan on developing a new contract developing a new contact based upon a requirement? • Could the way the work is being done be improved in any way?
Set 3: Identifying Issues • Are your customers having issues with exiting solutions or technologies? • Can you describe them? • How would you fix it? • Do you have a specific vision or solutions in mind?	**Set 4: Scoping the Work** • Can you describe your requirement? • What is the most important outcome for the project? • What issues remain unresolved that need to be addressed before putting out a request?
Set 5: Strategizing • Is there a formal requirement? • Are there available funds? If not, when do you expect to have funding for this requirement? • Are you considering a COTS solution? Or are you thinking of developing/creating something from scratch? • Does the planned funding align with the type of solution you're looking to purchase or develop?	**Set 6: Talking Time** • When would you like the project to begin? • When do you expect to get the procurement approved? • Have you defined the key project milestones? • Is there anything we can do to expedite the process for you?
Set 7: Talking Money • What is the budget for this opportunity? • Has this budget been approved and funded? • What are the milestones for approval and funding? • What is the risk that the project will not be funded?	**Set 8: Talking Personnel** • Where will the work be carried out? Onsite or offsite? • Are there any personnel specific requirements on the contractor side? Do they need specific qualifications or clearances?

TAFE INNOVATION ANALYSIS

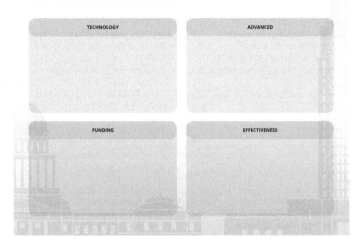

| TECHNOLOGY | ADVANCED |
| FUNDING | EFFECTIVENESS |

YOUR GOLDILOCKS INNOVATION AREA

Your Goldilocks Innovation Area is the intersection of your target agencies' REQUIREMENTS and the innovation FUNDING sources that play into your TECHNOLOGY vertical.

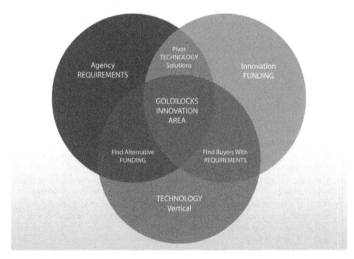

List the agency REQUIREMENTS of your target customers from Broad Area Agency Announcements, potential Innovation FUNDING Sources, and your preferred TECHNOLOGY verticals.

Then list areas where there is FUNDING available for REQUIREMENTS in your TECHNOLOGY vertical in the GOLDILOCKS INNOVATION AREA.

Where you have a FUNDING and REQUIREMENTS match, but you would need to PIVOT your TECHNOLOGY, list alternative technology options.

Where there is an agency REQUIREMENT for your TECHNOLOGY, but FUNDING is not available, list ALTERNATIVE sources of funding.

Where there is FUNDING available for your TECHNOLOGY, but your target agency has no current REQUIREMENT, list alternative BUYERS.

PITCH PERFECTION PROGRAM
Strength Analysis

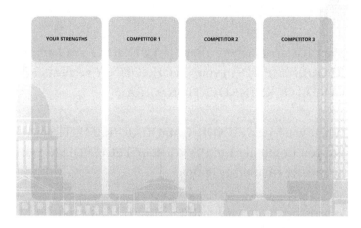

PITCH PERFECTION PROGRAM
Unique Strengths

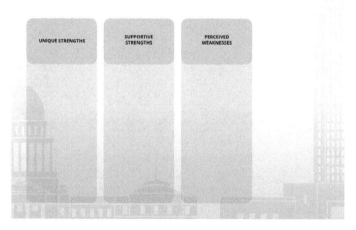

WIN THEMES

Use your Unique Strengths to create DISCRIMINATOR statements

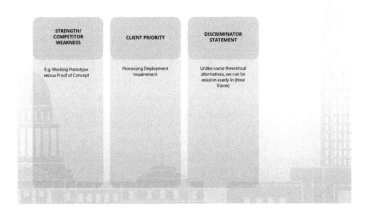

STRENGTH/ COMPETITOR WEAKNESS	CLIENT PRIORITY	DISCRIMINATOR STATEMENT
E.g. Working Prototype versus Proof of Concept	Processing Deployment requirement	Unlike some theoretical alternatives, we can be mission-ready in [time frame]

BENEFIT STATEMENTS

These are often the bullet points in sales literature, and they will make up a large part of your business capture literature too. Benefit statements package a feature of the proposed solution, service, or product, with the stated benefit and an element of supporting proof.

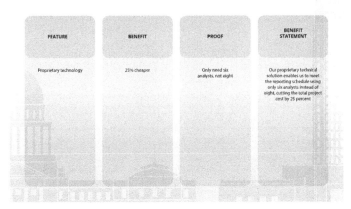

FEATURE	BENEFIT	PROOF	BENEFIT STATEMENT
Proprietary technology	25% cheaper	Only need six analysts, not eight	Our proprietary technical solution enables us to meet the reporting schedule using only six analysts instead of eight, cutting the total project cost by 25 percent

VALUE-ADDED PROPOSITIONS

A value-added proposition is an unasked-for extra. It's your promise to over-deliver. This proposition needs to be something that isn't in the government's specs or request, but that you will deliver naturally.

Ideally, these need to speak to one of the three major points of the Project Management Quality Triangle, which states that the quality of any project is constrained by the intersection of time, money, and scope of the project.

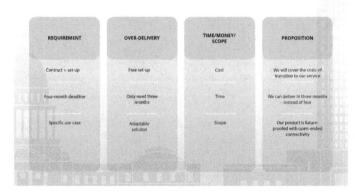

REQUIREMENT	OVER-DELIVERY	TIME/MONEY/SCOPE	PROPOSITION
Contract + set-up	Free set-up	Cost	We will cover the costs of transition to our service
Four-month deadline	Only need three months	Time	We can deliver in three months instead of four
Specific use case	Adaptable solution	Scope	Our product is future-proofed with open-ended connectivity

WIN STRATEGY
Walkback

For each Win Theme, walk backwards through what must happen for that to happen until you reach where you are now. Then create deadlines and assign your action steps to individuals or departments.

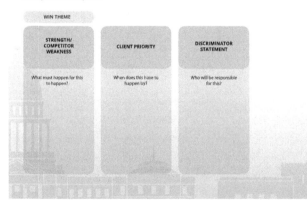

WIN THEME		
STRENGTH/COMPETITOR WEAKNESS	CLIENT PRIORITY	DISCRIMINATOR STATEMENT
What must happen for this to happen?	When does this have to happen by?	Who will be responsible for this?

WIN STRATEGY
Chronology

When you have completed your walkback for each Win Theme, combine your action steps chronologically to complete your Win Strategy.

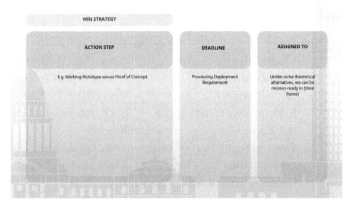

WIN STRATEGY		
ACTION STEP	DEADLINE	ASSIGNED TO
E.g. Working Prototype versus Proof of Concept	Processing Deployment Requirement	Unlike some theoretical alternatives, we can be mission-ready in [time frame]

PROPOSAL SET PIECES—CAPTURE PLAN

Set up a slide presentation with the following sections and slides. Consider making your own Capture Plan template and use a copy for each proposed bid.

- Summary
  - Client History
  - The Requirement introduction
  - Relationship with the client
  - Past/current performance
  - Recent interactions
- The Client
  - The Requirement in Detail
  - Hot Buttons/ Priorities
  - KPIs/Metrics
  - Procurement team
  - Decision-making process
  - Influencer map
- The Capture Team
  - Team roster roles and responsibilities
  - Meeting schedule
  - Action points
  - Project leader
  - Operations
  - Technical
  - Business Capture
  - Legal
  - Financial
  - Bid writing
- The Competition
  - Map of the Federal Procurement Arena
  - TAFE/SWOT Analysis per competitor
- Intelligence
  - Data collection
  - Data interpretation
- Strategy
  - TAFE Analysis
  - Unique Value Proposition
  - Win Themes
  - Win Strategy
- The Proposal
  - Outline
  - Rough draft
  - Technical draft
  - Operations draft
  - Sales draft
  - Legal draft
  - Financial draft
  - Final draft
  - Post award
  - Debrief
  - Contract
  - Implementation
  - Lessons learned

THE PITCHING PROCESS CHECKLIST

☐ Unpack the RFP—decode the language and write the request in plain English.

☐ Make a Master List of Requirements you can use as your guide to check things off at each stage.

☐ Start a spreadsheet with the requirements listed in column A.

☐ Title Column B "Win Themes" and then enter your win themes and phrases everywhere they fit in the requirements.

☐ Title Column C "Evidence" and enter your supporting facts, figures, past performances, etc. where they fit.

☐ In column D, write rough descriptions of each requirement.

☐ Use proposal writing software to transfer your proposal win themes and evidence into a proposal document template in rough draft form. Your template should include from your Capture Plan:

- Executive Summary
- Key Personnel (short bios & resumes)
- Past Performance (customer testimonials)
- Statement of Work (as requested in the RFP)
- Charts and Graphs (as requested in RFP or for ease of reading)
- Quality Control Plan, Subcontracting Plan, or other required appendices

☐ Have technical staff run through the proposal to check the language, facts, specifications, etc.

☐ Have operations personnel run through the draft to ensure the business can meet the deliverables.

- [ ] Get your sales and business capture experts to run through it and ensure the customer pain points and buzzwords customers use are incorporated into the language appropriately.
- [ ] Get your pricing experts to run the numbers and make sure everything is priced properly.
- [ ] Run the draft past a legal professional to ensure you are not creating obligations unintentionally or breaking any rules.
- [ ] Write the proposal in polished form.
- [ ] Get the graphic designer to create any graphics and do a first check on the formatting.
- [ ] Smart businesses, especially those who are just starting out, hire a professional proposal writer, if not to write the entire proposal, then at least to edit and format it. RFPs are dense and complicated, and your proposal must hit every note. Get someone who "speaks the language" to tidy yours up at the very least.
- [ ] Review the proposal against the master checklist one last time, ensuring nothing has been edited out that could disqualify it.

PROGRAM MANAGEMENT PRACTICE
Work Report Practice

When you have completed your walkback for each Win Theme, combine your action steps chronologically to complete your Win Strategy.

COMPANY

Daily Work Report: Please complete daily and return to Project Manager for compilation.

Remember, accurate and timely information allows us to over-deliver, and ensures client delight, business excellence, and personal satisfaction.

Contract		Agency		Site		
Employee						
Surname		Forename		ID#		
Date					+/-	
KPI1	Target		Actual			
KPI2	Target		Actual			
KPI3	Target		Actual			

Comments:

PROGRAM MANAGEMENT PRACTICE
Work Review Practice

COMPANY

Enter data from the daily work reports visually, with red figures representing underperformance, green representing acceptable results, and blue representing over-delivery.

Contract		Agency		Site		
Employee	KPI1	KPI2	KPI3	Emplyee Comment	Manager Comment	

REFERENCES

PREFACE

Department of Health and Human Services. "HHS Announces Ventilator Contract with GM under Defense Production Act." HHS.gov, April 8, 2020. https://www.hhs.gov/about/news/2020/04/08/hhs-announces-ventilator-contract-with-g-m-under-defense-production-act.html.

GM Defense. "History." GM Defense, accessed May 5, 2020, https://www.gmdefensellc.com/site/us/en/gm-defense/home/about/history.html.

Loten, Angus. "Startup Funding Dwindles Due to Coronavirus Slowdown." *The Wall Street Journal,* March 25, 2020. https://www.wsj.com/articles/startup-funding-dwindles-due-to-coronavirus-slowdown-11585175702.

INTRODUCTION

Bova, Tiffany. "Innovation from the Battlefield to the Boardroom with Pete Newell." *What's Next! with Tiffani Bova*. October 25, 2018. Podcast, 00:35:00. https://whatsnextpodcast.libsyn.com/innovation-from-the-battlefield-to-the-boardroom-with-pete-newell.

CNBC. "Jeff Bezos at the Economic Club of Washington." Video Recording, Washington: *CNBC* YouTube Channel. September 13, 2018. Video, 01:09:57. https://www.youtube.com/watch?v-=xv_vkAojsyo.

Coleman, Adam. "Matthew Boling Turns in 9.98 in 100-Meter Dash, Strake Jesuit Takes 2nd Straight Regional Title." *Houston Chronicle*, April 27, 2019. https://www.houstonchronicle.com/sports/highschool/article/Matthew-Boling-turns-in-9-98-in-100-meter-dash-13801284.php.

Goldwater-Nichols Department of Defense Reorganization Act of 1986, Public Law 99-433, 10 USC 663, 99th Congress U.S. Congress, 2nd session (1986).

Isaacson, Walter. "How America Risks Losing Its Innovation Edge." *Time*, January 3, 2019. https://time.com/longform/america-innovation/.

Lafontaine, Dan. "Army Honors Top Inventions of 2010." US Army, October 13, 2011. https://www.army.mil/article/67077/army_honors_top_inventions_of_2010.

Munro, Ethel M. *The Short Stories of Saki*. London: J. Lane, the Bodley Head, 1930.

National Defense University. Accessed May 26, 2020. https://www.ndu.edu/.

RAND Corporation. *Assessment of Joint Improvised Explosive Device Defeat Organization (JIEDDO) Training Activity.* Research Paper, Washington: RAND, 2013. https://www.rand.org/content/dam/rand/pubs/research_reports/RR400/RR421/RAND_RR421.pdf.

1. THE FEDERAL PROCUREMENT ARENA

Aaf.dau.edu. "Contracting Cone | Adaptive Acquisition Framework." Adaptive Acquisition Framework - Defense Acquisition University, accessed 6 July 2020. https://aaf.dau.edu/aaf/contracting-cone/.

AcqNotes. "Contracts & Legal: Broad Agency Announcement (BAA)," AcqNotes, last modified September 7, 2018. http://acqnotes.com/acqnote/careerfields/broad-agency-announcements.

Aida.mitre.org. "Other Transaction Authority (OTA)." Aida, accessed on 6 July 2020. https://aida.mitre.org/ota/.

Amazon Web Services. "Contract Center." Amazon Web Services, accessed on January 7, 2020. https://aws.amazon.com/contract-center/.

Amazon Web Services. "Govcloud." Amazon Web Services, accessed on March 7, 2020. https://aws.amazon.com/gov-cloud-us/.

Andrzejewski, Adam, and Thomas W. Smith. *The Federal Government's Use-It-or-Lose-It Spending Spree*. Oversight Report, Burr Ridge: Open the Books, 2019. https://www.openthebooks.com/assets/1/6/UseItOrLoseIt_Final1.PDF.

Apple Inc. "Apple Store for Government." Apple Inc., accessed on May 15, 2020. https://www.apple.com/r/store/government/.

Boeing. "Boeing History Chronolgy." Boeing, accessed on March 17, 2020. https://www.boeing.com/resources/boeingdotcom/history/pdf/Boeing_Chronology.pdf.

Brewster, Thomas. "$20 Million On An Unproven Malaria Drug, $650 Million On A Coronavirus Cure: How Trump's Government Has Spent Over $3 Billion Fighting COVID-19." *Forbes*, April 15, 2020. https://www.forbes.com/sites/thomasbrewster/2020/04/15/20-million-on-an-unproven-malaria-drug-650-million-on-a-coronavirus-cure-how-trumps-government-has-spent-over-3-billion-fighting-covid-19/.

CB Insights. "12 Early- And Mid-Stage Startups Backed By The CIA, Pentagon, And US Army." CB Insights, September 16, 2016. https://www.cbinsights.com/research/intelligence-military-startup-investors/.

Central Intelligence Agency. "The World Factbook." Central Intelligence Agency, accessed on August 7, 2019. https://www.cia.gov/library/publications/the-world-factbook/.

Cherney, Max A. "Here's What 20+ In-Q-Tel Investments Said About Taking The CIA's Money," Crunchbase, July 17, 2017.

https://news.crunchbase.com/news/heres-20-q-tel-invest-ments-said-taking-cias-money/.

Cornillie, Chris. "Pentagon OTA Spending Could Top $7 Billion in FY 2019." Bloomberg Government, August 8, 2019. https://about.bgov.com/news/pentagon-ota-spending-could-top-7-billion-in-fy-2019/.

DARPA. "DARPA Guide to Broad Agency Announcements and Research Announcements." DARPA, November 2016. https://www.darpa.mil/attachments/DARPAGuideBAARA.pdf.

Federal Acquisitions Regulations. "Subpart 6.1 - Full and Open Competition." Acquisition.gov, 2020. https://www.acquisition.gov/content/part-6-competition-requirements#i1120051.

Fleming, L. H Greene, G. Li, M. Marx, and D. Yao. "Government-funded research increasingly fuels innovation." *Science* 364, 6446 (2019): pp. 1139-1141.

Fortt, Jon. "Microsoft Wins Pentagon's Jedi Contract, And the Cloud Wars Heat Up." *CNBC* , October 31, 2019. https://www.cnbc.com/2019/10/31/microsoft-wins-pentagons-jedi-contract-and-the-cloud-wars-heat-up.html.

Human Paragon. "The 10 Greatest Space Programs Inventions." Human Paragon, June 5, 2017. https://humanparagon.com/space-programs-inventions/.

Good Jobs First. "Subsidy Tracker." Good Jobs First, accessed on December 8, 2019. https://www.goodjobsfirst.org/subsidy-tracker.

Grants.gov. "Grant Programs." Grants.gov, accessed on September 4, 2019. https://www.grants.gov/learn-grants/grant-programs.html.

Manuel, Kate M. "Competition in Federal Contracting: An Overview of The Legal Requirements." Congressional Research Service, June 30, 2011.

Mazzucato, Mariana, and Gregor Semieniuk. "Public financing of innovation: new." *Oxford Review of Economic Policy*, 33, 1 (2017): pp. 24-28.

Mehta, Aaron. "Pentagon turns to new buying tools 10 times more often." Defense News, April 1, 2020. https://www.defensenews.com/industry/2020/04/01/pentagon-turns-to-new-buying-tools-10-times-more-often/.

Microsoft. "Cloud Computing for Government | Microsoft Industry." Microsoft, accessed on June 10, 2020. https://www.microsoft.com/en-us/industry/government.

Mihalisko, Steven. "Other Transaction Authority (OTA) Trends, Points of Interest, and Entry Points." GovWin, September 7, 2018, https://iq.govwin.com/neo/marketAnalysis/view/3008?researchTypeId=1.

Nash, Ralph C. Jr. *The Government Contracts Reference Book 4th edition*. CCH Incorporated, May 3, 2013, supra note 1, at 414.

O'Connell, Johnathan and Dan Lamothe. "U.S. and Boeing have long had a special relationship." *Washington Post*, March 19, 2019. https://www.washingtonpost.com/business/economy/us-and-boeing-have-long-had-a-special-relationship/2019/03/16/abce-be8a-475a-11e9-aaf8-4512a6fe3439_story.html.

Rehn, Adrian. "Why Silicon Valley's 'Self-Made' Millionaires are Really 'Government-Made' Millionaires." *Mic,* March 25, 2014. https://www.mic.com/articles/86111/why-silicon-valley-s-self-made-millionaires-are-really-government-made-millionaires.

Schock, Aron. "Federally Funded Scientific Research Will Keep America's Economy Thriving." APS Physics, February, 2015. https://www.aps.org/policy/lawmakers/economy.cfm.

Shontell, Alyson. "The Greatest Comeback Story Of All Time: How Apple Went From Near Bankruptcy To Billions In 13 Years." *Business Insider,* October 26, 2010. https://www.businessinsider.com/apple-comeback-story-2010-10.

Ullman, Jeffrey D. "NSF Grant IRI-96-31952 Data Warehousing and Decision Support." University of Pittsburgh, 1997. https://db.cs.pitt.edu/idm/reports/1998/9631952.html.

United States government. "Introduction to Federal Government Contracting." USA.gov, accessed on June 10, 2020. https://www.usa.gov/government-contracting-for-beginners.

USA Spending. "Spending Search." USAspending.gov, accessed on May 3, 2020. https://www.usaspending.gov/#/search.

Williams, Joe. "Boeing profits soar to record on plane sales, more federal contracts." Fox Business, January 30, 2019. https://www.foxbusiness.com/industrials/boeing-profits-soar-to-record-highs-in-2018-on-more-federal-contracts-plane-sales.

YPulse. "The 'Startup Generation' Just Wants to Work for These Big Companies." YPULSE, June 1, 2018. https://www.ypulse.com/article/2018/06/11/the-startup-generation-just-wants-to-work-for-these-big-companies/.

3. PLAYING THE GAME

Army Research Laboratory. "Broad Agency Announcements." Army Research Laboratory, accessed on May 30, 2020. https://www.arl.army.mil/business/broad-agency-announcements/.

General Services Administration. "How to Sell to the Government." General Services Adinistration, accessed on September 15, 2019. https://www.gsa.gov/buying-selling/new-to-gsa-acquisitions/how-to-sell-to-the-government.

National Institutes of Health. "Widely Attended Gatherings (WAG), and Free Attendance," National Institutes of Health, Updated: 6/19/17. https://ethics.od.nih.gov/topics/wag.htm.

U.S. Navy Office of Naval Research. "Broad Agency Announcements (BAA), Funding Opportunity Announcements (FOA) and Special Program Announcements." U.S. Navy Office of Naval Research, accessed on May 30, 2020. https://www.onr.navy.mil/work-with-us/funding-opportunities/announcements.

4. THE STRATEGY ZONE

American Express Open. "Minority Small Business Government Contractors Investing More for Success but Efforts Pay Off, Finds New Study." *Business Wire*, March 2, 2012. https://www.businesswire.com/news/home/20120302005570/en/Minority-Small-Business-Government-Contractors-Investing-Success.

Armour, Mike. "What Revenue Goals Are Realistic." Startups After 50, 2009. http://www.startupsafter50.com/archives/realistic-revenue-goals/.

Carroll, Lewis. *Alice's Adventures in Wonderland*. Basingstoke: Macmillan Children's Books, 1865.

Cohn, Scott. "Amazon had it right: Virginia is America's Top State for Business in 2019." *CNBC*, 12 July 2019. http://cnbc.com/2019/07/09/virginia-is-americas-top-state-for-business-in-2019.html.

Funding Universe. "Westinghouse Electric Corporation History." Funding Universe, accessed on May 7, 2020. http://www.fundinguniverse.com/company-histories/westinghouse-electric-corporation-history/.

Hill, Simon. "Innovation Archetypes: What kind of innovator are you?" The Future Shapers, September 16, 2016. https://thefutureshapers.com/innovation-archetypes-kind-innovator/.

MacIntyre, Catherine. "Terry Fox's final push: 'I only think about the next mile." Macleans, June 29, 2017. https://www.macleans.ca/i-only-think-about-the-next-mile/.

Overfelt, Maggie. "The government track to a million-dollar business." *CNBC*, July 26, 2014. https://www.cnbc.com/2014/07/26/the-government-track-to-a-million-dollar-business.html.

WESCAM. "WESCAM's History in Hamilton." WESCAM Move, accessed on May 31, 2020. http://wescammove.ca/wescams-history-in-hamilton/.

5. PLANNING YOUR ATTACK

Koses, Jeffrey A. "Memorandum for GSA Contracting Activities." GSA Office of Governmentwide Policy, 2018. https://www.gsa.gov/cdnstatic/Policy_Initiatives/Class%20Deviation%202018-01%20MPT%20and%20SAT%20Increase.pdf.

NAICS Association. "SBA Size Standards." NAICS Association, August 2019. https://www.naics.com/sba-size-standards/.

National Science Board. "Science and Engineering Indicators 2018." *Science and Engineering Indicators 2018 Digest*. NSB-2018-2, January 2018. https://nsf.gov/statistics/2018/nsb20181/assets/1407/digest.pdf.

SBIR. Accessed on May 30, 2020. https://www.sbir.gov/.

Small Business Administration. "Is there an SBA Contracting Program for me?" SBA.gov, accessed on March 20, 2020. https://certify.sba.gov/am-i-eligible/.

Small Business Administration. "SBA Hubzone Map." SBA.gov, accessed on August 16, 2019. https://maps.certify.sba.gov/hubzone/map#center=39.828200,-98.579500&zoom=5.

Small Business Administration. "Size Standards Tool." SBA. gov, accessed on March 7, 2020. https://www.sba.gov/size-standards/.

US Department of the Treasury. "Policy Issues: Small Business Programs: Small And Disadvantaged Business Utilization: How To Do Business With Treasury: Part I: The Government Definition Of A Small Business." US Department of the Treasury, accessed on April 16, 2020. https://home.treasury.gov/policy-issues/small-business-programs/small-and-disadvantaged-business-utilization/how-to-do-business-with-treaury/part-i/the-government-definition-of-a-small-business.

U.S. Government. "Electronic Code of Federal Regulations." Electronic Code of Federal Regulations, accessed on April 2, 2020. https://www.ecfr.gov/cgi-bin/text-idx?SID=ee1595e6b-78f39b1563ab8a8440bc7cc&mc=true&tpl=/.

6. BUILDING YOUR TEAM

Cluster Mapping US. "U.S> Cluster Mapping," President and Fellows of Harvard College, 2018. http://clustermapping.us.

GovSearch LLC. Carroll Publishing, accessed on May 5, 2020. http://www.carrollpublishing.com/.

GovWin from Deltek. Accessed on May 15, 2020. https://iq.govwin.com/neo/home.

GSA, DoD, NASA. "Federal Acquisition Regulation." 2019. https://www.acquisition.gov/sites/default/files/current/far/pdf/FAR.pdf.

United States Department of Commerce. "Department of Commerce, Office of Small and Disadvantaged Business Utilization (OSDBU)." Commerce.gov, October 21, 2011. https://www.osec.doc.gov/osdbu/.

United States Government. "Introduction to Federal Government Contracting." USA.gov, accessed on March 15, 2020. https://www.usa.gov/government-contracting-for-beginners.

USA Spending. "Spending Search." USAspending.gov, accessed on May 3, 2020. https://www.usaspending.gov/#/search.

Office of Science. "National Laboratories." U.S. Department of Energy, accessed on 5 July, 2020. https://www.energy.gov/science/science-innovation/office-science-national-laboratories.

Office of the Under Secretary of Defense, Research and Engineering. "RTL/Labs." > Office of the Under Secretary of Defense, Research and Engineering . accessed 5 July, 2020. https://rt.cto.mil/rtl-labs/. Adapted from 2020.

7. THE TEAMING ZONE

Bloomberg Government. Accessed on May 27, 2020. https://about.bgov.com/.

Defense Contract Audit Agency. Accessed on May 15, 2020. https://www.dcaa.mil/.

Dun & Bradstreet. "Dun & Bradstreet Hoovers." dnb, accessed on March 17, 2020. https://www.dnb.com/products/marketing-sales/dnb-hoovers.html.

Government Executive. Accessed on May 16, 2020. http://www.govexec.com.

GSA Federal Acquisition Service. "GSA eLibrary." GSA.gov, accessed on May 27, 2020. www.gsaelibrary.gsa.gov/ElibMain/ElibHome.

NAICS Association. "SBA Size Standards." NAICS Association, August 2019. https://www.naics.com/sba-size-standards/.

Office of Small Business Programs, DoD. "Subcontracting for Small Business." Department of Defense, accessed on May 15, 2020. https://business.defense.gov/Acquisition/Subcontracting/Subcontracting-For-Small-Business/.

Small Business Administration. "All Small Mentor-Protégé program." SBA.gov, accessed on May 15, 2020. https://www.sba.gov/federal-contracting/contracting-assistance-programs/all-small-mentor-protege-program.

Small Business Administration. "Search Pro-Net Database." SBA.gov, accessed on March 17, 2020. https://pro-net.sba.gov/textonly/pro-net/search.html.

System for Award Management. "Advanced Search: Exclusion." SAM.gov, accessed on May 17, 2020. https://www.sam.gov/SAM/pages/public/searchRecords/advancedPIRSearch.jsf.

The Federal Contractor Network. "The Federal Contractor Network LinkedIn Profile." LinkedIn, accessed on March 17, 2020. https://www.linkedin.com/company/tfcn---the-federal-contractor-network/.

Washington Technology. Accessed on May 27, 2020. https://washingtontechnology.com/Home.aspx.

8. LISTENING FOR OPPORTUNITIES

Information Strategies, Inc. "Dynamics 365 for Government Contractors." 2019. infostrat.com/crm-for-govt-contractors.

JAMIS Software Corporation. "Jamis Customer Management Suite." 2020. jamis.com/products/jamis-prime-erp/customer-relationship/.

Salesforce.com, inc. "Salesforce Platform for Government." 2020. salesforce.com/solutions/industries/government/government-contractors/.

Government Contractors, LLC. "Government Contractors." 2019. governmentcontractors.co/crm-marketing-automation/.

9. THE INTELLIGENCE ZONE

Centurion Research. Accessed March 5, 2020. https://www.centurionresearch.com.

Congressional Budget Office. "Budget." CBO.gov, accessed on March 4, 2020. https://www.cbo.gov/topics/budget.

Federal Procurement Data Systems. "Federal Procurement Data System - Next Generation." FPDS.gov, accessed on May 23, 2020. https://www.fpds.gov/fpdsng_cms/index.php/en/.

Project on Government Oversight. "Federal Spending Report." FedSpending, accessed on March 4, 2020. https://www.fedspending.org/.

Under Secretary of Defense (Comptroller). "Welcome to the OUSD(C) Public Website." Department of Defense, accessed on March 5, 2020. https://comptroller.defense.gov/.

White House Office of Management and Budget. "President's Budget." Whitehouse.gov, accessed on March 5, 2020. https://www.whitehouse.gov/omb/budget/.

10. THE TECHNOLOGY ZONE

Atchison, M. *Department of Defense (DOD) Primer For Researchers*. [online] Research.utsa.edu, 2013. http://research.utsa.edu/wp-content/uploads/2015/02/Primer_for_DOD_Researchers.pdf.

Army Materiel Command. *Army R, D & A*. Michigan State University: Development and Engineering Directorate, HQ, U.S. Army Materiel Development and Readiness Command, 1983.

Congressional Research Service. "Federal Research and Development (R&D) Funding: FY2020". FAS.org, updated March 18, 2020. https://fas.org/sgp/crs/misc/R45715.pdf.

Espy, Walter Ellis. "TECHNOLOGY TRANSITION: GUIDANCE VERSUS PRACTICE." Thesis, Defense Acquisition University, 2006. https://www.dau.edu/cop/stm/DAU%20Sponsored%20Documents/Air%20Force%20Thesis%20on%20Technology%20Transition.pdf.

Moris, Francisco. "Definitions of Research and Development: An Annotated Compilation of Official Sources." National Science Foundation, March 2018. https://www.nsf.gov/statistics/rand-def/rd-definitions.pdf.

NASA. "Technology Readiness Level." NASA, August 7, 2017. https://www.nasa.gov/directorates/heo/scan/engineering/technology/txt_accordion1.html.

Office of Energy Efficiency and Renewable Energy. "Funding Phases for SBIR/STTR Programs." Energy.gov, accessed on May 27, 2020. https://www.energy.gov/eere/technology-to-market/funding-phases-sbirsttr-programs.

U.S. Department of the Army. "Department of Defense Fiscal Year (FY) 2019 Budget Estimates: Army Justification Book of Research, Development, Test & Evaluation, Army RDT&E – Volume II, Budget Activity 5B." February 2018. https://www.asafm.army.mil/Portals/72/Documents/BudgetMaterial/2019/Base%20Budget/rdte/Budget%20Activity%205b.pdf.

U.S. Department of the Navy. "Department of Defense Fiscal Year (FY) 2021 Budget Estimates: Navy Justification Book Volume 1 of 1: Weapons Procurement, Navy." February 2020. https://www.secnav.navy.mil/fmc/fmb/Documents/21pres/WPN_Book.pdf.

11. PLAYING TO WIN

O'Connell, Johnathan, and Dan Lamothe. "U.S. and Boeing have long had a special relationship." *Washington Post*, March 19, 2019. https://www.washingtonpost.com/business/economy/us-and-boeing-have-long-had-a-special-relationship/2019/03/16/abce-be8a-475a-11e9-aaf8-4512a6fe3439_story.html.

13. THE PITCHING ZONE

US Government Accountability Office . "Bid Protests, Appropriations Law, & Other Legal Work", US Government Accountability Office. Accessed July 5, 2020. https://www.gao.gov/legal/bid-protests/faqs.

14. THE PERFORMANCE ZONE

Ashworth, Will. "10 Best Value Stocks for Gritting Out the Downturn." Fidelity. May 25, 2011. https://www.fidelity.com/insights/investing-ideas/value-stocks-downturn.

Burke, Jim. "Harris Corporation Completes Acquisition of Exelis." L3Harris. May 29, 2015. https://www.harris.com/press-releases/2015/05/harris-corporation-completes-acquisition-of-exelis.